Threads of Gold

Frances A. Lewis

New Generation **Publishing**

Frances A. Lewis

Frances is from a very ordinary working class background. For the greater of her life it was generally considered she had no potential for achieving anything of worth!

She enjoys getting evolved with a wide variety of crafts, loves music, art, architecture plus the beauty of the flora and fauna around her.

She has an adopted son, three step-children, a foster son, grandchildren and three beautiful great granddaughters.

This is her first book with the hope for another to follow. One of her greatest wishes is to be a guest on 'Desert Island Discs'!

Frances lives near Bristol with her husband John.

I dedicate this book to my beloved husband John, who saw beyond the damaged, twice divorced woman with a difficult handicapped child, and filled our lives with unconditional love.

And to Ian, my very precious gift from God.

Acknowledgements

Chapter 1

- Historical background of Croydon...
  Personal and family knowledge
        Croydon Past by John Gent...
        Published by Phillimore Co Ltd 2002
    Shopwyke Manor Barn, Chichester, west Sussex
ISBN 1 860 223 4
- Lord Woolton
'Croydon Past' and the Internet
- Evacuation WW11
Mandy Burrows
Woodlands Junior School
Hunt Road, Tonbridge, Kent, TN10 4BB

Chapter 2
- Birdhurst Rise Murders
Julian Fellows
BBC TV Programme

Chapter3
- Commonwealth War Graves Commission
Head Office
2 Marlow Road, Maidenhead, SL6 7DX

Chapter 5
- Derek Bentley
BBC TV News Programme.
Personal and family Knowledge

Chapter 8 and Appendix
Internet and personal knowledge

Preface

"Threads of Gold" is a powerful, affecting memoir, telling the story of one woman's journey, growing up in post-war Britain, through illness and deprivation to faith.

Among the book's major strengths is its handling of her illness; in particular, her first hospitalisation. The reader gets a strong sense of her depression and pain without the portrayal feeling excessive or heavy-handed. The sense of objectivity, and the focus on the specific details of ulcerative colitis, gives the passage greater impact by inviting the reader to empathise, and thereby increasing their engagement with the story.

The challenges encountered with caring for a handicapped child are also explored.

The perspective offered on her faith, and on faith in general, is equally effective. By returning frequently to her relationship with the church, and addressing the problems she has in that relationship, the book avoids an overly neat conclusion and makes her eventual confirmation into the Mormon Church more satisfying for the reader.

Threads of Gold

❧❧❧

Chapter 1
"My War"
Croydon
England

1940 ------ 1945

Although I was happily unaware of it, at least as far as I can recall, a myriad of events were happening all around me during the most significant event of my life. As the bombs were dropping in and around Croydon, Surrey, on the 4 September 1940, I was taking my time about coming forth into the world of noise and mayhem. When I did appear I was promptly placed under the cast iron hospital bed along with my mother Maysie and the other mums and babies on the ward. I can only assume the staff at St Mary's Maternity Hospital felt an iron bed frame was the best protection they could give their mothers and new babies.

I was the first adorable bundle of joy born to my parents George Henry Overall and Maysie Emmaline Martin; they named me Frances Ann, in spite of a great deal of opposition from both grandmothers who wanted me named Grace Flora Rose. As I was growing up, I considered those names to be very old-fashioned. I didn't like them, and was very thankful Mum had stuck to her guns. I've grown a great deal older and wiser over the years, and now think they are very beautiful names; however, I know I would never have done them justice. I was in some ways a tomboy, and never considered myself as graceful. When I think of it now I do love all the flora and fauna around me and my favourite flower is most definitely the Rose, maybe my Grandmothers were inspired after all, however Mum's wishes took precedence over theirs and it wasn't to be.

I was born one year and one day after the Second World War was declared. On a bright and sunny Sunday 3 September 1939 Neville Chamberlain announced that Great Britain was at war with Germany. On the nights of 17 and 18 June 1940 the first bombs fell on Croydon and by the 15 August the onslaught had begun when the airport was attacked prior to the air-raid warning having been sounded. At that time Croydon Airport was a famous aerodrome which had been taken over by the RAF and inevitably became an integral part of the Battle of Britain. My parents lived on the perimeter of that aerodrome at 43 Westcombe Avenue; Mum was pregnant with me during what must have been a horrendous and nightmarish time. Although that was the address and house we lived in, the property belonged to someone who served in one of the forces and my parents were allowed to rent it until the owner was to be demobbed at the end of the war.

Between August and the end of the year Croydon experienced nearly three alerts a day, 399 in all, some of the raids were short, but some lasted eight to twelve hours or more. Many of the bombs fell on the town but the devastation caused was far less than in the City of London and the London Docks.

Prior to my entry into the world, and during the year of 1939, advanced defence preparations had been brought to the fore. In order to strengthen friendships with other countries King George and Queen Mary accepted a long-standing invitation for a seven week tour of North America, Canada and the United States, the diplomatic importance of the visit was fully recognised when the King and Queen returned to

8

Britain in June. My family, all Londoners, were staunch Royalists and would have been among the crowd of 50,000 people cheering and waving as the royal couple appeared on the balcony of Buckingham Palace.

Six months later on 23 December 1939, two days after my Mum's 21st birthday, my parents were married in St Agnes Church, Newington, London, just round the corner from Kennington Park. They had been engaged for a lengthy four years, I don't know exactly when or where they met, but they got engaged in 1935. Dad had presented his long term sweetheart with a white gold engagement ring with three Victorian cut diamonds set into it, the precious ring had cost him the princely sum of seven shillings and six pence, which was a great deal of money in those days. Their courting had mainly taken place in Kennington Park or at the Oval Cricket ground; they were both passionate about sport, or alternatively three nights at the local cinema which was a very popular pastime. They married against my Grandmother Martin and the local Priests wishes; Nan was a very strict practising Catholic and Dad had refused point blank to convert. They had consistently faced a great deal of opposition from both families and the Catholic Priest, hence the long engagement and marriage two days after reaching her 21st birthday, then of course no longer needing parental consent. Sad to say there were no photographs taken of their wedding day celebrations as it took place during one of London's notorious thick fogs or a peasouper (as they were known) that totally enshrined the city on a regular basis, bearing in mind it was many years before smokeless fuel was introduced. The only information I have of that special event was that granddad Martin was in hospital and as soon as the service was over they went to visit him to let him see Mum in her wedding dress and present him with her bouquet. I arrived nine months later, which was generally referred to then as a honeymoon baby!

During 1941 not only were we at war with Germany but also with the Japanese. When the Burma Campaign started, we lost many thousands of our men to appalling treatment, starvation and disease. America also received a devastating blow when the Japanese bombed Pearl Harbour in December of that year.

It doesn't take a great deal of imagination to recognize how uncertain every minute of each day was during those extremely difficult times but life did go on, indeed my brother David George was born two years after me on 20 August 1942, he came into the world during a pram shortage of all things. A baby carriage specialist had put an advert in the paper asking anyone for prams that were no longer needed. They were to either sell or lend it to someone else who was in need. People were advised to treat all war-time prams of all makes gently, owing to the restrictions of metal by the government; they weren't as strong as they used to be! They were also advised to take care of their prams because spares and repairs were difficult, a broken pram at that time was considered to be wasted material and labour. According to Mum we had a Silver Cross coach built pram; it must have been a second hand one as they were very expensive, or it could have been acquired by less honourable means as Nan Martin had 'connections' rarely spoken of in our hearing , but more of that later!

The earliest memories of my childhood are of sitting behind the settee with a group of children, I have no idea who they were, watching all the adults of extended family, friends, and neighbours having a whale of a time doing the Knees up and the Lambeth Walk etc, singing fit to bring the house down. My Dad would be playing the piano, my granddad Overall would be playing the spoons, Dads brother Walter, Wally or Uncle Wal as I called him, was a crooner and sang like Bing Crosby, who was a great favourite at that time, along with Vera Lynn. Someone else played the accordion and everyone who could sing or thought they could sing made as much noise as possible. They were typical Londoners, all the noise and energy of the parties were to let Hitler know that no matter how many bombs he sent over he wasn't going to stop them from having a good old sing song and knees up on a Saturday night.

I have no wish to deflect from the awfulness of the war that raged around us each and every day, especially considering it was the time of the Battle of Britain and the London Blitz, but as I reflect upon those times I stand in awe of my family, for me those were days filled with happiness, fun, excitement and plenty! As I have already indicated, our Nan, Emma Martin, had 'connections' and would somehow get all sorts of impossible to get treats, such as bananas and oranges. Her 'Boys' as she called them were based in the Surrey Street market in Croydon and we were never allowed to ask questions or tell anyone about her 'trips out'. Food Rationing had been introduced on 8 January 1940 and a 'Black Market' had developed. Shop keepers had 'under the counter items' they kept for favourite customers and Nan must have been everyone's favourite, as well as having the more dubious contacts to call upon.

As I got older I was occasionally taken up the market and most of the stall holders would call out their greetings asking how 'Emi and her nipper were' meaning me and Emi being short for Emma. At the top on the hill was a 'Sarsaparilla' man, it was a drink to die for in those days, I suppose you could loosely liken it to the cola of today. There was also an organ grinder with a performing monkey, he wore a very tiny red, Turkish looking, hat and green waistcoat that always looked the worse for wear, I can't remember exactly what it was but he always had a cane or a stick of some sort that was part of his performance. As children we thought he was so cute and funny, but truthfully he must have been a very sad pathetic little thing who had to perform in all weathers. The organ was painted bright red, green and yellow with touches of blue and gold in the lettering. It was transported around on, what to us as small children, were two enormous wheels, it never occurred to me at the time how it stayed straight and stable, I can only suppose there were some legs to it somewhere. The ones I have seen in later years all have four small wheels but the one of my childhood definitely only had two.

I vividly remember the times when we would be returning home after Mum had collected me from school when suddenly the air raid warning would go off, Mum would dump me on David's pram and run like mad with poor Monty the dog trying his best to propel us faster than Mum could run.

One often repeated story told by my mother, but not something I can substantiate one way or another, was that the blast from one of the many bombs blew off every other door all down both sides of the street. It was some years later that I came to realise that my mother tended to exaggerate any given incident, she didn't exactly lie she just stretched the truth a little to achieve a more dramatic effect. I hope it isn't something I've inherited, I want my story to be an honest and factual account of my life

In response to the introduction of food rationing imposed on the country in January 1940, in August the government launched an award for home grown vegetable production and the phrase 'Dig for Victory' was started by a London evening newspaper. Mum seemed to be a pretty resourceful person, she took up the challenge to grow her own vegetables and kept a few chickens as well. At the time a man called *Lord Woolton*, who had been appointed

as 'Minister for Food' and was the head chef at the Savoy Hotel, London, had been assigned to create a pie which came to be known as the *'Lord Woolton Pie'*. He urged people to be creative in their cooking with rationed food, and to use more vegetables, particularly potatoes.

Lord Woolton's Pie
Ingredients

1 lb (454g) potatoes	1 lb (454g) cauliflower
1 lb (454g) Swedes	1 lb (454g) carrots
3 or 4 spring onion	1 teaspoon of vegetable extract
1 tablespoon of oatmeal	Chopped Parsely

For the pastry:
4 ox (113g) Wholemeal flour and 2 oz (56g) lard (no sugar or egg),

Method:
Dice the potatoes, cauliflower, swedes and carrots, slice the onions and cook all with the vegetable extract and oatmeal for 10 minutes with just enough water to cover. Allow it to cool, then put in a pie dish, sprinkle with chopped parsley and cover with wholemeal pastry. Bake in a moderate oven until the pastry is nicely brown and serve hot with gravy.

Lord Woolton was also responsible for the verse
"Those who have the will to win,
Eat potatoes in their skin
Knowing that the sight of peelings

13

Deeply hurts Lord Woolton's feelings."

All the vegetable peelings were fed to the pigs, poultry, and rabbit clubs that were organised by local groups of enthusiasts.

Much of *Lord Woolton's* success was due to his business skill; he only rationed items of which he was certain he had enough to go around, however small the quantities. This built up a sense of fairness and trust: he also believed that ***the public should be educated and helped, not just instructed***. This he did by means of advertisements starring *'Dr Carrot'* and *'Potato Pete'*, they were broadcasted by 'Gert and Daisy' the music hall artistes Elsie and Doris Walters, by then the war time cookery book *'The Kitchen Front'* had regular air time on the radio and *'Food Flashes'* in the cinema were also a daily occurrence. Nobody liked the diet, but by all accounts, by the end of the War the country's population was fitter and healthier than they had ever been.

Once the Battle of Britain and the Blitz had died down the raids were quite minor in comparison, until 13 June 1944 when the first pilotless planes launched an attack. They were known as V1s, Flying Bombs, Buzz-Bombs, or Doodlebugs and for 80 days and nights they were an all too familiar sound over London and the south east of England. They were a cheap, mass produced unpiloted weapon that had rocket propulsion and could travel between 80 and 100 miles, filled with one ton of high explosives, they fell randomly when the fuel supply ran out or they were brought down by fighter planes, anti-aircraft fire, or barrage balloon cables. They did a considerable amount of blast damage over a radius of 400 yards or so but left only a relatively small crater. Croydon was badly hit but escaped some of the most serious incidents. Hitler had decided to obliterate all the airfields in the South East as he realised that was where the fighter pilots were based and they were giving him a headache as they were giving his pilots a hard time. The Croydon and Biggen Hill airfields were amongst those that had to be obliterated

However in July 1944, within a few weeks of the attacks starting, an estimated 36,000 people left Croydon. That was the very worse period we had to go through as David and I, (aged two and four years respectively) were evacuated in response to the heavy bombing. 'Evacuation' had previously taken place in 1939 and many children, mothers, helpers and teachers were sent to Brighton and Hove, but fives years into the war the flying bombs had brought about a different and more deadly set of circumstances and we, unfortunately, were sent to Congleton, in Cheshire. I still find it hard to believe we were sent all that way without our mother, I have no recollection of the journey or how we got there; I only remember our time there.

What I do remember of that time has to be using an outside toilet that had rats running around it, we were so frightened we started wetting the bed and that brought about punishments we had never experienced before. I don't remember having a lot to eat either, all in all it was a nightmare which, fortunately, didn't last for longer than two weeks. Mum got it into her head to make the trip to see how we were settling down, she very quickly appraised the situation and decided she would rather we took our chances with the bombs and not the rats, packed our bags and took us straight back home again, it took us quite a while to recover from that experience, David in particular had nightmares for a long time after returning home.

In order to help us forget those unhappy weeks Mum did her best to make each day as exciting as circumstances would allow. As young children we were unaware of the dangers we all faced and the most exciting part of each day came with the sound of the doodlebug. It was a wonderful game of who would be the first to make it to the Morrison shelter (a steel table) in the dining room before the bombs dropped, Mum would have David tucked under her arm pushing me in front trying to get us under the table before Monty the dog dived in. If he got there first it would take more than a few threats to get him to make room for us, he would be shaking like a jelly and whimpering with his head hidden under the blanket, he was definitely more frightened than we were as Mum had the knack of making it all seem like a really fun game that we played on a regular basis. There were books, toys, drinks and food tucked away under the table and a blanket was pulled down so that we were completely enclosed, for many years after the war ended David and I always loved playing houses and all sorts of imaginary games under a table encased in a sheet or a blanket.

The Morrison shelter was first introduced in 1941, for people without gardens, although we did have a garden so I'm not sure how we came to have one. The shelter, made from heavy steel, could also be used as a table. The Anderson shelter, a corrugated steel structure that was sunk about three feet into the ground and covered with soil, was in the back garden, but Mum flatly refused to go down among the creepy crawlies, the damp and the cold. We used it as a playhouse and had a wonderful time using our overactive imaginations for all sorts of games and adventures, the fact that Mum disliked it so much made it a very daring and exciting place to hide.

During these exciting, albeit dangerous times, children enjoyed playing out in the street. On one occasion I was sitting on the pavement with my feet in the kerb watching the horse drawn milk float, I seem to remember it was Welford's Dairies! The milkman hadn't seen me, leaving the horse to its own devices. The next thing I knew the horse had walked past me, an excruciating pain jolting me out of my daydream, as the wheels of the float slowly ran over my right foot. The racket I made screaming must have frightened the horse to death, along with the neighbours who came running out of their houses to see what all the commotion was about. The poor milkman got a tongue lashing from some of the women, but Mum showed what I thought was very little sympathy, she quite rightly said I should have known better than to sit in the path of a horse!

Dad was one of the very few people who had a motorbike and sidecar and we had trips out on a Sunday to see various family members. Nan and Granddad Overall lived at 222 Tylecroft Road Norbury and our visits to see them were a mixture of excitement and dread. The excitement came from having a wonderful Sunday tea of shrimps, and winkles that you had to prize out of the shells with a pin, bread, a scraping of butter and jam followed by seed cake, when I was old enough to know anything about rationing I was always amazed at how Nan managed to give us all such a feast. As always, whenever the Overalls got together, there was the inevitable sing song with Dad on the accordion and granddad playing the spoons.

The part we dreaded was walking around to Northborough Road that ran parallel to Tylecroft Road in order to visit Nan's sister Elsie (I think that's who it was). They had an overpowering Grandfather clock that chimed every fifteen minutes. It was situated in the 'best' front room, the room that was only used on a Sunday or special holidays. After the usual pleasantries were over and catching up on each others news all the adults would fall asleep and the noise would become deafening, the clock ticking, a great deal of snoring and Granddad's teeth making music to accompany all the different sounds and rhythms in the room. My brother David was another extrovert in the family, doing his best to wake them up and gain their attention by singing at the top of his voice *'Champagne Charlie is my name',* however hard he tried it didn't make the slightest bit of difference they never woke up until they were good and ready. I put it down to their having learnt to sleep throughout the bombings.

We would sometimes visit other relatives on Dad's side who lived in a flat somewhere on the outskirts of London, I don't know who they were or what part of London it was but we loved going there as we were allowed to go and buy blocks of ice off the back of an open topped lorry that toured the streets. Winkles and scrimps arrived in the same way and then the crumpet man would make his rounds on a bicycle, if we were very lucky an ice cream man would also turn up on his bicycle, the ice cream was stored in a box on the back of the bike. It was like heaven on earth to us kids. Those days out were the highlight of our week and it became even better if Dad hadn't been able to find any petrol for the motorbike he owned, as we would have to go on the open top tram and then a bus. You have no idea how exciting that was, made all the more fun by the conductors who were typical jolly Londoners, full of wit and wonder when they made a penny appear from behind our ears and made us laugh.

There were other people and places we visited, but sadly I don't remember who or where they were except there were two families in Brixton. One couple lived in an upstairs flat, being frightened of heights I wouldn't go anywhere near the window. We also visited a very large lady in a ground floor flat, I may be completely wrong but I would have said she was one of Nan

Overall's sisters; she had three sisters Hilda, Elsie and Grace. My most vivid memory was of us being a very close family who would have a song and dance whenever we all met up, Dad was always called upon to play either a piano or accordion whatever was at hand, the cry of '*Come on Georgie give us a song*' was all that was needed. Mum, bless her, was tone deaf, she sometimes got rather put out with Dad's neglect of her, but he was very popular and loved playing whenever he got the chance, the lure of the music took precedence over Mum's later dressing down!

Tuesday 8 May 1945 was declared V. E. day and impromptu street parties were organised. I remember tables being set up in our street and food appeared from everywhere, when you consider the restrictions of the ever present rationing the amount of food was amazing. Coloured flags and bunting adorned every house, garden fence and street lamp. Then rain was forecast so everything was moved to the local infants' school, it was the one I attended but I can't remember the name. Those parties continued for months in one way or another even into August and September when the end of the war with Japan was celebrated. Anyone who had a piano moved them out into the streets for many a knees up with lines of people of all ages snaked around dancing the Conga. The children's parties were held late afternoon then the adults would take over for the evening, I don't ever remember being put to bed we just joined in whatever was going on.

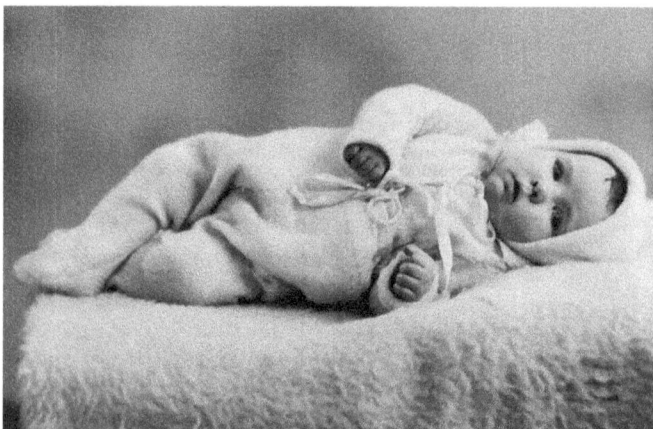

Frances taken on 19 February 1941

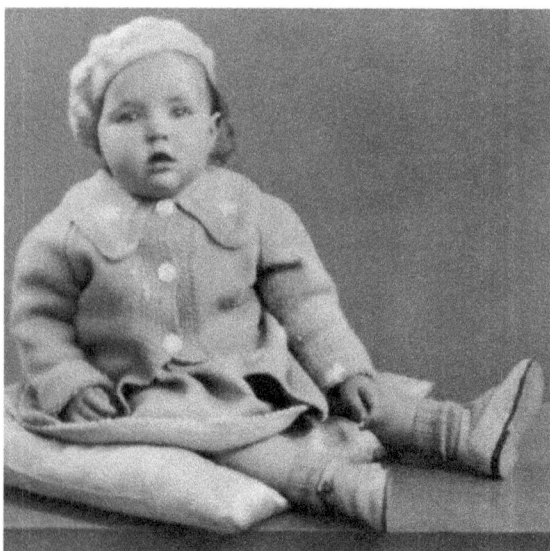

Frances 1942

Frances 1943

Frances and Brother David 1943

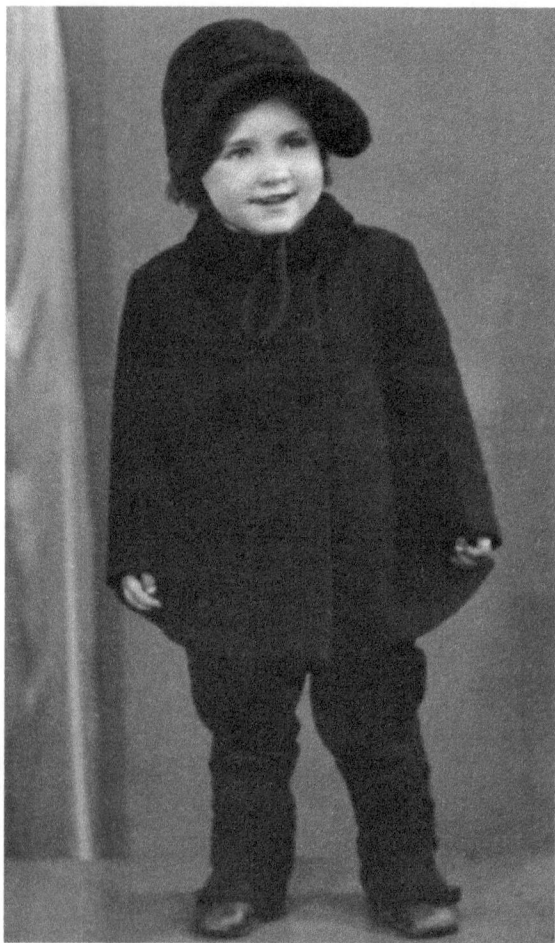

Frances 1944

Frances and David 1944

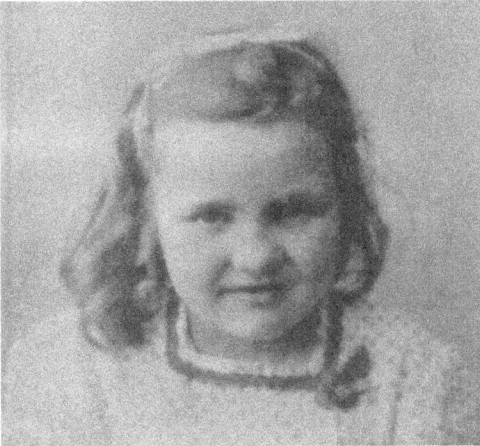

Frances 1945

Frances and David 1945

Chapter 2
"The End of My War"
Croydon
England
1946 ------ 1949

It wasn't long after all the celebrations had taken place that we had to move out of Westcombe Avenue, this was due to the owner having returned home from active duty. We moved into a massive house in Birdhurst Rise where Mum and Dad rented the ground floor flat. It was unthinkable in our family for the working class to buy a house, renting was the social level they aspired to, which was strange, I remember them as being a very contained and self assured couple.

The house was a very grand double fronted Georgian building with two flat sash windows on the ground floor, left of the tall front door. The door was made up of panelled wood on the lower half, with two vertical opaque windows that were above the central letterbox. Another larger opaque window was set on top of the door in order to let as much light as possible into the inner hallway. Above the door on the upper floor sat a smaller flat sash window with a larger one to the left of that. On the right of the door were two large bay windows again on the lower and upper floors with a small window above set into the apex of the roof. A deep white patterned plinth sat above the door and windows, looking as if a showering of snow had settled there. To the left hand side of the building was what looked like an extension but was an integral part of the original building, I can't say with total confidence but I'm sure as I can be that was where the huge kitchen was situated.

The front garden leading up to the main entrance was mainly trees and an assortment of shrubs, I don't remember any grass. I don't remember the back garden at all so can only conclude we weren't allowed to play out there. The entrance hall was spacious, light and airy with a number of quite large doors leading off it and a wonderful spiral staircase that went from the top floor to the bottom. David and I polished that staircase everyday to a very high gloss by sliding down it whenever we thought we could get away with it. The hardest restriction we had to observe was not screaming with delight on our way down as that would most certainly have alerted someone and our game would have come to an end. When I think about it now Mum must have been terrified of us falling off and killing ourselves as we were still very young, but to us it was so exciting sliding all the way down, knowing full well we were banned from such a dangerous activity.

We lived on the ground floor over the basement, that, believe me, was a very scary place, but scary things and scary places are like a magnet to most children. It was very dark, damp and cold down there and full of frogs or toads, I don't know who were the more frightened them or us, but there was always a certain amount of excitement in facing that fear. To make matters worse, depending on how you viewed it, the house was said to be haunted by a lady who had murdered one or more of the occupants. This alarming fact had been discussed at some length at the dinner table, giving rise to some anxiety to each one of us! Mum and Dad had not been made aware of this before taking up residency. Briefly three members of the same family were dispatched within about a year. The story goes as follows:-

The Birdhurst Rise Murders

Edmund Duff was poisoned via his evening bottle of stout, followed by his sister in law, Vera Sidney in 1929 (via homemade soup laced with Arsenic) and finally Vera's mother, Violet (via Methadone tonic). Incredibly it wasn't until all three were dead that someone realised that maybe something was a little suspicious! Despite numerous inquests no one was brought to trial, and it was thought that one of the surviving family members had to be the culprit, although one theory is Violet who committed suicide after killing off her daughter and son in law. Others entered the equation, including the grandson of Violet who was very young, and the doctor, who was supposed to be having an affair with Edmund's wife. In all, a quaint little English family!!! .

British TV reconstructed a documentary on the case, and the verdict, arrived by the presenter Julian Fellowes, was that Vera Sidney's son Tom was the murderer.

The whole affair was quite intriguing, there appeared to be no substantial motive, other than monies inherited from the demised, the amounts involved were little.

****

It isn't really surprising it was about that time when I started having nightmares; I was convinced my Mum had died or was being killed. Overall though, putting the nightmares aside, I loved our stay there as it was a large beautifully proportioned house with lots of fun things we could get up to! I'm certain it was while living in that particular house that a tiny seed was planted which over the years would flourish into my love of beautiful and artistic craftsmanship in all its various forms.

Our daily routine was planned around a very strict schedule each day, our behaviour was carefully monitored and if it didn't reach the high standard expected of us we didn't get to listen to the only programmes on the radio that mattered, *Children's Radio*, *Dick Barton*, and *Journey into Space*. *The Ovaltinies* for little boys and girls was also one of our favourites; there was nothing, as children, we relished more than having a secret or two. The makers of a famous bedtime drink *Ovaltine* realized this simple fact over 60 years ago and built success out of secrecy. Someone in the *Ovaltine Empire* had a winning gimmick when they hit on the idea of the *League of Ovaltinies*. The fun and excitement of having a membership card, badge and secret passwords was exciting stuff. Besides the badge and membership card we also used to be sent a regular newsletter and new password. And, believe it or not, we *Ovaltinies* had our very own programme on *Radio Luxemburg*. We had our own song too, which went something like: '*We are the Ovaltinies, happy girls, and boys. We share each other's troubles, and each other's joys, because we all drink Ovaltine, we're happy girls and boys.*' We would sit at the large scrubbed wooden table in the huge kitchen, this was the hub of the home, working on a variety of projects, eating our tea and listening to the radio. A cup of Ovaltine was one of our bedtime 'must haves' every night.

The Saturday Night Theatre, broadcast on the radio, helped develop our minds as each play was dramatised. I can't be absolutely certain when my love of reading as a child started, but I'm pretty sure it had something to do with that period of time when Mum was always encouraging us to use our imaginations, listening to the radio plays each week was part of that encouragement. The Sunday Evening Play was usually based on one of the classics, I came to love Charles Dickens through those adaptations and found his writing and story telling beautifully descriptive, I could always see in my minds eye the whole picture and circumstance he was endeavouring to portray, how I wish I had that talent!

I wouldn't have been able to vocalise my thoughts and feelings at that young age but deep down inside me I somehow knew they were there. I recently came across something that was reputed to have been said by *Carlos R Zafron* which fully explains my own sentiments *"I had never known the pleasure of reading, of exploring the recesses of the soul, of letting myself be carried away by the imagination, beauty and mystery of fiction, language, pathos and imagination, for me all those things were born when first reading the novel...."* Without my being aware of it at that young age, the 'Charles Dickens' stories were most definitely the catalyst that opened my mind to all those emotions. The other influence they had on me was a developing awareness of the social history of the ordinary working people, of the difficulties, deprivation and, above all, courage that so many people displayed through the most appalling conditions; it has continued to be of interest to me throughout my life. The wonderful thing about listening to the radio as children was, it encouraged us to use and develop our own imaginations, something I think is sadly lacking in some of today's children.

By now you may have noticed I haven't mentioned anything about going to school during this period of my life; I seem to have a complete mental block about the two schools I know I attended but they were institutions I disliked intensely. I certainly didn't fit in at school, I was an imaginative and creative child who lived in a world of my own making, I just couldn't get to grips with subjects like the dreaded arithmetic and set curriculum of the day, being also very shy and still am if truth be told. I didn't make friends easily, the exact opposite to my extrovert brother. I never seemed to be any good at anything that was expected of me, I was thought to be difficult, that stigma staying with me all of my school life, I don't ever remember getting a good report. All through those and the following years, school to me was like living in a monochrome world, it lacked colour and vibrancy and every school day was like living in a nightmare of inadequacy and lack of self-belief.

In October 1946 Uncle Wal married Auntie Vicky (Vera Hazel Howarth), way up North in Fulford, York. All the family travelled up there by train and were 'put up' by lots of strangers. I was quite worried about that, at the time, because I wasn't sure what 'put up' meant exactly, I suspect we were accommodated by family and friends of Auntie Vicky.

When we eventually arrived at the reception I became rather upset as, for the first course we were presented with a Yorkshire pudding with gravy. I thought that was all we were going to get to eat, not knowing that's how they do things in Yorkshire, it was their way of filling you up before being given the 'not a lot of meat' course. As far as I remember all went well with the usual song and dance going on, if Auntie Vicky's family hadn't met uncle Wal before, they soon found out what a very funny extrovert man she had married. I have no idea what the Yorkshire quests thought of the very loud, laughing Londoners deposited amongst them, but I can give it a jolly good guess!

Unfortunately when we arrived back at King Cross railway station in London Nan Overall fell over heavily on an uneven platform, she was a very large lady and the shock to her body was tremendous. She passed away five years later in November 1951 with cancer which, the family were told, was as a direct result of the shock to the body after that fall.

After their honeymoon came to an end Uncle Wal and Auntie Vicky moved into one of the other flats in the house in Birdhurst Rise and there followed a time of fun and laughter as Uncle Wal was the family extrovert and was always joking around. Dad was a serious and rather intense person at times, but having his easy going brother around ensured each day was filled with fun and laughter.

I don't remember the year exactly it could have been either 1947 or 48 but whichever it was I had the very best Christmas ever. We had made lots of paper chains out of coloured paper strips; they were stuck together with a paste made out of flour and water, which had been achieved with everyone's help around the huge kitchen table. I had two, never to be forgotten, presents that year. Jennifer was a beautiful china doll that Mum had dressed with hand made and knitted clothes. Dad had also made me a three up and three down dolls' house that even had electric lights and wallpapered rooms, it had been furnished with presents from other members of the family, cotton reels and small matchboxes had been saved so that I could make some chairs and beds myself. To me that was my most magical Christmas ever, even now I can close my eyes and see the room we were in, the Christmas tree was very big as the ceilings in all the rooms were approximately nine feet high and a small tree would have looked out of place. I don't know where they got it from but I have no doubt Nan Martin had something to do with it. Dad had somehow managed to get some fairy lights and we decorated it with all sorts of items we had made. The paper chains were hung from a picture rail that went all the way around the room that had been positioned approximately two feet below ceiling level. The anticipation of Father Christmas visiting, all the Christmas decorations, special food, courtesy of Nan again, and those two most treasured gifts, made that time one of magic and delight, the day was brought to a happy conclusion with the inevitable family songs and knees up.

I didn't know about it at the time, but on doing some research I found out that buying or selling things on the black market during the war was illegal, I now wonder how Nan got away with so much under the counter activity. It must have been obvious to the neighbours we had more than the allotted amounts, or did she supply them as well in order to keep them quiet about it. In those days' neighbours, on the whole, were a much closer community and would always help each other out whenever needed.

It was sometime around that period there was a competition being promoted for any budding song writers to have a go and send in their own original songs, there was be a financial prize for the best entry. Needless to say Dad and Uncle Wal put their heads together and came up with a song called "*Castles in the Air*". In their naivety they didn't put a copy write on it, or keep a copy of their work of art. They were later astounded when first of all they were informed their song hadn't been suitable material, then, just a short while later, they heard it being played on the radio with slightly different words. The song was "*Cruising down the River*". The promoters vigorously denied any scam had taken place and as they were in possession of the original copy there was nothing Dad and Uncle Wal could prove. It was a very sore talking point during the following years, especially when they heard it being played on the radio.

Birdhurst Rise was one of the original 'Upstairs Downstairs' properties which in times past would have been home to a very well off family, as such it was situated in a leafy secluded part of Croydon. As children we were blessed with having the beautiful Wandle Park, or it could have been Lloyd Park, to play in, which was just down the bottom of the road. Although we weren't allowed to go there on our own as we had to cross the very busy Coombe Road, Mum would take us there to run around and explore all the park offered, until we finally wore ourselves out, which I'm sure was the general idea!

Our whole lives up to that point had been centred on family and there were times when I practically lived with my Nan and Granddad Martin who lived in 185 Sumner Road South, Croydon. My most favourite person in the entire world was my Mum's sister Dorothy, she was twelve years older than me, and I always called her Doll. The story most fondly related, with a lot of laughter interlaced with the telling, was that on the day they were bombed out in London, Dorothy was down the bottom of the yard sitting on the toilet when the blast of the bomb blew the door clean off, leaving her in full view with her knickers down. The fact that she was frightened and screaming her head off was dismissed as of no consequence, it was far more important that Dorothy and the rest of the family were unhurt, they had lost their home but not their lives.

We spent a great deal of time together, throughout her life she was always the one I would turn to in my hours of need. When her fiancé Len married her in August 1947 I was a bridesmaid and very put out because my dress was different to everyone else. Their carefully thought out plan had been that I was to be the 'special' bridesmaid but I didn't appreciate it at the time. My dress had rose buds adorning the front and the others had open daisies, I cried and threw a tantrum because mine was different!! Something Doll could certainly have done without on her special day! The expression on my face in all the photographs gives a very good indication of how hard done by I felt.

Poor Len not only took on his beloved Dorothy, but he had to put up with me as well. I must have put the damper on many of their dates as I invariably went along as well; I very soon came to love him just as dearly, he was a lovely patient man. From him I learnt to enjoy cheese and jam, and beef or pork dripping sandwiches, which in today's society would be considered a dietician's nightmare, but with a little salt sprinkled over the dripping they were delicious. Doll and Len started off their married life living in Nan and Granddad Martins house and whenever I was staying there, which was frequently, Len would sit me at the table in front of the fire, after making me his wonderful sandwiches, and then tell me some of his exciting stories. He had the gift of story telling that fired my imagination. Bedtime would eventually creep up on us, my tummy would be full, my mind active in a world of make believe, but however hard I would fight it, eventually sleep would overtake me and that dear man would carry me up to bed and make sure I was tucked in nice and warm. When their daughter Pearl was born I was overjoyed, she was so tiny, like a little doll with fine blond wisps of hair, I have loved her like a sister from that day to this.

Some of my most vivid memories are centred within my Nan's house, I can still see it now in my minds eye; the kitchen was cold and sparse with the standard Corporation dark green and cream painted walls, there was a tall green and cream free standing cabinet with a drop down section that became a surface on which to work, a four ring gas cooker with a plate rack situated above it to keep the plates warm, the oven and grill were underneath the hob and were very small in comparison with today's big and glossy all singing, all dancing varieties, however that cooker was the luxury of the time for a working class family like ours. The stone sink and wooden draining board was under the window and a small table stood in the centre of what was a very small room. The side door into the kitchen opened off from an alleyway shared with the next door neighbour; just inside the door was the coalhole. I'm not certain if that is what it was meant to be but it was certainly used to house the coal and wood. The front room had a range with a high mantle piece above it, there were two armchairs either side of the fire, but I can only remember sitting around the 'best' table which was in the middle of the room. The bedrooms were up a narrow flight of stairs and each had a bedside table made out of wooden barrels, which I think had once served as fruit (orange) containers, the barrels had been cut in half and painted dark green with a shelf fitted half way up. The beds each had a thick cosy feather eiderdown, covered in a shot satin, on top of the sheets and blankets; the linoleum on the floors was always so cold. The really strange thing is I cannot remember a toilet or if there was a bathroom, I certainly don't remember having to go outside to a toilet so can only assume there was one inside. We had to wash in the kitchen sink, sitting on the draining board with our feet in an enamel bowl. The gas ring was lit to take the chill off the cold room in order for us not to get too cold.

Mum's youngest brother Michael John (Mick) was a redhead and tormented me mercilessly; his favourite trick was tying me to the table leg then going off somewhere and leaving me. He always got into trouble for doing it but, as trouble was his middle name, it was like water off a ducks back, he didn't seem to have a care in the world except for having massive boils on his neck; I remember Mum heating a milk bottle and putting it over a boil in order to bring it to a head and it would burst inside the bottle, it was utterly revolting to see, but like all children we loved to be horrified out of our wits, I don't know why that is, is there some sort of macabre button within each of us I wonder?

One of the highlights of my year was when Nan treated us all to the Pantomime on Boxing Day; The Pantomime goes back to the middle ages but really became an English tradition in the early 1700. The annual Christmas 'Panto' is as much our heritage as roast beef and Yorkshire pudding, the reason a woman always plays the main male part was because in those early days women were not allowed to be seen on a stage, hence the men playing the part of the Dame and the ugly sisters. All the Pantomimes are made up of the same basic format, but that is an essential part of the whole wonderful experience. Everyone in attendance gets involved and loves every second of being there. The outrageous and colourful costumes, the plushness of the décor, in those early days my child's eye didn't see anything beyond the richness and beauty of it all. The corny jokes that everyone laughed at which I, more often than not, didn't understand, the Nasty King was the bad man, who was always a bit scary and we all booed at, the good fairy Queen weaving her magic, and last but not least, the singing and dancing. We would arrive home with little or no voices due to having sung all the songs and shouting so much at all the 'Oh! No you can't' and 'Oh! Yes you can's'. We were always treated to ice creams or sweets; I never knew how Nan managed such luxuries. I still enjoy going to the pantomime every year and shouting myself hoarse along with all the children, the jokes are still corny with some being carried over from many years ago, but they are great fun and a fabulous family time together. I always saw Nan as the generous and giving person, she was, after all, the one who gave us the best ever treats. I remember her taking us to the London Zoo and seeing my first elephant and wild animals, we also went to the circus on Mitcham Common where we saw more animals and clowns etc., seeing it all through a child's eye was breath taking and magical.

It must have been approximately 1949/50 when we left Croydon for pastures new and a completely different life style. For Mum it must have been like going back into the dark ages but for David and me it was the beginning of an exciting adventure, as all will be revealed in a later chapter.

Frances and David 1947

**Dorothy (Doll) this was taken 15 November 1942,
she was almost 15 years old**

Dorothy (Doll) Leona Martin who was my Aunt, for me, the most favourite person in all the world

Leonard (Len) David Winchester, the kindest man I knew

Len and Doll's Wedding 2 August 1947

**Me in the special Bridesmaid Dress I had a
tantrum over**

ༀ৯৵৵

Chapter 3
"My Family"

I've wondered how I can introduce the members of my family who are no longer with us in this life who are responsible for passing on to me their genes, attributes, characteristics, attitudes, nurturing, talents and an abundance of love down through the ages, all those building blocks making me who I am, both good and bad. After learning about some of their backgrounds, the conclusions I eventually came to left me with a desire to acknowledge them in some small way. Some characters I have already included, nevertheless after a lot of thought I have decided to give my parents and grandparents, plus a few others of interest, their very own chapter.

My DAD
George Henry OVERALL
7 September 1916 – 18 January 2001

I know quite a lot about my Dad; he was born on the 7th September 1916 (see Appendix) at 196 Penton Place, Newington, London, the eldest son of George Overall and Rose Edith Jackson.

Brothers Walter Joseph arrived on 8th August 1920 and, after a big gap, James Harold on 9th July 1931 by which time they had moved to 276 Penton Place, London

Dad attended the St Paul's Primary School then started attending St Paul's Church of England school when he was nine years old; he left School on the 24th October 1930 (see Appendix) with an excellent school report after having been there for five years.

As they didn't have bathrooms in the flats the family would all have to make their weekly outing to the Manor Place Communal Baths, Dad told us he used to go on a Saturday evening to be clean for the Sunday and ready for school or work on the Monday.

At 14 years of age he was expected to find work to help with the household expenses. Dreadful unemployment affected every city all over the country; it must have been a worrying time for any school leaver needing work! Dad was extremely lucky to secure a job as a bell boy at the famous Kit Kat Club in London's West End. It was a well-known establishment where many notable people of the time frequented; he worked there for two years. Unemployment may have been exceptionally high but many of the better classes had a great deal of money to spend. I have to ask myself what has changed over the last eighty odd years.

Dad was fanatical about sports, he could be found regularly glued to the radio for the tennis and test matches. He also attended the Oval Cricket Ground, cricket being his outright favourite; he was totally mystified why anyone, including me, would find cricket boring!

It was some time during the period of 1931 to 1939 the family moved to 222 Tylecroft Road, Norbury, unfortunately I don't know the reasons behind the move but move they did.

In 1932 Dad became an apprentice sheet metal worker in E.A. Brown & Co (Ironworks) Ltd, Manor Place, Walworth, London qualifying in early 1939. On 3rd March 1939 he moved on to The Ranalah Ltd, Merton, London SW19 and stayed with that firm until 27th August 1942.

While learning his trade at 'The Ranalah' his work consisted of the manufacture and repair of cowlings, fairings, petrol tanks and aircraft bodywork, all of which had an important part to play later on when he was called up into the Fleet Air Arm, on 5th April 1943, he entered as Air Mechanic 2nd Class; and qualified as an Air Mechanic 1st Class on 5th November that same year.

It was around that time I began to take notice of the fact that Dad didn't come home every day and when he did it was like having a holiday, birthday and Christmas all rolled into one. His first assignment had been on 'HMS Gosling' but later on was assigned to 'HMS Jackdaw' 'Barracuda Aircraft'. He would come home looking wonderful in his navy uniform although we did have to be careful when sitting on his lap as his trousers were full of creases that all went the wrong way! Excitement would reach red zone level as soon as he walked through the door; Mum didn't get a look in with Monty the dog, David and me all fighting to be the first to command his attention.

On 21st February 1944 he was found to be "Below Naval Physical Standard" and was invalided out with stomach ulcers. He had repaired planes on the aircraft carriers but never went on a boat or flew in a plane and was never sent abroad during his wartime service; he was based in Scotland and was one of the lucky ones! On his discharge papers it says he was issued with an order form for a civilian suit and one shilling and nine pence for rations (Pre decimal days of course).

For years Mum would tell some incredible story of why he was medically discharged, she claimed it was because of him seeing so many pilots killed as they took off from the deck of the aircraft carriers that he developed stomach ulcers. It wasn't until just prior to his death in 2001 that I found out the truth, he had never been on an aircraft carrier or out at sea! Obviously as far as Mum was concerned being invalided out for just stomach ulcers wasn't historic enough, she must have felt the need to enlarge upon the circumstances as was her want.

Dad had an all-consuming passion for music; he had learned to play the piano in the conventional classical style as a child, but was eventually given up as a hopeless case by his teacher as he turned everything he played into swing and jazz. He had an incredible ear for identifying a subtle change of cord or particular style adopted by the different musicians and was tops at picking up all the latest tunes and playing them in his own individual style. He would be overjoyed when hearing any new song and quickly added it to his repertoire of favourites. Some of his idols were Duke Ellington, Benny Goodman, Count Basie, and Louis Armstrong, to name but a few. Between him and Uncle Wal they had a blend of the crooner type songs and the music of the day, whatever that happened to be.

Visiting the cinema a number of times a week was another great pastime, not only were the films good but it was also a visual way of keeping up with the latest news, seeing the stories on the 'Pathe Newsreels' put substance to the same stories they were hearing on the radio and reading in the newspaper.

As we were growing up Dad would sometimes forget himself and tell us stories of how he used to sneak out after his mother had gone to work in order to get up to all sorts of tricks, he never enlightened us as to what those tricks were he always made it out to be a bit of a mystery.

I would safely surmise that Dad's biggest fault was he always seemed to see greener grass somewhere other than where he was at any given time, as that thought always appeared to be at the forefront of his mind he moved around a lot seeking that elusive pot of gold. He was also a great debater, constantly on the alert to argue about anything he felt passionate about. His favourite statement or advice to us was *"you can argue the point but never the person"*. Unfortunately not everyone saw him taking his own advice; you could very easily feel nailed to the ground after one of his onslaughts. His leanings were towards the Labour Party by choice and over the years worked hard in the trade union movement fighting for the cause of the worker, I did at one point accuse him of being a communist as his idealism appeared to go along those lines, he was very upset when I told him that!

Just before he passed away he admitted to me that throughout their married life he never once told my Mother how much he earned, he gave her the housekeeping and she had to manage on that. I must admit to being pretty appalled when he told me as I had seen mum either go without because there wasn't enough food to go around or she had numerous part time jobs to earn just enough to make ends meet. But that was how it was in those days.

I loved my Dad dearly but he wasn't an easy man to get along with, he didn't suffer fools gladly and could be quite aggressive in his approach if he thought anyone was trying to get one over on him. Having said that he had a heart of gold underneath it all and would especially get upset when hearing of a child being neglected in any way and would always fight for the underdog. He was a difficult man but a good man for all of that.

≈≈≈≈
MUM
Maysie Emmaline MARTIN
21 December 1918 – 24 July 1999

Sadly I don't know a great deal about Mum's background, she didn't talk a lot about it and was a person who threw things of any interest away, so no records have survived that I know of. What little I do know is she was born on 21 December 1918 (see Appendix) at 100 Faraday Street, Newington, London, the second child and sister to Charles Francis born on the 2 June 1914, children of Charles Martin and Emma Churm. Two more children followed much later, Dorothy Leona born 29 March 1928 and Michael John born 26 May 1933.

I know Mum went to a Catholic school at some stage but have no idea where. I imagine it would have been connected to St Agnes RC church where she was married. She was a bright student and went on to work in the finance department in the Army and Navy Stores, in London, or Derry and Toms I think it was called at that time. As a child she was very ill in hospital with diphtheria and had to have her throat cut in order to help her breath, she had a scar all around her throat as a result. Her most lasting memory of that time centred on her father as all she could remember of him was being there all the time holding her hand. Of all the reading I have done about that period of time I don't think he would have been allowed into the ward, parents were thought to have an unsettling effect upon the child. I may be wrong of course, but if it brought her comfort to think he was with her who am I to say otherwise! She always spoke with fondness about her father but it was her mother who ruled the family. Mum's school life appeared to be good on an educational level as she left with very good grades, however she didn't have a good word to say about the Nuns who ran it, according to her they were very cruel and spiteful.

By the time she married her family had moved to 149 Lorrimore Road, Walworth, Kennington, Mum and Dad must have met up well before Dad had moved to Norbury. I think they moved to Croydon as newlyweds, sadly that is all the background I have of my Mum.

48

She is a difficult person to describe without my appearing too harsh. I loved her dearly but she wasn't an easy person to live with. There always seemed to be a power struggle going on between Mum and Dad as they were both very strong willed, but Mum was very dominant in the home just as her mother had been, Dad was equally determined not to be dominated by her or anyone else.

She was of an extremely jealous disposition and found it difficult to accept that some people could give of themselves without expecting anything in return; consequently she was very critical of my friends. On the reverse side she could be extremely generous and was very outgoing, she would meet anyone on the street, on the bus or wherever and within seconds be in conversation with them. She laughed a lot, exaggerated stories and incidents to a fine art and everyone thought she was wonderful. The darker side to her nature i.e. the jealousy, scepticism and bigotry were kept behind closed doors, it makes her sound an awful person which, of course, she wasn't, we couldn't have wished for a better mother. Towards the latter part of her life she became quite deaf and would misunderstand much of what was being said around her and would come out with the most hilarious statements that would cause us many hours of laughter. She would get things every which way but the right way, but always saw the funny side of the situation once we had explained why we were laughing so much. She was inordinately proud of the fact she still had all of her strong white teeth right up until the day she died. Unfortunately I didn't inherit her strong teeth.

There were times when she was very controlling and we didn't get on, however she shaped my life in ways that would prove to be invaluable as I embarked upon my own journey, this you will see as my story unfolds.

❧❧❧

GRANDDAD OVERALL
George OVERALL
4 December 1885 – 25 March 1955

Granddad Overall had been a driver in the Army South Corps (Motor cab driver) during the First World War. If you can picture him he was an exact copy of old man Steptoe in 'Steptoe and Son', a television comedy show, he was small and skinny, and for Sunday best wore a flat cap and white silk scarf. He had a full set of extremely loose false teeth that could easily have passed as the lead percussion soloist in any prestigious orchestra whenever he fell asleep. He had been born on 4 December 1885 at 22 Swan Street, Newington, London, the eldest son of parents Walter John Overall and Emily Craddock. His siblings were Maria Louisa born 31 January 1887, Lillian Emily born 26 August 1891, and James Henry born August 1893, more about them later.

Granddad always maintained he was a cockney but I'm not sure that Newington was within the sound of the Bow Bells situated in the East End of London, which qualifies an individual to be a true cockney. He had started work as an apprentice bookbinder but for some reason became a London Taxi driver after having gained the 'Knowledge' (which was a memorised map of all the streets in and around London), required of all taxi drivers before they were given the seal of approval and allowed possession of the famous black cab.

My main memory of him was someone who was a work-shy extrovert with teeth that noisily clacked together; he loved playing cards and would also play the 'spoons' on his knees at the drop of a hat. For the benefit of those who won't know what that means he would have two spoons, mostly dessert spoons, place the handles between his fingers and tap out a rhythm on his knees, it was amazing the vast amount of tunes he could produce and he was very fast. With Dad on the piano or piano accordion and granddad playing the spoons there was never a dull moment.

I have in my possession a common prayer book presented to granddad on 10 October 1896 from St Alban Holborn Sunday School. I shall be sharing more about granddad as my story progresses.

∂૭∂૭

Maria Louisa OVERALL
31 January 1887 – 9 June 1962

For years Dad and I used to visit granddad's sister Auntie Lou, she was in a hospital or nursing home somewhere in Thornton Heath. She'd had a number of strokes and couldn't speak but she always knew who we were and in her own way showed how pleased she was to see us. She had been born Maria Louisa on 31 January 1887 and died on 9 June 1962, which meant she lived for 75 years spending the greater part of her life confined to a bed in hospital

I have in my possession a common prayer book presented to Auntie Lou on 19 July 1896.

∂૭∂૭

Lillian Emily OVERALL
26 June 1891 – 15 October 1918

Auntie Lou and granddad Overall were the only surviving siblings, their sister Lillian Emily, born 26 June 1891, died on 15 October 1918 aged 27 years from the Spanish influenza that was sweeping the country just as WW1 ended. She was a *dressmaker* by trade and never married. The interesting thing about Lillian to me was I hadn't known of her existence until 2005 when I found her on the 1901 Census. It's a complete mystery why no one had spoken of her, we were such a close family, but her name had never been mentioned. The only conclusion I can come to is in days gone by when a death or tragedy occurred you showed the stiff upper lip, typical of the English, so it was never mentioned, you just had to get on with life.

❧❧❧❧

James Henry OVERALL
1894 – 8 April 1918

Granddad's brother James Henry, the youngest in the family, was born in 1894, he died in France on 8 April 1918 aged 24 years, was it because he had served and died in the war that he was mentioned in family conversations? Whereas Lillian was never referred to, I will never know! Henry, as he was always called, is buried in the Duisans British Cemetery Etuin, France. My very grateful thanks goes to the War Graves Commission as the information gained from them gave me the exact details of where he died and was buried. In December 2004 I was privileged to go and visit his grave, it was a very moving moment and one I will always treasure.

I have in my possession a medal and a tin box presented to him Christmas 1914, it contains a small Y.M.C.A book (which is a small copy of the New Testament) inside is inscribed a message to the troops from Lord Roberts which reads:-

25 Aug 1914

I ask you to put your trust in God. He will watch over you and strengthen you. You will find in this little book guidance when you are in health, comfort when you are in sickness and strength when you are in adversity—signed Roberts.

If more people in the world today, especially in Great Britain, would live by that creed there wouldn't be the inequality there is today, having said that it didn't do much for the many millions who have given their lives in all the wars. The people at the top running the show didn't appear to think that way judging by the appalling mistakes that were made by them. However I digress.

Of the four siblings granddad was the only one to marry and have children, which is quite sad when you think about it, without him I wouldn't be here to tell the tale!

෯෯෯෯

Grandmother OVERALL
Rose Edith JACKSON
12 August 1894 – 11 October 1951

Nan was born Rose Edith Jackson, always known as Edie, at 3 Exton Street, Waterloo Road, Lambeth, London on 12 August 1894, the eldest daughter of Joseph Jackson and Rosina Honoroh Reardon. Four sisters followed; Hilda born 3 May 1898, Elsie born 10 July 1901 followed by Kathleen in 1904 then Grace in 1910 (Kathleen is spelt with a C on the 1911 census). Great grandmother Rosina had been present at the birth of my father.

Nan was the complete opposite in size and temperament to granddad; she was a very large, quiet lady who was the mainstay of the family and a bookbinder by trade. Unfortunately I haven't been able to find out where she worked but it must have been close to where they lived in Clerkenwell in London. After they moved from London to Norbury she would travel back there every day to work, it was Nan who took home the wages each week. Granddad worked the night shift as a taxi driver and liked his game of cards! Dad told me how upset he would be when granddad arrived home in the mornings with little or no money pleading sickness of some sort, Nan would feel sorry for him, make him a cup of tea, then send him to bed before setting off for a full day's work. Sadly she died when I was eleven years old on 11 October 1951 after a long illness with cancer and I never really got to know her.

Before I close the accounts of the Overall side of my family I want to just add a few more items of interest as they in their own way are part of the genes I have inherited.

ঙঙ্গঙঙ্গ

James Marshall OVERALL
17 August 1858 - 17 May 1934
Born at 10 Thomas Place, Bow, London

James was the eldest son of my fifth generation great grandfather George Overall and Mary Marshall. His brothers were George William born in 1860 at Poplar, London, Walter John born in 1863 at Poplar, London and Henry Marshall born in 1865 at Poplar, London, all were true cockneys.

James worked as a tin smith, the same trade my Dad went into, near the Postal Sorting Office at Greenwich. He married Alice Charlotte Fisher and they had one daughter Alice, who had some form of disability and worked as a *music* teacher. James died in a coach crash at the 'Devils Punch Bowl' in Surrey; he was on a day trip with Timpson and Sons Coaches. Apparently the story was that the coach had reached a particular spot when the driver saw, what he thought was, a woman crossing the road in front of him, except it wasn't a live woman it was supposedly a ghost of years gone by. The driver swerved to avoid her and sadly great uncle James was killed. A shortened story of this event did appear on the front page of the Daily Express on 18 May 1934. I've included this story purely out of interest.

Brother Henry had a son Harold Osborn Overall who played the *piano* in a band; he married an Eve Martin, no relation to my mother, and sadly they were

54

unable to have children. I was privileged to meet and get to know Auntie Eve before she passed away, what a lovely person she was. It was her who gave me a lot of the background information and memorabilia of that branch of the Overall family.

I have done a lot of family research and know quite a lot about certain individuals, but I've chosen the ones mentioned because there is the theme of music running through and you will see why that is important later on in my story.

ৡৣৡৣৡৣ

GRANDDAD MARTIN
Charles MARTIN
16 April 1887 – 19 September 1947

Granddad Charles Martin was a very quiet gentle man who sadly didn't make much of an impression on me; I had only just turned seven years old when he died. He was the exact opposite of all the other extraverts in the family. He was born on 16 April 1887 at 52 Westmoreland Road, Walworth, London, to Scottish parents Jasper Martin and Janet (or Jessie as she was called) McFarlane. He was one of fourteen surviving children; the family story goes they had twenty-one in all. He was a horse handler during the war and was a Private in the Northumberland Fusiliers 55741(Post Office Porter) in 1918. He was killed in a car accident on 19 September 1947. The account was in one of the newspapers and read as follows:-

MAN'S FACE HIT WINDSCREEN:
Woman's Story of Road Tragedy

A woman described at Croydon Coroners court on Wednesday how, driving home with her husband in their car along Mitcham Road, Croydon she saw a man's face hit the windscreen in front of her and splinter the glass. The inquest was on Mr Charles Martin, builder's labourer, aged 60, of Sumner Road, South Croydon, who died from injuries received when he was hit by the car.

The wife, Mrs Emma Martin, said her husband was perfectly healthy except for a slight deafness in one ear. He went to work as usual on Friday and went out in the evening after listening to the 9 o'clock news to fetch beer from the off-licence in Mitcham Road. Later she was told of the accident.

Mr Charles Victor Gilbert, of Sutherland Road, Croydon said he was walking along the Mitcham Road towards Mitcham and said "I heard a bang in front of me, looked up and saw somebody lying near to the kerb. Somebody shouted and a car stopped just behind me" he continued "I helped Mr Beecraft to lift the man up"

The Drivers Story

Mr Stanley Harold Pithey of St Peter's Road, South Croydon, the driver of the car, said his car was a 10 h.p. Ford Saloon and his speed was between 22 and 25 m.p.h. He was driving at about three yards from the kerb and the road was clear in both directions. He did not see the man until his wife screamed out and a face came up against the windscreen and splintered it. He stopped the car and turned back. The spot where the accident occurred was badly lit.

His wife Mrs Hermione Pithey said she was sat beside her husband in the front seat of the car and was watching the road ahead. Suddenly a face came against the windscreen and she said to her husband. "O God, you have hit a man, you must turn back." She had not previously seen any pedestrians.

Dr Archibald Ray Anderson, senior casualty officer at Croydon general hospital, said Mr Martin was dead on arrival at the hospital.

*Dr David Haler, pathologist, said that Mr Martin died from a fractured base of the skull. He had face lacerations but no body injuries. Injuries were consistent with an impact and subsequent fall. The jury returned a verdict of "**Accidental Death**".*

Although I've said I don't remember a great deal about granddad Martin I do remember taking his supper to his place of work. He was a night watchman at a factory around the corner from where they lived in Sumner Road South and always had a fire going in a large drum outside in the yard; Nan always made enough for him to share his supper with me. He never spoke very much, maybe because he was deaf, but I loved being with him sitting around those fires.

જ⁄ક⁄જ⁄ક⁄જ

GRANDMOTHER MARTIN
Emma CHURM
28 January 1891 – 3 May 1959

Nan Martin was born Emma Churm in Wolverhampton on 28 January 1891 and was the illegitimate daughter of Susannah (Annie) Churm and Michael John O'Hara. Because of religious differences they weren't allowed to marry even though Annie fell pregnant in the hopes the families would change their minds. Not long after Emma was born they left her with her grandparents William and Susannah Churm at 53 Pearson Street, Wolverhampton and eloped to Boston Massachusetts USA. They went on to have a son and five more daughters but never lost touch with Emma. To my knowledge she did get to meet her father just once during her life as he came over to England around 1950/52 with the express wish to take all the family back to America. By that time all of Emma's children were married with families of their own and didn't want to go. My Dad was very tempted but the

57

stipulation was that he converted to Catholicism. As he was totally against being dictated to he decided to stay in this country, I never did find out why Nan didn't go back with her father as she had already converted some years previously. I've always thought it sad that she never got to see her Mother and siblings even though they constantly kept in touch with each other over the years; we often received massive parcels from the USA. The only sibling to marry was her youngest sister Leona, she married a 'Finnegan' and had three children, Susan, Joseph and Thomas, sadly the family have lost touch with them over the years and although I have gone through many channels to find them I've had no success. One of the stories in the family was that great granddad Michael John was a Tea Taster in Boston but when I eventually found them on an American Census he was a manager in a Pool-hall. The other family story, that has also been dispelled, was that John, her brother, became a catholic priest. After writing numerous letters to the Catholic Church etc. out in the USA, again no success, I eventually found out that he too was an assistant manager of a Pool-hall. Mary, Florence, Jennie, and Annie never married. They always seemed to be very well off, had a holiday home on Cape Cod and sending expensive parcels over to, not only Nan, but other members of the family as well. Now that I know that great granddad started off by managing a pool hall I've wondered how he got on during the prohibition in the 1920s, was that when he made his money; don't forget he was an Irish American Catholic by then, however I am only speculating but it has made me wonder!!!

Nan was still living with her grandmother at the same address in Wolverhampton in 1901, how she came to move to London I have no idea. I did eventually find her on the 1911 Census and she was a domestic in some sort of convent where she met the person who was to become her future sister-in-law Isabella Martin. It was also said that she worked for a Jewish jeweller but I cannot confirm that, she did refer to herself as a Silver Cleaner (Jewellers) so there may have been some substance to the story. On doing some of her family history research a few years ago I spoke to a number of people from Wolverhampton and came to realise she hadn't had an accent like they did. I rang cousin Pearl and asked her but she said the same thing, Nan did not have a Wolverhampton accent so how, why or when did she lose it?

Apparently, according to my mother and confirmed by her brother-in-law Len, Nan owned a cinema, presumably near where they lived in Newington London. How or why she came to own it I have no idea, was she financed by her father? Granddad Martin certainly didn't have that sort of background or money!

When I think about it, her background of working in the Jewish community and being close to the East End, owning a Cinema and later having so many dubious contacts during the War, she strikes me as being a very resourceful individual. She was certainly a dominant lady and a good strong Catholic; Mum would often say that the Church for Nan came before anything else.

I've thought long and hard about including this next bit of information, but it did actually happen and was part of who she was. For many years she was in love with her cousin Harry Williams and ended up having his love child. It was many years later but she did eventually marry him in May 1951, approximately four years after granddad died. The marriage turned out to be a disaster as they had both changed a great deal over the years and it finally ended in a divorce.

After Nan left Harry she separated her time between her children, living with them for a few months at a time, unfortunately she was skilled at playing one off against the other. Prior to her death in 1959 she made Michael, the youngest, the executor to her will, according to other members of the family he kept most or what was left for himself, needless to say that caused a rift between his brother and two sisters which was to last throughout the rest of their lives, I cannot substantiate the details but no family member had anything more to do with him after her death.

There will be more about the various individuals as my story progresses, but I do hope I have given a small insight into who I am and where I came from. The various traits, skills and temperaments you will see manifested in me as we go through the journey of my life.

My Dad as a Baby, with his mother Rose Edith Jackson and father George Overall in 1917

Mum and Dad in 1936, the year they got engaged

Mum and Dad in 1938 another Day Out, Mum loved her two toned shoes

Dad 1943 when he was in the Fleet Air Arm

Mum would have been two years old

**Mum 1934 with her Sister Dorothy (Doll) and
their Lodger Nancy**

**Mum 1938 at Ramsgate with her friend Kitty
with their very becoming Swimming Costumes**

Nan and Granddad Overall

**Nan and Granddad Overall again, see what I
mean about looking like 'Old Man Steptoe'**

**Granddad Overall's Sister Louise (Auntie Lou),
who spent a large portion of her life in Hospital**

James Marshall Overall 1934, who was killed in a Coach Crash, after the Driver had reputedly seen the Ghost of a woman in the road at the 'Devils Punch Bowl' Surrey

**Granddad Charles Martin who was a Private in
the Northumberland Fusiliers (55741)**

Me with Nan Martin, the staunch Roman Catholic, who tried to get me to become a Nun!

Chapter 4
"A Cottage in the Country"
Royston and Noon's Folly
Hertfordshire
1950 ------ 1953

This period of my life was to be a very interesting and challenging time for all involved, because it was like stepping back into a past century, especially as far as Mum was concerned.

In his line of work as a sheet metal worker Dad had met a man who was looking for a partner to set up a Car Body Repair Shop in Royston, Hertfordshire. I'm certain Dad had gipsy blood in him, he was always on the move to wherever he thought the grass was greener, and at that particular time, Royston had the greenest grass in the country.

He had terminated the rent on Birdhurst Rise and moved us lock stock and barrel to Royston. The first home he found for us to live in was a broken down caravan on a farm. I cannot begin to imagine what Mum thought or how she must have felt as it had no mod cons, running water or indoor toilet! Thankfully it was the summer; those were the days when we had seasons we could rely on, to David and I it was a great adventure. We had never seen cows or geese before and there were dogs and cats to play with as well, I don't know what happened to Monty our dog but he wasn't with us. My first taste of a goose egg wasn't particularly pleasant, mainly because the taste was very strong, but that was all we had on some days and we simply had to get used to eating them. Because of rationing and the general shortage of food during the war being fussy about what we ate didn't enter into the equation, we ate what was put in front of us or we went without.

Nan Martin was no longer around to supply us with any of the extra titbits or treats we had taken for granted but we did have a plentiful supply of fresh eggs and milk from the farm.

Up to that point, at each meal, we had always sat around the dining room or kitchen table as a family, especially for the main meal of the day which always proved to be a very lively occasion as everyone had an opinion about something and everything, we were encouraged to participate as long as we had some knowledge of what we were talking about. As young as we were we soon learned to listen to the news every day as invariably the topics under discussion were centred on the main items of the news. I could never understand why my parents and extended family weren't up in London running the country, they always had an answer for any given situation, as far as they were concerned the country was being run by a load of blind idiots and fools! If they were alive today I'm certain they would still be saying and thinking exactly the same thing! Sadly that is a trait I have inherited, I can rarely, if ever, understand the thinking of the heads of our government as the solution to any given problem is always crystal clear to me. However I digress once again.

The caravan didn't have a table, the extended family were no longer calling in and the dinner time discussions took on a different form as we had no radio and the newspaper didn't arrive until Dad came home from work, which was invariably after our bedtime. Because of the situation Mum found herself in, their relationship was somewhat strained and the interest in putting the world to rights became secondary to their present situation.

Before the winter had set in, Dad found us a 'Cottage in the Country' called 'Noon's Folly', this was reached by a dirt track leading to a farm with three farm labourers' cottages. The one we were allowed to rent was a palatial affair after the caravan, two rooms up and two rooms down, dirt floors, no electricity or running water, an outside dirt toilet, accessorised with cut up squares of newspapers joined together at the corner with string and hung on a nail on the wall. The lighting supplied was a '*Tilly Lamp*', which had to be pumped up to give out sufficient light, candles, and a small gas lamp on the wall; where the gas came from I have no idea. An open fireplace was situated in the 'front room' with a rusty, supposedly black leaded, stove in the kitchen. This less than ideal residence was also situated in the middle of nowhere. Our adjoining neighbours a Mr. and Mrs. Andrews were typical country folk and were life savers as far as Mum was concerned. Mr. Andrews would bring home rabbits and Mrs. Andrews showed Mum how to skin and cook them. We had approximately half a mile to walk every day to collect buckets of drinking water from the farm; we had a rain barrel outside the door which was used for everything from washing clothes, our Sunday baths, and anything else that water was needed for with the exception of cooking and drinking. As I've said, lighting came mainly from an oil lamp but we did have small ones to show us the way upstairs, they were very much like the Genies lamps in Aladdin only smaller, I also remember the gas mantles that were so incredibly delicate they could disintegrate at the slightest touch.

In Croydon Mum had been used to nice homes with all the mod cons of the day, she was most definitely a town girl having lived in London then Croydon all of her life and here she was living a life that was worse than when living through the war. She was extremely lonely, missed all the family and all the shops and to make matters worse Dad's business wasn't doing too well. Causing more difficulties was the fact he belonged to the 'Buffs' - (*an ex-serviceman's organisation which originated in a company of 300 men raised from the trained bands of the city of London and paraded on 1 May 1572 before Queen Elizabeth 1. The Company formed the nucleus of a body of British troops which, with many reinforcements, fought in Holland for the next 75 years, assisting the Dutch in their struggle against Spanish domination.*) - how Dad got involved in this organisation is beyond me. He spent quite a few evenings with his 'mates' arriving home at all hours, sometimes the worse for drink. It wasn't too long before Mum took matters into her own hands, packed our bags and the three of us went back home to Croydon to stay with Nan Martin. I remember it being a bit of a tight squeeze, with Doll & Len, Pearl, Mum's brother Mick who were all still living with Nan, but somehow we managed. Mum got herself a job in the local gas works, I don't remember going to school I can only conclude it was during the school summer holidays.

During the ensuing weeks our special treat for the week was going to the Saturday morning pictures at the top of Sumner Road South, I think it was called the 'Savoy' on the Mitcham Road; we loved every minute of it and never wanted to leave. The Saturday morning cinema in those days was totally children orientated, mainly I suppose because there wasn't television or any of the technology children have today. Saturday mornings were for children only and the camaraderie between us all was brilliant and we must have driven the management insane as shouting and missiles were part and parcel of the experience, and pity the projectionist if the film broke down, his life wasn't worth living, he was booed and hissed until he got it going again.

The man with the gong and the lion's head roaring at us indicated the start of the proceedings a hush would descend and the adventure began. The main attraction was an ongoing adventure story that always stopped at the most breathtaking and heart stopping moment 'To be continued next week' would produce loud groans but it was all part of the wonder of it all.

One of my fondest memories of our stay, at that time, are the visits we made to Len's parents house, they had a games room up in the attic where we could play an assortment of games, the favourite being table tennis, we always found it difficult to leave we had such a fun time. There was invariably Len or his brothers to play with and his Mother would always have some tea laid out for us all afterwards, they were unquestionably a different class of people as they owned their own house! As I have mentioned before, it wasn't considered to be the done thing for the ordinary working man to own their own house; I had often heard it said, 'you would be stepping out of your class' and staying within your class was very much a way of life in those days although it had greatly improved since the end of the first World War.

We were still staying with Nan in Croydon at the time of the "Festival of Britain" which was held at Crystal Palace in 1951. I remember going there and being in awe of the many objects never seen before, displays from all over the world, so many extraordinary things to see. Nan and her new husband Harry had taken us, but I'm as certain as I can be that Dad wasn't there. The day we attended was bright and sunny and we managed to find a cool spot to eat our picnic sitting by the very large central fountain. We were all happily exhausted by the time we arrived back at Nan's. It had been the most thrilling, out of this world day, or a more accurate terminology could be an 'embracing the world' day.

I don't know how long it took before Dad swallowed his pride and turned up to persuade Mum to return home with him, then once again we found ourselves back living in our 'cottage in the country'! I didn't miss being squashed in like sardines while we stayed at Nan's, but I did miss our Saturday mornings at the cinema and being thoroughly spoilt with all the special treats, for that period of time away it was as if we had been back living the good life again.

I believe the 'Car Body Repair Shop' business went into bankruptcy or liquidation, whatever it was; it brought about another change of direction for Dad. I don't know where the money came from but we suddenly had a car and Mum and Dad decided to start selling china on a circuit of market stalls, Royston, Newmarket and Haverhill to name the three that I can remember. Mum was a natural and could sell anything to anyone; conversely Dad was a different kettle of fish. I loved him dearly but he could be very temperamental and difficult and had the knack of easily upsetting the customers, especially if they couldn't make up their minds whether to buy or not. He invariably lost the sale because of his attitude and Mum would get so cross with him, the ensuing row would last all the way home. Needless to say that little business didn't last too long either; I've no idea what happened to all the left over china that didn't get sold!

One particular winter, it must have been 1951/52, was an extremely difficult one as it snowed heavily, deeply and for a very long time. The snow seemed to be totally different out in the middle of the country as everywhere was a wonderful pristine white wonderland, as opposed to the town where it always looked like grey slush. It caused Mum a lot of pain and hardship as she struggled with the frozen water, it was treacherous going down to the farm to collect the drinking water and the wood and coal were difficult to get hold of to keep the stove and fires burning. We slept with all our coats as well as blankets piled on the top of the beds as the icy winds found their way through every crack around the door and windows.

We were dressed every day in a 'Liberty Bodice' a very thick jacket like vest that had rubber buttons all down the front, we wore it under our top clothes to keep in the warmth, the only trouble was it made you itch when you got warm. If Mum thought we were developing any signs of a cold she would smother our chests with an evil smelling jelly like substance then wrap sheets of brown paper over the top kept in place with string. I'm not sure it did any good but, as a softener to the indignity of it all, we would have a twice daily spoonful of 'Cod Liver Oil and Malt' now that was something we did enjoy.

To add to our distress David and I were laid low with the measles just before Christmas of that winter and had to miss out on all the children's parties, we felt pretty miserable and sorry for ourselves. Dad had somehow got into Royston and purchased food for Christmas but we weren't expecting a great deal as we couldn't see how Father Christmas could find his way to us in the snow drifts (we still pretended to believe, it was more fun that way). Christmas wasn't like it is nowadays with hundreds of gifts, we were lucky if we got one present we had asked for, however, that Christmas Mum and Dad went out of their way to make it as special as they could, seeing as we were confined to bed in a darkened room. When we woke up on Christmas morning there were two brand new bikes at the bottom of our beds, I have no idea how they got them up the stairs as they were very narrow, steep and winding. By fair means or foul they somehow managed it without waking us, when we did eventually wake up we were excited and dismayed in equal portions, excited at having those wonderful new bikes and dismayed at not being able to go out and ride them, the snow was too deep and we weren't allowed out of our bedrooms, we didn't get to ride them for well over two months.

On another Christmas holiday I remember travelling back to Croydon on the bus and train, we split the holiday and stayed with either Nan Martin or Uncle Wal and Auntie Vicky who by that time had a small daughter Valerie. It must have been a Christmas back in 1949 as Valerie had been born the previous July and was still quite small. They had rented a flat somewhere, I don't remember where but it wasn't in Birdhurst Rise; I only remember what we did. Dad had bought a wind up trumpet gramophone with a dog on it, I believe it was called 'His Masters Voice', and a set of 78 inch records called "*Sparky and his Magic Piano*". Listening to Sparky's story with Dad was absolutely magical and cemented my love for classical music and the piano that has lasted me throughout my life. *RACHMANINOFF'S 18TH VARIATION on a theme by Paganini* has been my all time favourite from the moment I first heard it on that wind up gramophone. Dad also managed to get another set of records called "*Tubby the Tuba*" which again I loved; sadly neither of them has been available for a number of years now which is such a shame as they were a wonderful way to introduce children to music. Many years ago I managed to acquire a much shorter version of them and my son Ian and I spent many happy hours listening to them together. I recently found a cartoon version of Sparky and Ian and I got the same pleasure watching it. As the years have progressed and my enjoyment in listening to a wide variety of music has developed I have come to realise that certain pieces of music have the capacity to touch the inner most core of my emotions. There is something unexplainable and liberating about perfect music and all forms of art, I sometimes feel sad when I'm with another person who doesn't hear or see what I can hear and see, but what an incredible amount of joy I feel when I can share those feelings with another likeminded person.

Thinking back over those years it was a surprisingly happy time for David and I as we enjoyed a freedom we hadn't had before. In the summer Mum would pack us up a sandwich and a bottle of water and off we would go out on our bikes to explore the surrounding countryside, we didn't have any restrictions, as such, as long as we were home in time for tea.

During the summer holidays we had a wonderful time 'helping' the local farmer with the hay bailing, riding on the tractors or farm carts and getting thoroughly dirty, tired and sun tanned.

One of the people we used to hang around with was a boy called Maurice Mailing, he was local to the area and knew all the best places we could go to on our bikes; he would help us 'townies' to find bird's nests and many more interesting things we didn't know about or had never experienced before. It was quite a long cycle ride to get to where he lived but it was worth it as he was the one who added adventure to our days even if at times that adventure was questionable! I vividly remember playing in a wood fairly close to home when we disturbed a wasp's nest, they were all in my hair and I couldn't get rid of them, I ran home screaming and Mum threw a bucket of water over me. My face and head were stung and I was in a mess for a number of days but fortunately I didn't come to any major harm, I've disliked wasps and bees ever since, on second thoughts using the terminology dislike is perhaps too strong it would be better to say I am still a little afraid of them.

While on the subject of playing, considering some of the dangers we occasionally encountered we had a couple of children's cane chairs that Nan Martin had given us one Christmas. We used them all the time for the basis of a variety of games wherever our imaginations took us, we could be pirates, cowboys, even racing car drivers, the list was endless. One day David was using his chair tipped on its side as a horse and somehow I knocked him over, I hasten to add it wasn't deliberate; he tipped over the chair falling face down, knocked one front tooth out completely and broke another tooth in half which imbedded itself into his bottom lip. Dad must have had the car then as David was rushed into Royston to a dentist. They managed to put the tooth back into the socket again but could do nothing about the broken one. I can't even begin to imagine the pain he must have gone through and I was utterly mortified at what I had done even though it had been an accident. I believe the tooth piece did eventually work its way out of his lip!

Although our life was carefree and fun filled, one thing I really was scared of was the dreadful outside toilet. It had a double hole to sit on, as it was meant for two people to be out there together. At first we all thought how disgusting that would be but when it came to the night time we could easily see why it had been made that way, it had to be the most scary place on earth, even Dad didn't like it out there on his own; cleaning the toilet buckets out was one of the jobs we could do for a shilling (a great deal of money in those days) Dad had to dig incredibly deep holes at the bottom of the back garden, the contents of the buckets had to be tipped in and soil shovelled over it, it was the most revolting task we had to do. Once again Mum kept chickens and grew her own vegetables, the soil was rich and fertile, due to the many years of the disgusting compost I've no doubt, but we were too naïve to put the two together at that time.

We had the most delicious apple/cross pear tree just outside the door and to this day I have never tasted anything to match it in taste, totally impossible for me to describe but unique, both in looks and flavour. In the back garden we had a huge walnut tree that would be tantalisingly covered in unripe shells, coming from a town we weren't knowledgeable enough to know they took a long time to ripen, it was hard to let them mature and we frequently tried to eat one but the outer shell was disgusting, however they came in abundance and were a great treat at Christmas. We also picked fruit from the hedgerows and Mum taught me how to cook and feed a family from whatever we could either grow or find around us. That turned out to be one of the best things she ever did as, not long after their reconciliation, Mum became pregnant with her third child. In spite of experiencing two pregnancies, she was unaware of having a rare rhesus negative blood group; Dad's was positive, which meant their blood groups weren't compatible. Because of this Mum became very ill and had to be taken into the Cottage Hospital in Royston. David and I were sent to stay with Uncle Wal and Auntie Vicky who by that time had moved to Southend-0n-Sea in Essex where Uncle Wal was the manager in a Newsagents shop.

We had a brilliant time staying with them although it must have been hard on Auntie Vicky as she had two small daughters, Valerie was approx three years old and Lesley was only a few months old. One of my favourite pastimes each day was trying on Auntie Vicky's hat that she wore at her wedding, it was a wonderful fluffy creation of pink feathers and I absolutely adored it. I've always loved wearing hats and I'm certain it was that beautiful hat that started me off. It has been said that children only remember the sunshine of their holidays and that is how I remember that summer, sand, sea and sunshine, an indoor flushing toilet, and plenty of sweets to eat that were a treat at the end of each day for having been good.

Mum was still in hospital when we returned home, which must have been the end of the school holidays, and I had to take over the cooking and running the house. At the start Dad and I had a few difference of opinions over the cooking but Mum had taught me well and I was confident I was on solid ground, I knew exactly how long to cook cabbage or how to make a stew etc. Dad soon learnt that my meals were better than his dishes of either raw or over cooked meals and turned the job over to me. Mr and Mrs Andrews were a wonderful support system to me as well as I was still only eleven years old.

Although we had dirt floors Mum had insisted on a carpet square being laid in the front room and the only way we could get it clean was by scattering wet tea leaves all over it and brushing vigorously with a hard broom. The tea leaves kept the dust down and the carpet always looked a picture after it had been done, until that is, the dirt started to seep through again. Layers of newspapers were underneath but the dirt still seeped through. We could earn another shilling for cleaning the carpet as it was extremely hard work, however I don't remember being paid during that time after all I was then the acting lady of the house! I'm sure I must have been given some pocket money, but not having anything to spend it on i.e. my Saturday trips into Royston, my memory tells me otherwise. The other hard jobs were black leading the range before the fire was lit and filling the copper up, which was in the corner beside it, with rain water from the barrel outside ready to do the washing or having our Sunday night baths in the tin bath in front of the fire. Last, but not least, was collecting the drinking water from the farm every day. When I think about it now I wonder how on earth I coped but I did and was none the worse for the experience.

Mum had instilled in me the need to keep everything as clean as possible, she used to say that however poor you may be a small bar of soap and a lot of elbow grease would always make you feel worth something and never feel ashamed of what you did have.

On the 4 September 1952, my twelfth birthday, Mum gave birth to my baby brother Keith Henry. I was ecstatic and couldn't have wished for a nicer birthday present. Mum and Dad had been going to call him Paul but David pointed out he would be called 'Pullover' at school if his name was Paul Overall, they saw the possibilities in that and named him Keith instead, years later he was nick named 'Og' at school!!

Because of the different blood groups, Keith was born as what was then called a 'Blue Baby' and was extremely ill. He had to have his blood drained and new blood put back. I don't remember how many times they had to do that before he started responding positively but eventually both Mum and baby were allowed home and I fell passionately in love with that tiny wizened buddle of joy, effectively becoming his second mother. They hadn't been out of hospital very long when we all went down with chickenpox and Dad got shingles, he was the worst possible patient and drove us all mad with his complaining and feeling sorry for himself. Mum still wasn't very strong and didn't have the energy to cope with him and us so once again I had to carry the load even though I wasn't well myself.

However it soon passed and we all started to get stronger.

Keith was what one might call a difficult baby, particularly during the night. Mum, Dad and I would each take turns in seeing to him during the night and there was a lot of bed swapping in order for the one on duty to be as close to him as possible. Thinking back we must have been either approaching, or in, the grips of the cold winter weather and, believe me, the winters were very cold in those days. However much we tried to keep him and ourselves warm it was always worse during the night, I would guess it was the cold that woke him up so many times every night.

Keith was only a few weeks old when we received an extra large parcel from the Aunts in America, in it were the most beautiful romper suits for Keith, food parcels full of all sorts of things we had never seen before and, my most treasured present of all, a number of books to read. Aunt Leona's daughter Susan was about my age and we had became pen pals and there was a long letter from her as well. I don't know when or how it happened but I've always regretted losing touch with her.

I loved reading those books but as we only had paraffin lamps, candles or one gas mantle we could only use one at a time. I found my eyes would get very sore and I ended up needing glasses, having arrived at the age of being very self conscious I rarely wore them and now have to wear them all the time. That was vanity for you, but if you had seen the sort of frames they had then I'm certain you would understand why I had felt that way.

Saturday was still the special day of the week when we would catch the bus into Royston, it was market day and the place would be crowded. I used to buy a small bunch of Anemones to take home to Mum, it was one of the first purchases I made until I came to realise they were wilted by the time I got them home, as soon as that lesson had been learnt I left them until the last possible moment before buying them., they were still wilted but not quite as much. There would always be a group of Jockeys from the local stables all dressed up in their finery, making a tour around the town. I had just turned twelve years old when I fell hopelessly in love with a jockey called Peppy. I wasn't very big at that age but he was even smaller than me and we must have made a comical pair, but I didn't care, as I thought he was wonderfully handsome and dreamed of him all the week until I saw him again. David and I used to separate and go our own separate ways most of the time, but would meet up to go swimming in the outdoor swimming pool although David wasn't very keen, for some reason he didn't like it there. Then it was on to the cinema, where our last stop and treat of the day would be. If the film was late in finishing or we stopped talking for too long we would miss our last bus home which meant a walk of approximately three miles up a steep hill with no street lights, then down the dirt track where there were always bats flying about over our heads. Whenever we missed the last bus we would always be in big trouble and grounded for at least a month which, in a way, we didn't mind as it gave us the opportunity to earn more pocket money. We never gave a thought about Mum being frantic and on edge until we arrived home, we just accepted that the punishment had to be endured. You must remember we were still only 10 and 12 years old.

There was a list of jobs we had to do before we got a penny of our pocket money, but we could earn more by doing more jobs that were priced from a penny up to a shilling depending upon the difficulty or the amount of dirt involved. My heart was always pining not seeing

Peppy during that time but practicalities usually won me over, the more money we could earn meant the more we could do when we were allowed out again.

One Saturday feeling confident in the knowledge I wouldn't be seen by anyone I knew, I bought a lipstick to wear while I was out. Peppy and I were walking in the park when who should came up behind me was my Dad, I was mortified as not only had we been holding hands but I was wearing lipstick as well and I was still only twelve years old. Yes, you have guessed it, I was grounded again, but for much longer that time, I had broken all the rules, the main one being I wasn't looking after my ten year old brother! When you think of the conditions of today where you can't let your children out of your sight for fear of what could happen, we had an incredible amount of freedom and opportunities to explore and develop our imaginations to the full.

Not long after Keith was born one of the main things that caused me the greatest sadness was the breakdown of my relationship with David. We had always been very close and done everything together but my joy and devotion to Keith drove us apart, I suddenly didn't have any time to go off on adventures or do the things we had always done, with the exception of our Saturday trips into Royston. Understandably David was jealous and I got cross with him if I thought he had deliberately made Keith cry.

In the winter months our Saturday evening pastime of listening to the radio had continued, except that we didn't have electricity, the radio had two quite large batteries that constantly ran low. Dad would put them in the oven to warm up and on most occasions they would take us through one program or two if we were very lucky, which meant we had to be very selective; the only sure way to listen to our favourite was to have been extremely good or particularly nice to someone during the week.

Another of my lasting memories of the radio was Mum and Dad sitting in front of it late on a Saturday afternoon checking their football pools. I don't know how many years they each had a card to check, but to my knowledge they only won about £10 throughout all the years they paid in. If they had put the money they spent on it each week into a savings account they would have been well off. Their mentality must have been rather like doing the lottery of today there was always the chance to win big, except that they never did.

Another treat for me happened on a Wednesday when a baker's van used to call and Mum would buy a chocolate cake which was my all out favourite in those days. I have a vision of me eating it all but I think that must have been a happy illusion on my part, I'm absolutely certain there was no way Mum would have allowed that to happen. I said previously that we ate well, but when I think about it now everything we had was intended to fill us up at a minimal cost. A crusty suet pastry with a soft centre made any meat go a long way, and there were wonderful fluffy dumplings on top of the stews; bread and dripping sprinkled with salt; and potatoes in all their forms. The favourites though, were egg and chips with lots of vinegar, fluffy mashed potatoes with milk and butter, or crispy roasted ones that were wonderfully soft in the centre.   Jam tarts, bread puddings that were made from the left over stale bread soaked in water which would then be squeezed out, followed by lots of spices, suet, dried fruit, and beaten eggs added to the mixture before being baked in the oven (I have never tasted any as delicious as my Mum made). The smell as it was cooking made your mouth water, we eagerly waited for it to come out of the oven and cool down slightly before devouring every wonderfully delicious mouthful, we would have it cold the next day with custard. Then there were pancakes smothered with either treacle or lemon and sugar; suet was also used for mouth watering puddings steamed with treacle, jam, lemon or sultanas, then there was a jam or fruit roly-poly either steamed or cooked in the oven. There isn't anything today that can equal those incredibly delicious, comforting meals, in today's society they would all be considered a dietician's 'diet from hell', however in those days they were all designed to fill the tummy and bring comfort in a time of want.

I had our next door neighbour to thank for teaching me about the food we could collect from the hedgerows, blackberries, hazel nuts, and wild strawberries, if you knew where to find them; it was an education in itself having come from a town and never having seen any of them before. My first experience of finding Sloane's which looked like small plums wasn't very pleasant as they are extremely bitter, they are great as a jelly and, I was told, they made a good drink for Christmas, but we didn't like them at all. Mum had no way of preserving any of the fruit in those days, even had she have known how to, so we ate what we managed to find, when they were in season, whilst we were out on our travel's exploring the surrounding countryside.

At some point during our Noon's Folly internment Nan Martin came to visit with us for a while, not many days had passed before I found out that the purpose of the visit was to set about 'saving' me, within hours of her arrival she quietly began working on my attending a Catholic school with the long term aim of me eventually becoming a Nun! Mum had been brought up a Catholic and Dad a Protestant and there had been many a battle against them marrying, but they had successfully weathered the storms and, regardless of the opposition, went ahead and married without Dad having converted. When, or if, any children came along they had decided not to have them christened, they felt each child should choose for themselves when old enough to make up their own minds. That was a very hard cross for Nan to bear, she was determined I would be taken out of the paths of evil and guided into the paths of righteousness, then to get me into a convent. By achieving that end she felt it would be restitution for my having no legality or heresy as she viewed it. I don't know why but she didn't appear to be as concerned about David.

She organised a day out into Royston for just the two of us and took me to visit a very beautiful convent on the outskirts of the town. It's incredibly difficult to adequately describe with words the feelings and atmosphere the interior of that building generated, all I can remember about the visit, was the stillness, silence, tranquillity and peace I felt there. There were statues of Jesus and his mother Mary and various Saints placed in alcoves along the corridors, and the Nuns appeared to glide across the floor without their feet touching the ground, with just the barest swish of their long black gowns breaking the silence. After a lengthy discussion with the Mother Superior, none of which can I remember, Nan went ahead and booked me a place to attend the local Catholic school. In my untutored, non religious mind it had no significance to me whatsoever; neither did the warning of not telling my parents. I was far too excited at having spent such a lovely and extraordinarily different day with my Nan to recognise the importance of secrecy.

When we arrived back home Mum found out by me relating the day's events, having completely ignored the need for secrecy. All hell broke loose, it was as if WW11 had started all over again. Mum was beside herself, she was so angry, it made matters worse when Nan insisted we were bastards; we had been born out of wedlock in the eyes of the Catholic Church as Mum and Dad hadn't been married in the sight of God. The atmosphere became even more vocal and heated after Dad arrived home, Dante's Inferno comes to mind as the heat of his temper radiated from him. After the most horrendous argument imaginable, Dad immediately packed her bags then drove her into Royston, presumably to put her on a coach back to Croydon. I cannot begin to imagine what the conversation must have been like during that journey, the colour 'blue' comes to mind! The volume created at home was loud enough to carry all the way through to London, what it must have been like out of our hearing I can only guess. Nan was suitably ejected with what was described as having a flea in her ear and told never to darken his doorstep again; personally I was rather disappointed as I always enjoyed being with Nan mainly I think, because she spoilt me rotten. At the time I often wondered if I would have been happier at Nan's chosen school, but Mum and her brothers and sister had all been sent to a catholic school and both Mum and her older brother Charlie, in particular, had many unhappy and unfortunate experiences at the hands of the Nuns. Charlie had a broken ear drum at one point because of a beating about the head he had received. Some other often told horror stories are not worth repeating; suffice it to say Mum was adamant I was not going to be sent to a Catholic School. I think it must have been at that point in my life when I started to think about God and wonder if he really did exist; it certainly sowed some seeds and started me off on a journey of discovery that was to take me along many different roads.

One long hot summer I remember an incident occurring which involved the local farmer's grandson who used to stay with his grandparents during the summer holidays. He was a big sissy in front of his grandmother who treated him like he was something fragile and was certain he could do no wrong, but truth to tell, he was a bully and very sly. I must have upset him on one occasion, the next thing I knew I was being called back home and given a grilling for using bad language. I can honestly say I hadn't, but Mum didn't believe me, even though I had unthinkingly sworn on the bible as to my innocence. What had possessed me to say that I do not know but I should have known better, religion at that time was a very sore point in our house, it only made matters worse and I suffered the indignities of a good hiding and bed without anything to eat? He most definitely paid for it the next time I caught him away from the watchful eye of his grandmother!!!

During all this time Dad had a number of jobs, but the one I remember the most was when he worked for a factory making Caravans. It was beginning to be a growing industry at that time, families were starting to be able to afford a few days holiday in a caravan by the sea. Dad's job was putting in all the fitted cupboards etc. He would bring home all the off cuts of wood and metal that were being thrown away and set to and started assembling them into something quite creative. We must have been the first family ever to have a smart fitted kitchen, built on a dirt floor with no running water or basic utilities. However it looked very smart and at last Mum had somewhere to keep her food and cooking utensils out of sight.

We didn't have fridges or freezers, even if there had been electricity, food was kept cool and mice proof by a number of innovative methods. A bucket of cold water kept the milk from going off; biscuit tins were used to store anything from bread, cakes and pastries, to cooking fats and the like. We did have a cupboard that was on the coldest side of the cottage with a cold stone shelf and a small mesh covered, air vent, it was very basic but worked quite well, very much like the old fashioned larder with a marble slab, except ours was a lot more primitive.

Hygiene was paramount as far as Mum was concerned; however it involved a lot of hard work. She insisted we had a strip down wash every night before bed and every Sunday night we all had a bath, in a galvanised tin bath beside the fire, all using the same water. When I think of it now with the luxury of showers it must have been dreadful. David and I took it in turns as to who would go first each week, then after drying our hair by vigorously rubbing it hard with a warm towel, checking for any signs of lice and my hair being brushed dry in front of the fire we would be sent up to bed. By that time Dad would be ready to have his bath which had been topped up with hot water from the boiler, then last of all Mum would have hers. Dad would drag the tin bath out into the garden and ladle out all the dirty water while Mum dried her hair in front of the fire. Every Sunday afternoon the boiler beside the grate had to be filled up with rain water using a bucket, this made it extremely heavy work taking up quite a lot of time, it was then heated up for our bath with enough over for top ups for Mum and Dad. It's no wonder they used the same water as the filling and emptying the one tub was a major task every week. During the summer the water in the rain barrel had to be used sparingly as well especially if it hadn't rained very much.

It was during bath time we listened to the Sunday evening play, I think it lasted for the half an hour it took David and me to have our baths. Just prior to our Sunday evening baths the fire in the front room was built up and we were allowed the final treat of the day, toasting slices of bread or crumpets on the end of a three pronged toasting fork. By the time we had finished our cheeks were glowing red and our mouths covered in melted butter and a selection of jams and golden syrup, courtesy of Mrs Andrews. Our tummy's were full, our minds still dwelling on the radio play we had heard, we were clean and scrubbed and ready to face the oncoming week, or that was how Mum saw it.

Our time of living in our 'cottage in the country', was coming to an end and despite the hardships and lack of amenities etc. My overall memories are happy ones as the freedom we enjoyed and the new things we learnt stayed with me during a time when I had little else to think of, but that story comes later on.

Once again I have resisted mentioning anything about school as my memories are ones I really don't want to think about, however as those experiences are part of my development as an individual they must, therefore, have a place in the narration.

There was a big field we had to cross in order to get to the main road where the school bus stopped to pick us up. No matter what the weather, wind, rain, snow (I can never remember sunshine during school hours) we trudged across the field with Mum standing by the door watching us in the distance to make sure we caught the bus. I tried all sorts of delaying tactics in spite of all the dire warnings of the punishments I could look forward to if I missed the bus.

The main source of any threatened punishment was a large thick wooden stick; Mum used it to transfer the washing from the boiling water in the copper beside the fire into the tin bath that had the cold rinsing water in it. The stick was bleached white, just over two feet long and thick and knobbly, she only had to pick it up and we would run for our lives. Funnily enough I can't ever remember her using it on us, the threat was enough.

While my thoughts are on the washing, when I was about ten years old Mum had decided I needed to learn the basic skills a girl needed to have, in preparation for growing up and becoming a wife. With that in mind she made me do my own washing in order to teach me how it was done. I felt I was very hard done by and decided I wasn't going to do it, the lesson I learned from that decision was one I will never forget. After having worn all my underwear and blouses, the day very quickly came when I didn't have anything clean to wear, which of course meant I couldn't go to school, or so I thought. Not so, Mum quietly explained that having no clean clothes was no excuse for not attending school and made me go with a dirty blouse plus, horror of horrors, a dirty pair of knickers which, I was convinced, smelt of stale fish. I had the most dreadful day, certain that no one wanted to sit next to me because of the smell (there was a girl from a gypsy site who smelled and we all avoided her). I couldn't wait to get home and do my washing, the lesson had been well and truly taught. Judged by today's idea of bringing up children, some could say it was a harsh way of teaching, but Mum knew how particular I was and that it would only ever happen once, which of course was. That, and all the subsequent harsh lessons (as seen in today's society) she taught, has stood me in good stead throughout my life. Her daily maxim of cleanliness was to wash our face, feet and 'furry bits', the latter I will leave to your imagination! We used the rain water to wash with and when it was time to have my hair washed Mum would add a teacupful of vinegar to the rinsing water. The combination of the soft rain water and vinegar made my hair shine with deep auburn tints; it was very soft and silky for days after.

There was one thing she did that I found extremely hard to get over as it was very personal to me. After returning home from school one day I found she had given away my beautiful Jennifer doll and my dolls house. There were other toys as well, but they were the ones I treasured the most. There was a family who lived on the main road on the other side of the field where we caught the bus, they had a young daughter who wasn't very well and the family, in Mum's opinion, were not very well off, deciding the little girl needed the toys more than I did. She had done it with the best of intentions, but I wished she had asked me first. It took me a long time to get over that incident but from it I learned two things, 'there are people a lot worse off than ourselves, and to never take anything for granted' The latter I've had to learn a number of times over but eventually, over the years, it has sunk in.

When Nan Martin married Harry Williams in May 1951 a truce was called and we had to travel to Croydon as I was to be one of the bridesmaids along with cousins Pearl and Ann, Charlie's daughter. Harry was a very large man and not someone I liked, he was ex-army and a member of the Free Masons, who in those days were considered to be a strange group of people. I've since learnt over the years that the general public get very edgy about things or people that are different and the masons fell into that category.

After the wedding they lived in Nan's house at Sumner Road South but sometime later went to live in Brighton, I don't know if it had been Harry's home before they married or that they had got a transfer through the Council whatever is was, it started off a train of events that effectively brought to an end the happy times spent in that crowded and happy refuge. Doll and Len had been allocated a brand new two bedroom house in Addington on the outskirts of Croydon and at last had their very own home to live in.

Shortly after Nan and Harry had moved into their home in Brighton, I remember Mum putting David and me on a coach from Royston to London where Doll met us and put us on a train to Brighton to be met by Nan at the other end; we were approximately 9 and 11 years old. What trust in other people Mum must have had and what confidence we must have had, I cannot begin to imagine anything like that happening in today's society?

Now here I need you to use your imaginations as it's a picture that is difficult to explain. The Brighton house they had moved into had the front door in the centre of the building; the toilet was at the top of the stairs, parallel with the front door. As I've said Harry was an extremely large man and there was no way he could get into the toilet and shut the door on himself, the picture he made while sitting on the throne was pretty obscene as there was flesh hanging over the sides and his trousers would be draped around his ankles, a horrible sight to behold, but like all children we were fascinated and revolted in equal measure. Because of his size it was impossible to see anything of the toilet pedestal itself and Harry appeared to be suspended in mid air! To his credit though Harry was a brilliant cook and made wonderful soups, meal times were always like having Christmas every day, I loved his food even if I didn't like him.

On one of our visits to stay with them when I was slightly older, I must have been coming up for thirteen/fourteen; I met up with a young man at the local cinema. Unfortunately Mick, who was still living with them, saw me, the teasing I endured at each meal time after that was unbearable and he carried it on for the rest of that holiday!

As you can see, I've avoided recalling my time at school yet again, but I must make a concentrated effort to come back to the dreaded, rather be forgotten, school issue. I wasn't what you could call academically clever, whereas David was, so much so he was more often than not in the same class as me. The teachers would ask me questions I couldn't answer and then ask David to tell me, and the class, what the answers were. I was embarrassed and humiliated and at that age when every child is trying to find out who they really are, my feelings of self-worth were at an all time low. Although I had dark brown hair I was more often than not referred to as the dumb blond and I hated every minute of my time there. The dumb blond issue had been affectionately directed at me by my family for many years as I was, and still am, hopeless at spelling. Affection it may have been and I'm certain it wasn't meant unkindly, but the inner feelings of ignorance and inadequacy that terminology engendered stayed with me right through to my mid/late thirties.

However there was one special teacher who was able to bring out the best in me at school, a Mr. Ogden. He seemed to see something in me that no one else could and I loved his classes, he introduced me to more literature, art and poetry that I had hitherto not known about. Attending his classes were the only times I could honestly say I felt anywhere near happy. Another teacher was a Mr Marshall; his family owned a market garden and Mum used to do some 'home work' for him writing out envelopes connected to the business. I have no idea how she got the job I just remember being surrounded by hundreds of envelopes at home. There was another lesson I enjoyed but I don't remember who taught it and that was learning all about bookbinding, it was quite messy but I took great satisfaction in following in my grandmother Overall's footsteps.

I was good at domestic science and needlework (all thanks to Mum having taught me well). The difficulties I encountered in both those classes were the items required to cook or sew and how much would it cost to buy them (it was extremely embarrassing if you had little or no money). In my case I had been taught to be more innovative in using different, cheaper ingredients, to produce the same dish. Unfortunately the teacher always thought I was being unreasonable when I arrived with something different to the set ingredients, I could never understand her lack of insight regarding why I was unable to take along the ingredients that cost much more than we could afford. I was also more advanced in needlework than your average child, I must have been seven or eight years old when I stared making my own doll's clothes on Mum's treadle Singer sewing machine, I could only just reach the pedal. I very soon progressed onto making my own clothes, consequently I was easily bored making an apron or tray cloth and quite often I was more skilled than the teacher gave me credit for. Unfortunately I tended to be rather outspoken, a trait I inherited from both my parents, it was never very helpful in those difficult relationships, needless to say, I was again considered to be an obnoxious child. The one skill the teacher did teach me was smocking and embroidery, I soon picked it up and enjoyed it very much as it allowed me to be creative, however I have never done any smocking since leaving school, I think it must have gone out of fashion. It was around that time Mum had decided to cut up her wedding dress to make some blouses and petticoats for me, as I was growing quite rapidly. I helped make them and used all the smaller pieces to make dolls clothes. As the years progressed I soon realized that Mum wasn't very good at sewing, she had taught me the basics and the skill from one of my ancestors passed over to me (Dad's Auntie Lillian was a dressmaker)

Another activity I was very good at, again all down to Mum's tuition, was cleaning out an assigned room from top to bottom, the domestic science teacher even checked the tops of the doors and windows but I never got marked down in any of those important areas. I think it a great shame that children leave school now without any idea of home management, budgeting and basic life skills to prepare them for entering college, university or setting up home etc.

I also enjoyed art and would have loved to have gone to art college, I'm not sure if they were around in those days, but even had there been my lack of skills in the set curriculum would have negated going on to anything as grand as a college. The only thing I did extremely well in was a handwriting test, each child was given a set piece of prose to copy out. Using ink from the inkwell set into our wooden desks and a nibbed pen, something like the fountain pen of today, I set to and using all the skill and confidence I could muster, doing my very best to be as neat and tidy as I could. Everyone was totally amazed I had done so well! Plus, miracle of miracles, I achieved a certificate for work well done, wow!

Some of the more dubious highlights of my time there in order to break the all consuming boredom of the school day, were visits by the 'Nit Nurse' checking for flea infestations in our heads, and a dentist, who was so awful I not only ended up with crooked teeth because of the work he did on them, but was left with an irrational fear of dentists.

Physical Education days were another nightmare as once again I was useless at everything I attempted. We were all expected to do a set of leapfrogs and no matter how hard I tried I could not get the hang of it. I was, more often than not, sent in to write an essay on how lazy or uncooperative I was being. Having an essay to write was a joy, even if the subject matter left a lot to be desired, 'the benefits of physical exercise'

I never saw it as a punishment as I was at my happiest in my own world of free thought and imagination. I usually got into further trouble when I handed it in as I never stuck to the subject assigned. My imagination would take me as far as seeing a frog jumping into his future life where he was free to be himself, I think that was a cry from the heart at the time. How I wished I could be that frog leaping over someone's back and getting away from school. I would always get a dressing down for being wilful. Needless to say, David was also very good at sports!!

Then there was the subject of our health!! We were expected to participate in attending school dinners; overall it was totally unimaginative, stodgy, heavy and filling. (I'm trying very hard to think of something positive to say, as I feel as if I'm being unnecessarily negative about everything). Have you ever eaten Tapioca pudding, or frogs spawn as we all called it, as it had that same glutinous texture with slimy round balls in it? Having come through the war and food rationing we were used to eating whatever was put in front of us and being grateful for any food we were given, but those school meals challenged even our hardened palates. We were very fortunate as when we returned home Mum would be there to greet us with the smell of something delicious cooking on the stove. One of my favourite meals during a school holiday was fried egg and chips, followed by pancakes covered in Golden Syrup and lemon juice; I can close my eyes and taste it even now, if that makes sense, I'm sure you will know what I mean!

Another good memory was the second love of my life (remember Peppy?), was a boy called Peter. He lived in an adjacent village, I thought he was wonderful. The crushes of silly 14 year old girls in those days were pure and innocent. We didn't grow up quite so fast back then and sex was definitely not thought of or spoken about.

I've made it sound as if every day at school was black and all the teachers were dreadfully cruel. They weren't of course they were all doing their very best, I just didn't fit into the mould of a perfect student of learning, in fact I was more of a tomboy, always getting into trouble. One particular incident that comes to mind, and one I am definitely not proud of, is the day I chased a boy, who was a little backward, around the school grounds. In an effort to get away from me he went to push open a door to the classroom and his hand and arm went straight through a glass window. I was more upset at what I had done than the punishment I received, I have no idea what happened to that child but it was something I bitterly regretted. When I hear of children today playing truant or displaying disruptive behaviour, I know I could have been one of them. I feel sad that schools aren't necessarily designed to reach all children. I cannot even begin to conceive what I would have been like had I been expected to stay on until I was 16 plus. I will always be exceedingly thankful that I was able to leave before my fifteenth birthday and go into an apprenticeship that gave me the chance to develop and stretch my creative nature, but more of that later.

One of the few very happy memories I have of my final year in school is a day trip to one of the London Museums with Mr Ogden and some of the girls in my year. Mum and Dad had bought me a mustard coloured, hip length, jacket; I loved it and wore it for the first time on that very special day out. He truly was the only teacher I have fond and happy memories of; he touched a spark inside me, that wanted to learn, and he was the only person who gave me the self-belief that I could, in fact, be somebody.

I vividly remember the day I left school, I was the only one who didn't cry, I couldn't wait to get through those gates for the last time. At the conclusion of our school years David went on to pass a scholarship to go to a prestigious school in Cambridge with one of the highest marks ever achieved in the school, while I failed my eleven plus and it was generally felt I wouldn't make much of myself during my lifetime! On that school leaving day I felt as if I was entering a Technicolor extravaganza. Suddenly every day was a kaleidoscope of colour, each day was something to look forward to, a day to enjoy and to savour all the wonderful light that had suddenly filled my life and my mind, I was free to be myself!

Even so one thing I did enjoy during those school years were friendships, I had two close friends, Joy who was blond and petite and Sheila who had the most beautiful auburn hair, the three of us used to do all the usual girly things together. They both excelled at sport especially hurdles and running, why they had me for a friend I will never know, but they did and we had some fun times together. Joy was the 'rich one' who shared all she had, I can't remember what they were called but she used to get a weekly magazine aimed specifically at young girls, I couldn't wait for the next one to come out and, in a fever of anticipation, wait for her to read it so that I could lose myself within its pages. Joy's father owned the electrical shop in Melbourn, they lived in a lovely cottage and Joy had a special retreat in the back garden that we used for playing 'house' in. To my knowledge they were the only ones in the village to own a television at that time. In June 1953 Queen Elizabeth's Coronation was televised and Sheila and I were invited guests, amongst others, who were privileged to watch it on the television. What an incredible day that was, I enjoyed every minute of it and can picture it in my mind today. I was still living in Noon's Folly then and had to cycle quite a distance into Melbourn, but it was worth the effort as I had an enormously magical day. As Londoners my family were inordinately patriotic and would never allow anything detrimental said against the Royal family, to have the chance to see the Queen on this wonderful new invention of technology, a television, was an absolute privilege.

I revisited the school in 2006 and found it had hardly changed, except that the large building beside it, (which I believe had been some sort of church or church hall in earlier years) had been knocked down, and turned into a car park. We used to have some of our classes in there, one of which was our geography class, not a subject I was interested in, surprise, surprise! The building used for domestic science and needlecraft lessons is still there, it reminds me of an old army Nissan hut. I'm not absolutely certain, but I seem to remember having our school dinners there as well. I find it very strange that some things stick in your mind as clearly as if it were yesterday and other things like where we had our dinners don't.

The only school day I remember in any great detail, which had a massive impact on me, was the finale of an incident being discussed in nearly every household in the country. This was the trial and sentencing of Derek William Bentley and Christopher Craig. Derek who was considered to be slightly backward, he had received an injury to his head during an air raid in 1941; this had left him with epilepsy and mentally rather slow, consequently being an easy target for the wrong type. In 1948 he got mixed up with a group of boys who got him into trouble, he was the only one caught and subsequently sent to an approved school. Because of his seizures and low intelligence he was released in 1951. Continuing to be an easy prey to unsavoury elements of society, he was singled out by Christopher Craig who was approximately three years younger, a nasty piece of work! Under Craig's influence Derek stole some keys to the local butchers shop and a robbery was planned. Unfortunately it all went wrong; Craig shot and killed a policeman. Because of having been in an approved school and the subsequent withholding of evidence by the police, Derek, who was 19 years old, was sentenced to hang. Craig, who was 16 years old, by law a juvenile, was sentenced to a term of imprisonment.

The hanging took place at 9am on 28 January 1953 (my Nan Martin's birthday) for a murder he did not commit. I know exactly where I was, I can picture it even now, at school about to attend a geography lesson, when hearing a Bell toll, we all knew the hanging had taken place! It had become very personal to me and my family as it all took place in Croydon and Derek's family lived very near to my Nan and Granddad Overall. Derek was the last person to be hanged in England. We had followed the events throughout the trial and I had come to think of Derek as a member of my family, consequently I was very upset and sad for a long time afterwards. It made school work for me even more irrelevant, as even at that young age my sensitivity to the social injustices of the less fortunate were heightened! I think there were a great many people all over the country who went through their own grieving process after that tragic event.

Me nearly 10, looking a bit scruffy

**Me as Chief Bridesmaid at Nan Martin's
Wedding**

Me again, this time with cousins, Pearl Winchester next to me, and Ann Martin.

❧❧❧❧

Chapter 5
"My Teenage Years"
Melbourn,
Cambridgeshire
1953 ------ 1956

Keith must have been a little over a year old when we were allocated a three bedroom council house in 30 Fordham Way, Melbourn, Hertfordshire. After Noons Folly it was pure luxury, running water, gas and electricity, a bathroom with flushing toilet and, downstairs in the kitchen, an Aga type cooker that heated the house and all the hot water. The sitting room at the back of the house was covered with black floor tiles and the windows over looked the garden and adjoining fields. But most important of all, Mum felt she was back in civilisation again, people could be seen from the kitchen window which was in the front and overlooked the road and houses opposite. Never one to be a shrinking violet, within minutes she was chatting to our next door neighbours over the chain link fencing that separated each of the back gardens. I seem to remember the very first thing she did was hang the treasured carpet square over the washing line and bang it all over with her own specially made carpet beater her copper stick, she hadn't been able to afford a proper carpet beater, she set to and beat that carpet near to death in order to get the dirt and dust out of it, when she was satisfied not one speck of dirt remained it was laid out over the floor and given the customary clean with the saved up tea leaves. She then set too with my help and polished the black tiles until they shown so brightly we could see our faces in them, it was then the turn of the few bits of furniture we had to be cleaned and polished. By the end of the day we were exhausted, my fingers were sore and my back ached, but what a feeling of pride and joy we both felt seeing the end result. Everywhere we looked our new home gleamed and sparkled and smelt fresh and clean and joy of joys, we were able to have a bath before going to bed with our very own clean hot water and we felt as if we had surely gone to heaven!

Melbourn as a village was, and still is, quintessentially English, thatched cottages, narrow lanes and a babbling brook. St Mary's church was in the centre of the community, as was the village school. At the time of our moving into the area a growing population of council houses were sprouting up. As a village it dates back to the Stone Age and a book written and compiled by the Melbourn Village History Group for the 2000 millennium is a delightful record of the village through the ages. When we visited Melbourn in 2006 I made some enquiries and to my delight was able to find my special school friend Joy, we spent a very happy couple of hours talking nonstop about our school days and looking through the village history book. I was thrilled when Joy pointed out a photograph of me, with a group of girls I remember from my school days, standing outside a coach ready to leave on a brownie outing; interestingly though I don't remember being in the brownies! Once again it's strange how our memories can be very selective sometimes!

By the time we had moved to Melbourn I was already familiar with most of the village, owing to my many visits to spend time with my friends Joy and Shelia, but I very quickly set to out to fully explore the surrounding area and find all the places of interest that only children seem to appreciate!

Now that we were living back in civilisation, the dinner time discussions started up again, all of our favourite radio programmes were avidly listened to, with no need to warm up any batteries in the oven any more. One of my favourite events of the week was on a Sunday afternoon, when Dad and I would sit at the piano playing duets. I had started taking piano lessons in Royston but wasn't very diligent with my practice; I have learnt over the years that piano teachers are no different from school teachers you either take to them or you don't, at that time I had a very low self-esteem and belief in myself and my abilities. Sad to say the piano teacher seemed to endorse those feelings of inadequacy and no matter how hard I tried she was never satisfied, I gave up trying in the end. However I did enjoy those Sunday sessions with Dad. After a great deal of discussion they eventually decided their money was being wasted on me and the lessons came to an abrupt end. Needless to say, now that I'm a great deal older and wiser I wish I had been more dedicated and carried on or they had found another teacher.

We hadn't been in our new home for very long when I became friendly with the Cutter family who lived a few houses along the road from us. I'm not at liberty to name names, but there were two sons, older than me who were very handsome and available. Sadly the one I was mostly interested in didn't see me as anything other than a friend of his sister, I was, in truth far too young for him! I found many reasons to be at their house when he was at home, but to no avail. I must have been a great embarrassment to them, having a silly thirteen year old mooning over them all the time. I was invited to join the family on days out and had a brilliant time with them all. Mrs Cutter wasn't English and had a beautiful, soft, gentle accent, far removed from the loud brash Londoners I was used too; I don't remember Mr Cutter at all I can only imagine he was out at work most of the time, I do remember being sent home before they settled down for their evening meal.

By the time I had arrived at the grand age of fourteen I had reached the stage and awareness of being a *woman*. I naturally needed extra money to purchase those items essential to a girl's self image, make up to experiment with, accessories, hair slides etc. My pocket money was never enough, so Mum encouraged me to get myself a job during the school holidays; I was eventually taken on by Palmers, the local fruit growers. Apple picking was hard work, the trees weren't very high, but it was rather precarious climbing the ladder, especially as I was scared of heights. Stabilizing the basket was an art in itself, added to all that was the requirement of making sure the apples didn't get bruised in any way. I used to take Keith with me sometimes, he had a *Silver Cross* coach built pram that had a false bottom to it, I used to pinch the apples and stash them away safely under him. My heart would race ten to the dozen whenever the village bobby approached as I was certain he would catch me out and arrest me. Although I was scared to death I still carried on doing it. Mum used to go mad and threatened to tell him, but somewhere deep inside me, I always felt he knew about it anyway. It never struck me at the time but Mum never made me take the apples back! Keith got taken for a lot of walks for many more of those underhand activities, scrumping was the terminology used in those days for stealing fruit that didn't belong to you!

I was the member of the family who always got sent down the road to buy tomatoes and a cucumber for our tea. There was a family who had a large greenhouse in their back garden who grew the said items and much more besides. The gentleman of the house in particular, liked to talk and I remember being lectured, on a regular basis, about the need for male and female cucumbers and how each were required for cross pollination, to stop them from being bitter, I've never grown cucumbers, but that information has stayed with me all these years. I believe that over the years science has now produced a cucumber that is somehow self pollinating I still don't grow them so don't know how true that is.

The local bobby used to visit our house occasionally as David used to get it into his head to leave home. I remember one occasion when he packed his bag and set off up the road certain that Mum would call him back, but she had decided not to. He got to the top of the street, stopped, looked back to see if she was following him or watching him through the kitchen window, she wasn't, at least he couldn't see her, so he turned around, returned home and as he came through the back door was heard to say in a very loud voice "I'll go tomorrow!" at the time there always seemed to be a lot of tomorrows, I don't remember him ever getting beyond the top of the road at least not until he was a lot older!

I must have been a real pain on the quiet, as I used to get involved in the game of 'Knocking down Ginger'. I've no idea why it was called that but it was great fun. At that stage I was in with a group of tearaways and tended to be leader of the gang. There was this particular house whose front door was very close to the pavement and had a large bush outside that proved to be very convenient. We would knock on the door; hide behind the bush stifling our giggles, until the dear old lady who lived there would open the door. After the third knock or so she would get either annoyed or upset at finding no one there, which we thought was hysterically funny. After a few times of harassing that poor woman she must have contacted the police as, unbeknown to us, the village bobby laid in wait for us to turn up again. I was in big trouble that time and was grounded for what seemed like forever. Mum and Dad had very strong views on how we should behave, and had made it crystal clear that, if we got into trouble with the police, we would be in even bigger trouble when we got home. A good hiding and sent to bed without any tea or supper was the punishment of the day, but that was nothing compared to having to stay in for any length of time and not being allowed out to play. After that incident whenever I went out the village policeman always seemed to be in evidence, or maybe that was my guilty conscience playing tricks on me!

A very painful incident happened one bonfire night. A huge bonfire had been made on some waste area a few yards from our house; it was intended to be a real community event, with baked potatoes and sausages etc. Fireworks were to be set off at a distance but the usual idiots, who think they are very clever and funny (I forgot at that stage I had been one of them), started throwing bangers into the crowd and one landed on my hair and set it on fire. Fortunately a man standing beside me very speedily threw his jacket over me to put out the flames. Although I was terrified at the time I fortuitously didn't lose much hair, only a relatively small piece in the front which took quite a while to grow back: even today I 'm not that keen on fireworks, except when watching through the safety of a window or at a great distance.

We did the usual normal childish things like getting into trouble on a regular basis, exploring the countryside during our holidays and when Christmas arrived we went carol singing, raking in a fortune, or so we thought. It was during that period of time I had started attending the various churches in the village, not any one in particular at first, but I did seem to frequent the Methodists more often than not, as the singing was always more jolly, at least that was how it appeared to me at that tender age. I had taken my first tentative steps of searching for something I wasn't very sure about at that time. My parents only found out about those Sunday visits when I started to be more particular about what I was wearing, I had become aware that everyone always looked rather posh and I felt the need to fit in or at least not stand out by wearing my play clothes.

Mum could never quite work out why it had to be, but for a number of years one or more of us, as a family, would be ill all over the Christmas holidays. One particular Christmas we all went down with a bad bout of influenza. In order to make her life easier, as she was ill as well, Mum took all the mattresses off the beds and laid them down side by side on the sitting room floor where we could then all suffer together. That way Mum didn't have to keep running up and down the stairs and we could all be kept occupied by listening to the radio, in particular the '*Queens Speech to the Empire*', we would never miss listening to her Majesty's message and still don't today, she is a wonderful woman who is greatly maligned and underestimated by so many of today's generation. Over the years Christmas dinner has always been cooked, and eaten, in time for us to sit and either listen too, or watch the Queens Speech. Christmas would not be the same without our sharing fifteen minutes with her Majesty. I wouldn't mind some of her money but most defiantly not her life as some of the media, society and even politicians give the royal family a ridiculously hard time.

During the summer months we had various members of the family visit us at regular intervals. Uncle Wal, Auntie Vicky, Valerie, Leslie, Doll, Len, Pearl, Nan Martin, Dad's youngest brother James with his first wife Dot and son Christopher, who sadly was very disabled, and last, but by no means least, granddad Overall. Whenever anyone visited we always seemed to end up in Cambridge to have lunch in the Corn Exchange, I remember it was a huge hall set out with what appeared to be dozens of tables and chairs, it certainly wasn't posh as it was aimed at the working classes but the food was always plentiful and tasted good. The meal was followed by a tour of the shops, and sometimes a visit to the cinema, finally, before catching a bus home, we would gather around the bandstand to listen to the band. They were always in the park next to the bus depot, we would all make a rush for the deckchairs and, whenever possible, sing along to the music. I'm not sure our presence was altogether appreciated, but it was always good to be singing together as a family again.

Granddad Overall was the funniest, although I think he gave Mum and Dad a hard time on the quiet. He used to send David and me down to the local shops to purchase ten Woodbines, Turfs or Craven A cigarettes. It was always done on the quiet as Mum didn't agree with us buying cigarettes, however the promised treats were too tempting to turn down. As payment for running the errand, we were allowed to buy whatever sweets we wanted with any change that was left over, who could resist, certainly not us! Every afternoon Granddad had his nap in one of the armchairs and that was when the fun started. David and I were mesmerised with his teeth. As I've already stated the sounds that his teeth created would have given any qualified percussionist a challenge, on two counts. One, to reproduce the decibels of sound they made, along with the deep throated snores, and two, to keep in time with the erratic rhythm produced by snores and teeth that worked independently of each other. We loved it and would rush home from school to ensure a front row seat.

Our regular radio programmes were Family Favourites, Workers playtime and Forces Broadcasts all people and music based which somehow gave a warm family feeling to the people all over the country. We always felt part of each family mentioned and we rejoiced with them all. There certainly wasn't the feeling of separation as there is now, we had come through the war and proud to be called British, the feelings of solidarity were still predominant then.

Mum, bless her, was a great one for teaching me the hard lessons of life, most of which I didn't appreciate at the time. As the years passed by I did eventually learn, and appreciate the value of the lessons, as they did, without a doubt, set me up for all that was destined to take place in my life. One such lesson that occurred involved my school friends, Joy and Sheila. Mum had been into Cambridge shopping and bought me some very pretty underwear. In an effort to show off in front of my friends I showed a certain amount of disdain and said 'I didn't think they were that special.' Without saying a word Mum immediately turned to Sheila and asked her what she thought of them. Needless to say Sheila thought they were wonderful, Mum promptly gave them to her, insisting that she have them. I was absolutely mortified and stood glued to the spot not knowing what to do or say. The dressing down I got after they left instilled in me a true appreciation for any gift I have ever been given over the years, I also learnt never to take anything for granted, I was well and truly chastened.

I was into my teenage years and experimenting with my self image etc. when I decided I needed a change of style. I didn't feel the need to consult with anyone else and followed my instincts and cut my hair. It was quite long and very fine, on that particular day of experimentation, I decided a fringe would look good and duly set to and cut it. Mum went mad, said I looked dreadful and called me all sorts of names, but it was one of the few times I was determined to stand up to her. I didn't go through the usual teenage rebellion as such, but that was one time I stood my ground, besides which, it was too late by then, my hair had been well and truly cut.

Suddenly those carefree summers were drawing to an end and it was time for me to start work.

Dad had managed to secure me a post as an apprentice hairdresser, I had no idea of how he went about it and to this day it's still is a mystery to me. Dad, bless him, had been listening when I said hairdressing was what I wanted to do and he helped me achieve my dream. Although I was terrified at the time, I thought I was going to get into all sorts of trouble as up to that point there had been only the one person, Mr Ogden, who believed I could achieve something good, nonetheless here I was taking those first tentative steps into unknown territory.

The Hairdresser's where I was about to enter the real world of people and experiences, was in Russell Street, Cambridge. It was a very small establishment with an outside toilet. Mrs Schmeler was the boss and owner and incredibly we liked each other immediately upon meeting, something I had been somewhat worried about, owing to my years of non acceptance at school. I was just a little over fourteen and a half when I first started working and I was paid the princely sum of £1.2s.1d per week. It cost Dad £1.6s.3d (pre decimal days of course) for my return bus fares from Melbourn to Cambridge, he used to say it cost him more to send me to work than have me stay at home.

Mum and Dad had bought me a set of new clothes for starting work, those clothes made me feel very special. It felt a little like a chrysalis emerging from the confines of the casing it had been in, suddenly emerging into becoming something beautiful and individual, I unexpectedly began to feel grownup and beautiful from within. Mum and Dad had always bought new outfits for us every Easter and Christmas but this was to mark a special event, their eldest daughter was starting work and entering the world of adulthood. The mid green skirt was a complete, seamless circle; the material had the appearance and feel of a soft felt, a bit like the suede of today only heavier, the waist was cut from the middle of the circle. The blouse was sleeveless, a very pale lemon and white silky fabric, with a little white peter pan collar. I felt absolutely wonderful wearing them and very ladylike.

From the very beginning I loved my boss, the work and the customers. I was keen and eager to learn all that I could. I attended collage one evening a week and enjoyed all the learning that entailed. As part of the contract of apprenticeship I had been made aware that I would be encouraged to attend college where I would be taught to make wigs and learn the science of colour and chemicals etc. the thought terrified me as I was so used to being an under achiever, however I suddenly found that I wasn't quite as dumb or difficult as commonly believed. I loved learning about the intricacies of wig making, hair colouring and permanent waving, along with the many other necessary skills to become a hairdresser. At last I had found my niche in life.

There was a small flat above the shop occupied by a single lady who enjoyed listening to all of Slim Whitman records, I don't know where she worked but she seemed to be home a lot as all we could hear was her playing his songs. We used to think she had been let down in love, as some of her favourites were of the sad, melancholy kind.

Being the only help she had, Mrs Schmeler soon initiated me into permanent waving as she knew I was leaning about the theory at college, what a terrifying experience that was. Very strong chemicals and electric curlers were used and you had to get exactly the right mixture for the different types of hair. Each section was soaked in this evil smelling lotion, rolled onto the special curlers, and then the customer was seated under this machine with lots of wires protruding from it, rather like an octopus. Heated clamps were put onto each curler and left for a set amount of time. As the heated clamp touched the chemical, vapours of steam would erupt and the smell very nearly choked you, your eyes and nose would run for a few minutes. How on earth the customers could stand it I don't know, but they did and went back for more. The task I enjoyed the most was cutting hair and again Mrs Schmeler gave me every opportunity to learn and practice. The customers were wonderful and very trusting; it was them who taught me how to give the best hair wash. They would tell me if I was rubbing too hard or missing parts out etc. until in the end I perfected the hair shampoo they all felt was the best. Some of them would arrive half an hour before their appointment so that I could shampoo, then practice setting their hair, before Mrs Schmeler took over. Oh how I loved those wonderfully trusting and supporting ladies.

My first winter there was a major challenge as everything became frozen up. Every day as soon as I had arrived for work my first task was to try and thaw the frozen pipes outside which serviced the shop and outside toilet. I had to use a paraffin blow lamp and be very careful not to do it too quickly, otherwise the pipes would burst. I suffered badly from chilblains on my feet and standing outside in the freezing cold didn't help. However, I survived it all without mishap and, in doing so, got to know a young man who worked in the cycle shop on the opposite side of the road; he would come over and help out if we had any major problems to resolve.

Michael was tall, had dark hair and was very good looking and we soon became firm friends, wanting for nothing more than to be in each other's company whenever the opportunity arose. It wasn't long before we became inseparable and spent many happy hours together; I would even go as far as to say we were in love, that special first love we all go through and always remember. We had Sunday afternoon tea at either his house or mine and spent all our free hours together. One of the popular songs of the time was Max Bygraves singing *'I'm a blue tooth brush, you're a pink tooth brush'* it was a particular favourite of Michael's mother. They were a wonderfully kind and loving family and I enjoyed being with them very much.

Mrs Schmeler's husband Paul was a refugee from Czechoslovakia and worked in the government offices, not very far away from the shop. We would meet up in the Cambridge University's Botanical Gardens for lunch, Mr and Mrs Schmeler, Michael and I, it was a time of sunshine, gloriously bright and warm, all my memories of that period of time are exceptionally happy ones. Paul had a son in Czechoslovakia and they were constantly concerned for him. I seem to remember them trying to get him out, but to my knowledge they weren't successful, at least not at that time.

For a very short period of time I was blissfully happy as I loved my job, my boss and Michael, but sadly it wasn't to last for very long because I suddenly started to have serious bouts of ill health. I'd been having problems with my monthly 'curse' as Nan used to call it; everything was very erratic and very painful. I had reached the stage when I found it difficult to eat, was in a lot of pain and bleeding heavily, not from a period but from the back passage, I was also losing weight rapidly. Mum took me to see the Doctor on more than one occasion; he said not to worry as everything would eventually sort itself out. He diagnosed piles, due to my having sat on the radiators at school! I got progressively worse until finally the day came when Mum was so worried she called the Doctor, but he refused to make a house call. I eventually passed out and Mum and Dad called the police to see if they could convince the Doctor to make the visit, he still refused saying a fuss was being made about nothing. The village bobby, who knew me quite well, assessed the situation and rang for an ambulance; I was rushed into Addenbrooks Hospital in Cambridge as an emergency. I was fifteen and a half years old, extremely ill, had gone into a coma and stayed that way for quite a few weeks. After numerous tests, x-rays and blood transfusions I was diagnosed as having Ulcerative Colitis. At the time I had no idea what that meant or how it would affect my life, all I was aware of was the pain I had to suffer each day. I later learned that the same Doctor who had refused to visit me, had refused a home visit to another patient who had subsequently died. Because the police had been involved in both incidents he was later stuck off by the Medical Board.

I was completely bedridden and on a very low fibre diet which was tasteless in the extreme. Visiting hours were restricted in those days to only two afternoons a week, a Wednesday and a Sunday for two hours. I believe that policy was introduced for two reasons, it was felt that having visitors too often upset the patients, it also cut down the possibility of any infections being taken on to the wards. Mum, bless her, came on both those days leaving Keith with neighbours, she always brought with her something special to cheer me up, mostly it was a book or a new pair of baby doll pyjamas or a pretty nightdress. I never questioned at the time how they could afford both the presents and the travelling expenses; I was too ill and overwhelmingly pleased to see them to consider the issue of how much it all cost.

It must have been a horrendous time for Mum and Dad as coupled with the anxiety about me and constantly worried that I might not pull through; they were being accused of all sorts of things as to why I was so ill. It was said they had neglected me, underfed me, and so on. In today's society that would have amounted to child abuse, I dread to think what the social services of today would have done about it as I was still under age. In whatever form the dreadful accusations took, nothing could have been further from the truth, my poor parents suffered many anxieties and humiliations of that sort. The third degree became so bad at one stage they started believing themselves that it was their fault I was ill. As time, further research and learning has proved, there is no known cause for Ulcerative Colitis, and to this day there is still no cure.

Colitis is a disease of the colon, the large intestine, a potentially serious disease of unknown cause. In most cases it is a chronic condition as it causes severe diarrhoea, with as many as 15-20 watery and bloody bowel movements every day and it can be excruciatingly painful. The obvious side affects are total exhaustion of body and mind, due to the loss of blood, vitamins and minerals. The brain functions through a cloud of mist and fog and concentration is negligible. That was the condition I was in and without fail every visiting time I would need a bedpan. I was always mortified and upset as I made the whole ward smell appalling, but I didn't have a choice as I was not allowed out of bed. Because of the loss of blood and after numerous tests had been completed it was confirmed I had the same blood group as Mum, A Rh Negative, as I had already been given a number of blood transfusions, Mum said she was more than willing to be a donor. For some reason they turned her down, they did explain it at the time but I was too ill to understand any of the information we were given. For a couple of days after having a blood transfusion I always felt so much better, it was if I had the energy of two people. It was always referred to as being 'black man's blood', powerful and strong. I certainly wasn't racist, I didn't know what that meant, I just knew that for a few short hours I felt really good, God bless those generous and wonderful black men, whoever they were.

The worst and most distressing test of all was having a sygmoidoscopy put down my throat; it was a thin tube with a light and camera on the end that worked its way through the gut and intestines etc. in order to see what damage had been done to those internal organs. The first time the procedure was performed my body went into shock; my survival was in the balance for a few hours as my already weakened condition made it difficult for it to fight. It obviously did and in the end I came back to the land of the living. That first time I was awake but, thereafter, because of the shock to the system, it was done while under anaesthetic, for which I was extremely grateful.

Another administration I had to suffer was a Barium Enema, which was a chalk like substance injected into the rectum before having an X-ray. It shows up clearly any tumours, ulcers or any abnormal conditions that may be present. Alternatively I had to swallow a similar substance in order for the X-ray to show them another part of my gut/stomach. That was absolutely revolting and I heaved on every mouthful I had to swallow. I cannot find words sufficient to explain how ill I felt; on top of all those procedures going on I started to believe they were trying to kill me off with every indignity and torture they were putting me through!

The highlight of each week was receiving visitors. I can only remember David visiting me once during my stay in hospital and that memory will stay with me for ever. He had decided to accompany Mum on one of her visits and turned up in a bright yellow sweater with a big blue letter *E* on the front. Mum had knitted him that extraordinary creation, he was crazy about *Elvis Presley* at the time and the *E* was in honour of his idol, he also waxed lyrical about *Bill Haley* and *Lonnie Donnigan's* skiffle group. His whole conversation was full of all their music. As I didn't have access to any music whatsoever it was as if he was speaking a foreign language to me, I hadn't a clue what he was talking about!

Shortly after that visit, and completely unbeknown to me, hospital radio was just about to take to the air waves for the first time. Mum got to hear of it and made a request especially for me. She wanted me to be the very first person to receive a request on the new programme, that piece of music would be one of my 'must have' *Desert Island Disc* records, she choose *Grieg's 'Greensleeves'* knowing it was a favourite of mine. I never did find out how she knew that, I can only assume she'd heard Dad and me listening to it and the discussion resulting from it. Mum, bless her, was tone deaf and her choice of music was very limited, *Lonnie Donnigan's 'Does your chewing gum lose its flavour on the bed post over night'* and *'My Old mans a dustman'* were two of her favourites, skiffle music was about all she could understand. However, back to the night in question, there was a great deal of excitement on the Ward as a new venture was about to begin, imagine my amazement when I heard my name announced as requested by my beloved Mother. I spent the whole time crying and had to be given a sedative to settle me down for the night. It's another memory that is very dear to me and whenever I hear that piece of music I think of my Mum.

One of the daily treatments I came to dread was two particular injections, one of penicillin the other streptomycin. The penicillin was very painful as it went into the body and the streptomycin stung, which was just as painful but in a different way. My buttocks were so sore and covered with black and blue bruises, I cried as soon as I saw them, the nurses were so sweet and apologetic, but it was something they had to do. They did everything they could think of to make me comfortable, but nothing lasted for long as I wasn't allowed out of bed. I was also being treated with some sort of hormone to suppress the bleeding, the long term effect that had on me was horrendous as I started growing thick black hair all over my body, particularly my face, back and chest, they had to discontinue that treatment in the end as the side effects were too disastrous and extremely upsetting.

Setting all the pain and bruising aside, in all my time in bed I never once had a bed sore as each day the same routine was administered to my bottom, feet and elbows. The treatment consisted of, first and foremost washing each area at a time with warm water, and then, very carefully drying, before a soothing cream was gently massaged into the vulnerable pressure points. It lasted for quite a long time as it was felt the gentle massage helped the circulation. Finally a powder was then smoothed over. At the conclusion it left a wonderful combination of relaxation and a release from any soreness for a while. When my bottom was at its worst, as a result of all the injections, those wonderful caring nurses would administer that treatment to me a number of times throughout the day and night, it was always the last routine of the day before I was settled down to sleep.

Sadly things have changed and that treatment doesn't happen anymore, bed sores seem to be common place now and all you get is a cling film like covering placed over the sore and nothing else, after a short while the film starts to curl and creates even more pain which only adds to the overall discomfort. Whoever thought that idea up has obviously not suffered with bedsores or been expected to sit on the film for any length of time. In my opinion bed sores are no longer kept under control and patients are left to suffer unnecessarily. While I am on the subject of changes within the National Health, many things have changed for the worst. One without doubt was the discontinuation of the role and authority of the Matrons, there is no longer the strict discipline that the Matron had over her hospital. Whichever hospital I have been in as a patient I remember those days of Matron's weekly rounds, everywhere was a buzz of activity, the wards had to be spotless, beds made to exactness, patients staff or visitors were not allowed to sit on the bed, and nurses had to be as sharp and clean as a new pin with not a hair out of place. Once a week all the beds would be stripped and made then pushed to the centre of the ward, none of the patients were allowed out of bed while the walls, floor and all the bed frames were washed down with disinfectant. The beds would be pushed back into place then it was time for the lockers to be cleaned before they too were pushed back beside each bed. Last but not least the centre floor was washed then polished with a heavy machine. That all sounds very authoritarian but hospital bugs and unclean wards were unheard of. Sadly those days have long gone, germs abound in hospitals today, I am absolutely certain they can all be traced to uncleanliness and lack of care.

As a very sick patient with a head filled with fog, one of the things I didn't like was the sound of the floor polishing machine. In my sick mind it had a dreadful droning effect and I used to plead for them to go away and turn it off, but cleanliness was paramount and I just had to endure the noise, for what was, in reality, a very short space of time.

I had been in hospital for approximately six months when my sixteenth birthday arrived and what a day to remember that turned out to be. I had dozens of presents from family, nursing staff, Doctors and patients, I was in an adult ward as they didn't have a children's wing and was totally spoilt. The gift that had the most impact on me came from two nurses, Susan and Elizabeth. Their gift was a beautiful red leather bound Bible, the card that went with it said 'If you want to learn of God you will find him within these pages'. I had been given many opportunities to pursue my interest in that direction over the months with visiting clergy and nurses who were practising Christians, and that bible became something very special to me during the following years. I still have it today as a treasured memento. The real excitement of the day came when another couple of nurses turned up with a decorated wheelchair with balloons and streamers attached. Amongst much excitement and hilarity they took me into the centre of Cambridge to visit a restaurant for afternoon tea. It must have all been pre-arranged beforehand as other nurses and doctors were there waiting to welcome me. I was served with everything I was allowed to eat; the favourite of the day was fresh scones with strawberry jelly and cream. I hadn't eaten so much for a long time as the hospital food was dreadful. It turned out to be a lot like the 'Mad Hatters Tea Party' as everyone joined in the spirit of the celebrations.

On our return to the hospital Mum and Dad had been allowed to visit as it was a non-visiting day, the other patients had a bit of a party to as Mum had taken in some fancy cakes and goodies. It was a birthday I will never forget. I had a relapse and was dreadfully ill for a few days after but that was to be expected with all the excitement of that day. I treasured every single moment and would have been more than happy to end my days there and then, with the memories of so much love, laughter and happiness, I couldn't think of a better way to go.

I have no idea why it happened but acute depression set in shortly after that fabulous day and I began to deteriorate, after a great deal of consultation the treatment recommended was a possible visit home for a weekend. By this time I had been in bed for nearly seven months. It was felt necessary for me to be up and about before they would let me go home as there was no way my parents could have coped with me. Due to my not having used them for so long my legs collapsed from under me as soon as my feet touched the floor, fortunately two nurses were holding on to me, but my muscles had deteriorated so much I couldn't put one foot in front of another, like a baby I had to go through the process of learning to walk all over again.

The day finally came when I was taken home for the weekend by ambulance, but not to the home I had left. Dad had been on the move again and had got a job in

De Havillands Aerospace in Hatfield, Hertfordshire and my new home was to be No 1 Greencroft, Hatfield.

To add a little background information about De Havillands, in 1942-43 it had been the scene of a double cross sabotage raid by the Nazi secret agent 'Zigzag' Eddie Chapman, a famous pre-war safe cracker, he made his spoof attack on the power house in January 1943.

The comet flight test hanger was built in 1952-54, it was the largest aluminium building in the world and that was one of the areas Dad worked in. I think he later worked on the 'Blue Streak Missile' which was a British ballistic missile designed in 1955, as a skilled sheet metal worker or Tin Smith as was his official title.

Although I was obviously pleased to be with my family for the weekend and in different surroundings, all my friends were in Melbourne and I hadn't been able to say goodbye to any of them, I guessed then I would never see them again and I cried for the lose of those special friendships. As a four year old, Keith didn't seem to know me and wouldn't have anything to do with me at first, he hadn't been allowed to visit me in hospital and this tearful, thin, weakly creature before him certainly didn't resemble the big sister he had known. It was a weekend of enormously mixed emotions, I was happy to be out of hospital and with my family, but I was in the wrong place, everything was new and rather strange to me, there were no longer fields at the bottom of the garden, no pretty village to drive through and no friends to call in and say hello. I was still suffering the effects of the hormone treatment and was very conscious of the black hairs on my face. Understandably, taking into account all those scenarios, my depression intensified and I spent most of that weekend in tears and it didn't turn out to be quite the success it was hoped for.

Me, Summer 1955, with my best friend Joy, third from the left, and other School Friends

Me with my Teacher Mr Ogden, the only one throughout my School years who believed I had any potential.

Me in a New Outfit, I had made the Dress!

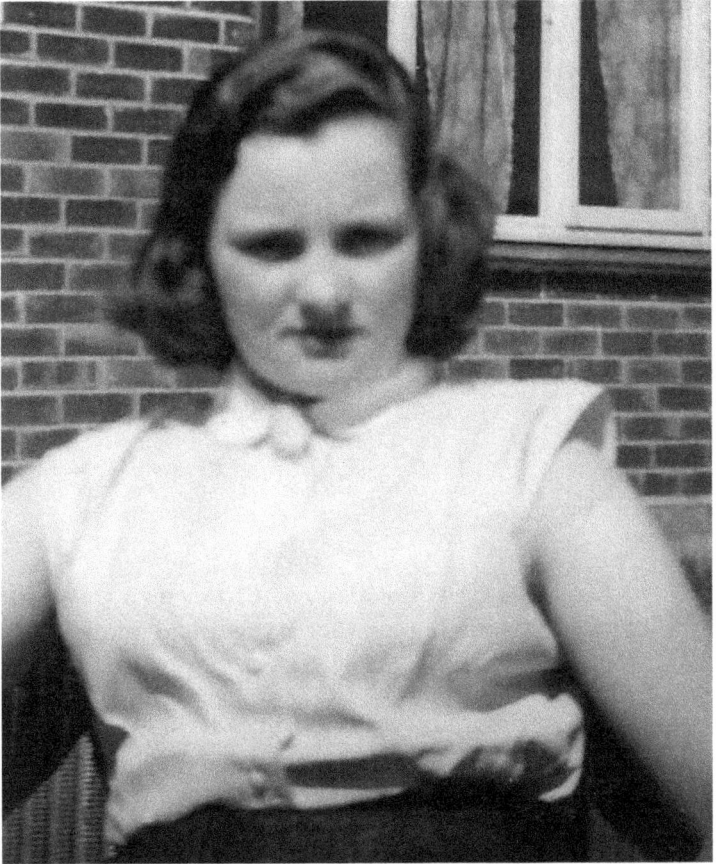

My new Blouse ready to start my first day at work

Me, 1955, with Cene Cutter on a Day out wearing another Dress I had made!

Me, age 16, wearing one of the few purchased Dresses I owned

Chapter 6
"Marriage & Divorce"
Hatfield
1957 ------ 1965

Because of the travelling costs and gifts bought for me every week my long term hospitalization had incurred, one of the most precious items owned by the family had been sold, the piano. I was devastated and felt exceptionally sad and guilty, that piano had been the heart of our family home all my life, no matter where we had lived. They had bought a television, thinking it would keep me occupied when I did return home for good. How could they think a television could take the place of seventeen years of the mainstay of our family activities, I so missed my Dad playing, and him and I sitting playing duets together. I obviously can't say for certain because I wasn't there, but I'm as sure as I can be it would have been Mum's idea, she had no appreciation for music and couldn't have conceived how much of a loss it would be to both Dad and me. From that time on our Sundays were never the same as the television became the dominant centre piece of our home.

Michael had visited me as often as he could for the first few months of my being in hospital but I had a lot of time to think about what his life would be like if we stayed together. My parents and I had been told there was no cure for ulcerative colitis and I would be a semi invalid for the rest of my life, I didn't feel it was fair to tie him down to what looked like a very uncertain future together. At first he refused to listen to me so in the end I refused to see him and thought that would be the end of our relationship. I think it was at that point the depression and feelings of hopelessness had started to take hold, I was losing someone I loved and being told my life wasn't going to amount to very much; both scenarios appeared to be hopeless situations and wasn't something I could easily dismiss from my thoughts. Michael kept in close touch with my parents and when he learnt I was going home for a visit he travelled over to Hatfield to see me. I was adamant that was to be the last time, I could hardly walk, wasn't able to climb the stairs or a roadside kerb, I was on a strict low fibre diet, most of my hair had fallen out of my head, but still covered with it over other parts of my body, I thought I would never be well again. I was deeply depressed, but seeing him waste his life on me was more than I could cope with, he finally, but very reluctantly, agreed and I sobbed my heart out when he left. It took me a long time to get over it, but I honestly felt it was for the best. On top of all that I had overheard a conversation between my parents and the local doctor; they were told I would be exceptionally lucky if I reached 21 years of age. That knowledge also went some way in my making the decision to terminate the relationship. I didn't tell my parents I had heard them talking about the possible outcome, I thought that would upset them even more. The strange thing is, it was a turning point for me, as very slowly it brought to the fore the fighting spirit that was inside me, I was determined to do all that I could to prove the doctors wrong.

That weekend home was the first, but not the last, as surprisingly, aside from the tears and depression I certainly did benefit from it. Mum and Dad went out of their way to make me as comfortable as possible, Mum cooked me all sorts of tasty dishes, even going as far as to peel and de-pip some tomatoes, which she cooked with some soft fish roes and mashed potatoes. It may not sound very nice but to me, who had hardly eaten anything for weeks, to be eating my Mother's wonderful cooking was as good as taking anti-depressants. Dad had to help me around as I still couldn't walk very well; he had to carry me up and down stairs and spent a lot of time during the night helping me visit the toilet. Fortunately there was a toilet downstairs; I don't think we could have coped otherwise.

My bedroom in Greencroft was freezing, it was so cold ice patterns would cover the windows and the lino floor seemed to have a film of ice over it as well, we are talking about the days of pre central heating, at least for our status in life. Mum and Dad were so worried about me; they put a runner on the floor and at bedtime would wrap the bedclothes around me like a parcel. The only problem was the number of times I had to get up during the night. I would have to call out, Dad would have to unwrap me and carry me to the bathroom and wait for me to finish in order to put me back to bed again by which time I had lost what little body heat I had and he would have to make me another hot water bottle and wrap me up again. That activity took place a number of times each and every night in those early days; I don't know how he coped. He must have collapsed with exhaustion by the time the ambulance returned to take me back to Addenbrooks Hospital at approximately 5pm on the Sunday.

Over the years I have felt guilty about something that happened many times although I wasn't actually aware of doing it. Every time I felt more ill and pain ridden than usual I always wanted my Dad, he spent hours with me rubbing my back when the pain was more than I could cope with. In my confused mind I was certain the nursing staff had done as I had asked and called him out to the hospital on the occasions when the pain and depression was so bad that only he could take it away. Thinking back that wouldn't have happened but they somehow made me believe he was there with me. He never complained or wavered in his administrations even when he'd had little or no sleep, but still had to be at work early the next day. I have often asked myself why I wanted Dad, and not Mum, but that was just the way it was. I seemed to recognise in them a different role they each had, Dad the protector, and Mum the one who had the greater burden to bear, with the constant visiting and all that involved, along with looking after Keith, David and Dad. When I think about it now I want to weep, when I think of the tremendous pressure they both must have been under, it was unrelenting for two very long years.

On one of my visits home Mum arranged a trip to the hairdressers. My hair had fallen out but was slowly growing back again; I had approximately an inch of baby's down covering my head. The hairdresser very gently gave me a bubble cut permanent wave and I was left with soft downy curls close to my head. I was very thin and the hair style suited me, even if it was a little on the short side. My hair has never grown back to the thickness of my childhood; it also lost its natural wave and auburn lights.

My stay in Addenbrooks had been a reasonably happy one when taking into account my illness and all that involved, but I had met some incredibly kind people, both on the medical side and in the other patients and their families. One of the patients, who occupied the bed next to me, had started me off smoking on one of my 'down' days. Smoking was allowed in hospital in those days, sadly that habit stayed with me for well into my thirties. However, my stay at Addenbrooks was coming to an end. Because of the increased travelling involved, both for Mum and Dad and the trips home by ambulance, I was eventually transferred to St Albans Hospital and entered in to what can only be described as a nightmare.

My first distressing experience happened within the first few hours of my arrival. The Doctor taking down all my background etc. started asking questions I had never been asked before, they all had a sexual overtone to them, questioning my relationship with boys, and pressing for details I couldn't give him. Most of the questions being asked I wasn't even sure what was meant, all I knew they were making me feel decidedly uncomfortable. When the physical examination started the questions being asked, while he was touching areas that had never been touched or spoken of before in all of my nine months in Addenbrooks, were very disturbing. Bearing in mind the only sex education I had ever been given was by my Nan who had rather cryptically told me to 'keep my hand on my halfpenny at all times'!! I found it frightening in the extreme. I was so unhappy that when Mum and Dad came to see if I had settled in I asked to see Mum on her own, I was too embarrassed to speak of it in front of Dad. When I had finished telling her what had transpired she rushed down the ward like a ship in full sail, shouting for my Dad and demanding to see someone in authority. On further investigation it transpired that this particular Doctor had been inappropriately examining female patients for some time and there had been other complaints made about him. My parents were adamant he wasn't going to get away with it. I was later given to understand, that he had been struck off by the Medical Board! That was the second Doctor to be struck off because of me, it didn't add to my popularity amongst the staff in that particular hospital!

Because of all the battles going on in the background the nursing personnel were very unhappy with me. One nurse in particular did many things to make my life very miserable and uncomfortable. On one particular occasion she insisted on giving me an enema which, at that time, was the worst thing she could have done. My parents turned up and found me in a dreadful state, very ill and incoherent, which meant I couldn't tell them what had happened. Fortunately for me one of the patients told them what had been done and who had done it. At that point everyone thought World War Three had broken out as all hell let loose, once again my parents were on the rampage. I remember the noise, but not what happened, which is probably just as well; the only thing I remember was never seeing that particular nurse again.

Shortly after that a Doctor from a London Teaching Hospital (sadly I can't remember his name) came to visit the hospital, apparently they used to make visits to outlying hospitals in those days, to give advice and support. That doctor got to hear of me, asked to see me and my parents, he assured them and me that I would be better off in his London Hospital. Arrangements were made for the move and after he had left, not one member of the staff spoke to me unless it was absolutely essential. That all sounds very dramatic and unbelievable but it did actually happen. As the years have passed by I often wondered what had brought so much hostility about, the only conclusion I have come to is it all stemmed from the dismissal of the said Doctor, they blamed it on me. The fact that there were other female patients who verified my observations of inappropriate behaviour was apparently overlooked, I had been the one to bring it to light.

On the day of the transfer to the London Hospital Mum turned up to travel with me, we were put into an ambulance, with what appeared to be, the intention of causing me further distress as it was the worse one they could conjure up. It had broken windows, was freezing cold and at first I had only been given a very old blanket and nothing else to wrap around me to keep me warm. Mum once again went on the war path; we were then supplied with an extra blanket. I had been in hospital for a year at that stage and was very ill, I was a stretcher case and Mum didn't think I would survive the journey in the best of conditions, let alone what I was being subjected to. By then all I wanted was to leave the 'hospital from hell' as I called it. I cannot begin to imagine what would have happened to me had I not been taken out of that hospital, I can honestly say I don't believe I would have been here now. I was so thankful my stay in Addenbrooks had, over all, been a very positive and largely happy experience, otherwise I would surely have died in St Albans!

We arrived at my new destination late that afternoon, The Gordon Hospital, Vauxhall Bridge Road, London and entered into paradise compared to what I had just left behind. After numerous tests and X-rays I became the patient of a wonderful man called Mr Aylett and his team.

Instead of a large ward I was put into a small four bedded room, something I hadn't come across before. Once again there wasn't a children's ward, although by then I was nearly seventeen. The other ladies in the room I shared kept dying off, mostly during the night. I would wake up in the morning and see another empty bed; it was all very depressing to say the least.

I don't remember very much of that period, I was very ill and progressively getting worse, what I do remember was a particularly kind and caring person, a Dr Samson. He seemed to take me under his wing and took over the role of my Dad at least that was how it felt. Dr Samson always appeared to be there when I needed the most comfort and understanding, even during the night he was with me. I think I must have been in some sort of half world of pain and insensibility to think he was always there with me, but I definitely felt a presence with me all the time. I'm very aware we do have selective memories and only remember what we want to sometimes, but I've tried to be as objective as possible about all I have written. However my memories of Dr Samson, as an individual, are perfectly clear I can close my eyes and see his face and jet black hair in my mind. He was the one person I trusted to cut down into my veins, on both my wrists and ankles, in order to give me the blood transfusions and drips I so desperately needed.

There was one nurse who didn't take to me at first, she treated me offhandedly, even unkindly, at times, so much so that on one occasion I became very distressed. The Ward Sister spent some time with me in an attempt to not only calm me down, but to find out what had upset me. Considering the unpleasant experiences I had already gone through in the previous hospital I was very reluctant to say anything, I was worried the outcome might be the same, however after a great deal of persuasion I did tell her what had been happening. The said nurse was taken aside and presumably told off; the result was more than I could ever have expected. We actually became quite close; she started taking me out in a wheelchair, on some of my better days, to St James Park on her afternoons off, a time which became precious to both of us. As I have been reflecting about that period of time I have often wondered how and why I was let out, even in a wheelchair, as it makes it appear that I couldn't have been as ill as I have made out, but I was. I did get very bad days of depression and having spent so long in hospital and my weekends at home had come to an end it was felt by the doctors that an afternoon out in the fresh air and sunshine could possibly do me some good, it certainly couldn't do me any harm. It was during those precious few hours out of the confines of the hospital that I discovered her personal life was in a great deal of difficulty and upheaval, she had been finding everything impossible to cope with. The upset with me, and with the Ward Sisters support, she had come to realize it was the catalyst that was to bring about a change of direction for both herself and her relationship with me and the other patients.

As I have previously said, I was very ill and not responding to treatment; throughout it all I was still reading the Bible on my occasional 'clearer' days and having long discussions with the visiting clergy. It was after one such visit I suddenly reached a point when realisation finally dawned on me that deep down I knew I wasn't going to live much longer and it had became evident to me, throughout all my reading and discussions, that I wasn't going to go to heaven! I hadn't been christened and couldn't be buried in consecrated ground. I had an overwhelming desire to return to the God I had found and felt the only way I could do that was to be christened. I had been visited by a variety of clergy of diverse denominations, all of whom were worthy in their own beliefs, but the time had come for me to make a choice. After a great deal of thought and pondering I choose the Church of England. The local minister was contacted and arrangements were made, the minister was very concerned about my decision, he knew my mother was a Catholic and was worried about how she would feel. A message was sent post-haste to my parents, via the police; we had no telephone in those days, to the effect that they needed to get to the hospital as soon as possible. They were informed I only had hours to live. Dad at that time didn't have a car so they had quite a journey to make in order to reach to me, using the Green Line bus service.

After speaking with the Doctors, who confirmed their diagnosis of my not responding to treatment and rapidly declining, then to the Minister, who relayed my wishes to be christened in the Church of England, Mum and Dad assured them that whatever made me happy and at peace was perfectly alright with them. I was christened from my hospital bed with two Doctors, a nurse, Mum, Dad and the Minister in attendance.

I have great difficulty in explaining what was about to take place, but it really did happen. I had been ill for a very long time, and in a great deal of pain throughout, but, as the service was being conducted, the pain left me. I felt as if I was floating above the bed, happy and at peace. Then I was certain a hand was stretched out to me and a voice said "Frances, you know that I'm here, now go and find me." The pain came back immediately and, instead of dying, I turned the corner and started to get better, much to the utter amazement of everyone involved. Some people questioned the original diagnosis, as to the severity of my illness, and the seemingly miraculous recovery, but, in the end, they had to come around and accept it as too many of the staff who looked after me were respected professionals.

The progress of recovery was very slow, but positive, and I was eventually sent to a convalescent home just outside Margate, run by Church of England Nuns, I think it was near Westgate-on-Sea. I weighed in at 5 stone 3 pounds (73 lbs) and was literally skin and bones. My stay there was a time of healing, both physically and mentally, for the second time in my life I had entered an institution where the peace and serenity of the place entered my very being, and unlike Mum's supposed experiences, those particular Nuns were so kind and gentle, I enjoyed the whole experience immensely.

Later whilst I was still there and had gained a few pounds and some added strength, one of the things I was able to do was visit the local cinema, what a wonderful experience that was; it was like an old time music hall, as you went through the doors you were personally welcomed and made to feel like royalty, it was all so exciting. During the intermission, tea and cakes were served and you were treated like a very special quest, I had never experienced anything like it before or since. My stay at the nursing home had lifted my spirits, calmed my soul, added a few pounds in weight and given me some inner strength, to continue fighting to beat the odds that had been stacked up against me. When I finally left to go back home, I felt like a different person, the sunshine, sea air, spiritual peace and the exceptional entertainment set me up to further progress along the path of recovery, or so I thought at the time.

As I was in remission and feeling reasonably well I decided I wanted to live as normal a life as was possible, I started going with David to the local youth club. After a while we dropped back into old habits and went our separate ways, we would meet up again when it was time to go home.

I have some very happy memories of that period of my life. Dad appeared to be determined to make up for lost time and would organise a lot of treats for us all to enjoy, trips out in the car to a variety of places where we would regularly end up having a picnic or pub lunch. We also went to the cinema on a regular basis although he sometimes thought it was a waste of time taking Mum as she would invariably fall asleep. I remember two incidents in particular, we had gone to see 'West Side Story' and on another occasion 'Porgy and Bess', Dad and I were enthralled with both the films as the music and acting was superb. Mum, bless

145

her, wasn't at all interested and within minutes of the films starting she fell asleep, that in and of itself wouldn't have been so bad but she started to snore, as she went deeper into the sleep the louder the snores were, in the end Dad woke her up, took us home. Later him and I went back on our own in order to enjoy the films, without the interruption or embarrassment of being told to be quiet!

As a special treat he took us up to London for the day where we did some sightseeing, had lunch at a posh restaurant before going to the cinema. It was the beginning of Cinemascope with the huge wide surround screens, I can't remember exactly but I think the film was 'How the West Was Won', it was a long film and they had an interval in the middle of it. We were upstairs in the front seats of the balcony and the second half of the film started with an ear-splitting sound and very visual cannon being fired straight at you, it frightened the life out of us all. Dad had bought each of us our favourite sweets and on the way home had stopped off for some supper. It had been a very special day out, I can only conclude the outing had been planned for a special occasion but I haven't any idea what it was.

Although I was in remission I still had to be careful as I was as thin as a rake and tired very easily. David decided I needed to get back into the land of the living and took me to the local roller skating rink; they were all over the country in those days as it was the in thing to do and were replacing some of the dance halls. However hard I tried I could not get the hang of staying up straight on the roller skates, I began to feel clumsy and totally inadequate just as I had felt at school. We gave up that idea and David took me dancing, the only trouble was everything I thought of as dancing had changed, it was all jive and rock and roll. Again feelings of inadequacy took hold as I didn't seem to have the aptitude or the energy to master any of it; the only place I could go where I felt as if I could fit in was at the local youth club so that became the regular thing to do.

I eventually met up with a young man who worked in the same place as Dad and he started walking me home. Dad had set a curfew for 10.00pm and one evening I pushed my luck too far and stayed out later with the said young man; David had got fed up waiting for me and had gone home. When I did eventually arrive home I found the doors locked and I couldn't find a way in. I threw gravel at David's window but he was dead to the world and didn't hear me, all I could do was sit on the doorstep and wait for something to happen. It took about half an hour before Dad eventually relented and opened the door. Needless to say the dressing down was much worse than the thrill of staying out late, it never happened again. I found out later that my poor parents were worried sick about me, not for being late in, but for being left outside in order to learn a lesson. I had been in hospital for such a long time they were worried it would set me back, but were determined that I had to learn once more, to abide by the rules of the house.

It wasn't long after that particular incident had occurred that the same young man asked me to accompany him to his firm's annual dance; I first of all approached Mum, I needed her to be an advocate on my behalf in getting Dad to agree. As was usually the case the subject was brought up at the dinner table and I was subjected to the third degree, who was the young man, how old was he, where did he work etc. I answered as best I could but had that sinking feeling that the answer was going to be a resounding NO! Mum and Dad decided to discuss the matter after Dad had declared he would think about it! A few days later it was agreed that as long as the said young man made a visit to our home in order for Dad to meet him, if he passed muster, then Dad would agree to me going to the dance. I cannot remember that young man's name but he did visit and Dad did proceed to put him through the third degree. He finally, and reluctantly I think, gave consent to him escorting me to the dance, on condition he returned me home by 11.00pm and no later. Dad's baby girl, who he was very protective of, was spreading her wings and he wasn't totally convinced it was something he was happy about.

I was in a fever of excitement, I was seventeen and a half years old and it was to be my very first dance, but what could I wear, all my clothes hung on me as I was so thin. Mum and I were pondering over that agonizing challenge, when an unexpected letter arrived in the post, asking me to call in at the police station. With a great deal of worry and trepidation we made our way there, I had no idea what it was about and could only think they had contacted the wrong person. When we arrived I was taken into a side room and presented with a purse that contained well over five pounds, a great deal of money in those days. I had found the said purse lying in the street three months previously, had handed it into the police station, then dismissed it from my mind. Apparently no one had made a claim and it had now become my property, purse and contents. I was absolutely astounded and thrilled in equal measure as it opened up the possibility of having a new dress for the dance. Mum and I spent a few happy hours in St Albans looking for something suitable and found the prettiest dress imaginable. I can see it now in my mind's eye, it had a round, full, ankle length skirt, a neat pinched in waist, a reasonably low top, front and back, edged with a pretty lace edging, the slightly gathered cap sleeves were edged with the same lace. The main, fine cotton, background was white and pale blue stripes, with sprigs of tiny pink flowers and green leaves, running down the half inch wide white stripes. It was beautiful and fitted me perfectly. There was enough money left over to buy new white underwear, and a pair of white shoes to wear with it. There wasn't much money left over from the five pounds but it did stretch to a new lipstick and Mum paid for me to have my hair done. I looked and felt better than I had done for years. I felt young, alive and very feminine; I was on top of the world and ready to party

On the night of the ball, so to speak, my very handsome escort arrived on time and presented me with a beautiful pink and white corsage; it's strange but I can't remember how we got to the dance, I can only presume we went in a taxi. I had a fabulous evening, it was wonderful and I felt like a modern day Cinderella. During the evening I was complimented a number of times, being told you were the prettiest girl in the room had the effect of too much champagne going to the head, after having been ill for so long and having a very low self image of myself it was exhilarating. My dashing partner was very protective and enjoyed being the envy of his work colleagues. That sounds very big headed doesn't it, but that was the type of evening it was. The music at that time was very romantic, some old and up and coming crooners of the day were popular, Bing Crosby, Frank Sinatra, Nat King Cole and my favourite Johnnie Mathis. The band played 'Some Enchanted Evening' and 'When I Fall in Love' along with many others in a similar vein, all of which ensured my evening was filled with an enchantment and magic that was my very own. All too soon the evening came to an end. I was very reluctant to leave, but my escort had promised faithfully to have me home by 11.00pm. My bubble of euphoria burst a few days later as I was rushed into hospital, I was no longer in remission. Sad to say I never saw that young man again. Although sadly I can't remember his name, he gave me the most magical evening of my life, to this very day I have never experienced another like it.

The months following were filled with intense pain and fluctuating emotions of hope and despair. Mr Aylett, my surgeon, had seen performed in America, a revolutionary new procedure to help people with my condition. I don't know the details; I only know we agreed to him trying out the operation on me, I had nothing to lose and possibly everything to gain. The first operation wasn't successful and I ended up with a gaping wound in my abdomen which continually seeped raw faeces, the smell was appalling and distressing in the extreme. I had to pack myself with dressings that couldn't adequately cover the open area, especially when standing up. My days were a constant worry and I became virtually housebound. I had been sent home to regain some strength before any more surgery could be thought of, I physically needed building up, but every day was faced with an overwhelming dread, the nights were even worse, as the packing would not stay in place, nightwear and bedding were in a dreadful mess as morning approached. Our washing machine was quite a big one with a mangle attached, but it still must have been exceedingly difficult for poor Mum to get all the soiled bedding, day and night clothes washed and dried etc. Some months later, although to me at the time it seemed like a life time, Mr Aylett performed a second operation which thankfully was more successful, however the intervening months had been like living a nightmare that was beyond imagination.

During my 'in remission' periods, I tried going back to work in hairdressing but it wasn't to be, for whatever reason, I always ended up unwell, or in hospital, I finally had to come to terms with the fact that I simply had to relinquish my dream of becoming a qualified hairdresser. I made one more attempt before coming to that final decision obtaining a job in one of the salons in St Albans, where I went to work as a receptionist. I felt that if I wasn't working as a hairdresser as such, but was still in the business, all would be well. However one evening on leaving work, after having been let off early because of the threat of the weather worsening, I stepped out into deep snow; it had only been snowing for a very short space of time but was already heavy and drifting. I managed to catch a bus back to Hatfield but had only gone a few of miles or so before the bus got stuck in a deep snow drift. The bus couldn't go either backwards or forwards and the only course open to me and the other passengers was to walk the rest of the way home. All I had on was a pair of high heeled shoes, a knee length coat, no hat, gloves or scarf. I don't remember how many hours it took me to get home; I only remember the sense of relief at having made it and Mum's tears of joy and relief as I literally fell through the door. She gave me a hot drink, ran a hot bath and warmed my nightclothes in front of the fire; insisting I eat a hot meal before wrapping me up in bed. A few days later I was once again taken ill, rushed up to the Gordon Hospital and was unable to work again for many more months. The final decision had effectively been made for me and I never went back to hairdressing.

After that particular hospital stay, as part of my convalescence, I went to stay with Doll and Len. It was approaching Christmas time, Mum and Dad weren't happy about me being away from home, but did, very reluctantly, agree to me to staying at Addington over the holiday, although they were upset I think they realized I desperately needed a change of scenery. It was a relatively easy journey on the train, with a change over in London and a short bus journey at the end. I knew that as soon as I arrived, there would be a lot of love and a hot meal waiting for me. After they had all made sure I was suitably replete there was time to catch up on all the news before being sent to bed to rest and recover from the effects of the journey.

Christmas Day arrived and Len took me out to the 'The Addington Arms', the local public house, while Doll and Nan were cooking the Christmas dinner. I can't remember who else was with us, however, while we were there I met a young man called Tony, who apparently knew Len, he lived in Addington not very far from their house. We hit it off straight away and before we left for home it was arranged he could call to see me. Nan Martin (or Williams as she was then) had split up from Harry and was staying with Doll and Len at the time. Tony duly arrived, amid much speculation, and was asked all the usual questions as to his worthiness and suitability in escorting me out for the evening. He obviously passed muster but, as we were going out of the door on our very first date, Nan counselled me, in all seriousness, to 'keep my hand on my halfpenny', meaning don't let him take any liberties with any of my private parts. I nearly died of shame; thankfully Tony saw the funny side of it and assured her that she needn't worry and he would take very good care of me.

That was the beginning of a very happy relationship. Even though we lived miles apart, we managed to keep in touch and see quite a lot of each other; poor Doll and Len were always having me stay with them during those intervening months.

Tony introduced me to his favourite jazz club in Croydon when he found we both had a love of Jazz. I remember it as a smoky pub that had, as their speciality, visiting bands and jazz singers. Pubs in those days catered for all types of music, skiffle, country and western, or a variety of performers etc. They probably still do but I don't frequent them any more.

Things were going really well when Tony was taken ill; I thought at the time he must have been in the services of some sort as I remember going to see him in, what I thought was a military hospital. I had to walk pass rows upon rows of Nissan huts to get to the one Tony was in. I'm not absolutely certain but I believe he had TB, although I wasn't aware of that at the time. It wasn't very long after he left hospital he sent me word to tell me when he was travelling over to Hatfield to see me, we didn't have phones in those days every communication between us was by letter. The post then was excellent as the letters arrived within hours of them being posted. It was quite an easy journey on the train and didn't take too long so I wasn't overly concerned about his health.

I was so looking forward to seeing him and being with him for the weekend, but as soon as he got off the train I knew there was something wrong. He told me he didn't want to see me again, and refused to go back to my house to talk it through. We were both in tears, but he felt it was the best thing all round not to prolong the agony, and caught the next train back. I was desperately upset and couldn't understand what or why it was happening. I found out, many months later, that Doll and Nan had talked to him and said they didn't want me to catch anything that was likely to make me ill again, as I was still very vulnerable. Tony agreed with them and that was the end our association!!

As I've already said, whenever I went to stay with Doll and Len I was totally spoilt, as soon as I walked through the front door, a hot meal and a great fuss would be waiting for me. Len spoilt me the most, always getting me a hot water bottle and night time drink and every morning he would wake me with a cup of tea and biscuits before leaving for work. I slept with Pearl and we would be awake for hours talking, how I loved being with them all.

The way I am recording this makes it appear that I wasn't happy being at home, I have thought long and hard about that period of time and have concluded that home was a place where I was always treated as an invalid. Looking back with a great deal of hindsight and maturity I can understand why they had felt the need to treat me that way, I had been seriously ill for approximately four years and Mum and Dad had carried that burden every single day of those very difficult years. On top of that they still believed the doctors prognosis of my not making it to my 21st birthday. They were scared, over protective and I felt smothered by them. My time at Addington was a time for freedom, and acceptance that I knew deep down inside me when I needed to be sensible. Mum and Dad had always given me an abundance of love, but it was coupled with a great many restrictions, Doll and Len's love was unconditional and they allowed me to find my own way through my challenging disabilities.

There was a short period of time when I worked at De Haviland's in Hatfield, the office building was situated on the outskirts of the airfield, set amongst trees and flowers which made it a pleasant and relatively peaceful place to work. I was employed as a comptometer operator; I worked on a machine that could perform all mathematical problems at high speed, for example addition, multiplication and subtraction, an early sophisticated calculator. I have no idea why I was given that job as I was hopeless at maths but I seemed to cope quite well as a trainee, high speed didn't come into the equation but at least I didn't make too many mistakes. I don't remember being there for very long before as once again I became ill and ending up in 'The Gordon'. During those months I was in and out like a yoyo.

Everyone at the hospital knew me, so going back in was very much like being in a home from home. There was a time when I used to bet on the horses, I studied the 'form' to pass the time away and placed my bets via a porter. I got quite good at picking winners and the porter soon became a regular visitor as, through me and my tips, he won quite a bit of money. I remember one particular win was enough to pay for me and another young girl patient to go out to the cinema, followed by afternoon tea. We saw 'Women in a Dressing Gown' with Yvonne Mitchell in the lead role. We didn't have far to go as the hospital was very close to the main shopping area at Victoria, we had a very nice afternoon out. I'm making it sound as if I spent my whole time going out somewhere but I was allowed out only very rarely and after a great deal of consultation. As I have said before I tended to get very depressed looking at the same walls all the time while in hospital, so as long as everything had calmed down and I was close to being sent home, I would be allowed the occasional afternoon out.

It was during all those years in hospital that I had to find things to do that would pass the time away and they all had to be crafts that I could do while sitting up in bed. I tried many things and became quite competent in a lot of things but have never become a master in any of them; I tend to get bored at sticking to any one thing for very long which isn't a character trait I particularly like in me.

My frequent stays in hospital caused Mum a great deal of stress and hardship, both emotionally and financially. On one of my returns home, I found Mum had been having added stress heaped upon her because she was having trouble persuading Keith to go to school. He used to plead with her not to send him, we didn't know why, at the time we never gave bullying a thought, Keith wouldn't tell us why he was so unhappy. In retrospect I'm pretty sure that he must have been bullied as every morning there were tears and pleading, he must have been absolutely desperate, if only he could have told us what was wrong, maybe, something could have been sorted out.

It became more and more clear to me during those weeks of convalescence how brilliantly Mum was coping with all the challenges she had to meet at that time. Due to her thoughtful caring administrations I realised I had the innate desire to return to a working life! I felt this would hopefully relieve her of some of the financial pressures. I had always enjoyed sewing and handling fabrics, so as soon as I was on my feet again I applied for a job in a fabric shop in St Albans, owned by a Jewish husband and wife. There was a lot of physical hard work attached to the job but I loved it, getting quite a few perks with discounted materials. I was very slim, or thin would be a better description, and could get away with quite small pieces of fabric to make a dress. I was also creative enough to put minuscule pieces of fabric together and end up with something totally different to anything you could buy. That was a time of feeling reasonable well, which was all down to the success of the surgery I'd had done.

It was whilst working in the shop I met Michael number two. I passed his house on the way to and from the bus stop every day. One day we got to talking, then eventually on to dating and it wasn't very long the relationship started getting serious. We were both eighteen and looking to fill a need in ourselves, rather than in each other. He had recently split up with a girl he was in love with; I was missing my first love, Michael number one, recovering from Tony's abandonment and I needed to feel like someone who could be loved, in spite of all my health problems. Not the best recipe for any firm foundation, but we blindly went ahead and continued with the relationship.

Michael had a Lambretta and worked in Welwyn Garden City, it wasn't long before I applied for, and gained, employment in the Welwyn Department Store, on the fabrics counter. We travelled to work together on his scooter. I didn't like travelling on it very much, especially after coming off a couple of times, but it was a cheap form of transport. I soon settled into my new job as I knew my way around fabrics, but I wasn't in that department very long before being transferred to the cosmetics counter. For the first time since leaving behind my friends Joy and Sheila at fifteen and a half, I made some very good friends whilst I was there; I was happy and feeling pretty good about myself at last.

Michael and I spent most of our Saturday afternoons at his parent's house where we would have tea and cake, or a particular favourite, freshly bought soft roes, fried in butter, on hot buttered toast, yummy! I can't honestly say I liked his mother. He was the youngest of her brood and in my opinion rather spoilt, nothing was too good for her son and she constantly let me know, in very subtle ways, that I simply didn't pass muster. As the relationship progressed, his parents went away on holiday and we had the house to ourselves, which was a dangerous situation to be in, the temptation became too great, our relationship turned the corner and we became intimate!! Bearing in mind I was incredibly naive and had received no sex education whatsoever, except for my grandmothers counsel, I had no idea what it all meant or where it could lead to. I thought it was what love was all about and I needed to feel loved.

Our thoughts soon turned to marriage, my Mum in particular, decided the sooner the better, before I became pregnant. I never could work out how she knew what was going on. The date was set for the 18 July 1959 just a few weeks short of my nineteenth birthday. At one point it was in the balance as to it taking place on that date as Nan Martin had sadly died on the 3rd May; however it was finally decided that she would have wanted the wedding to go ahead and the final arrangements were confirmed.

The day of the wedding was a beautiful, warm, sunny day, and everything went smoothly. My dress had been made by Michael's brother-in-law; for that period of time it was a very modern creation, a straight, fitted, knee length, white satin brocade with a skirt of white netting. My headdress was made by Phillip, a colleague I worked with, and was a beautiful, incredibly intricate and delicate creation, in the shape of a crown, covered with crystals and pearls. The wedding cake had been made and decorated by my lovely Len, I have never called him uncle in all the years I have known him; the bridesmaids were my four cousins Pearl, Ann, Valerie, Lesley and a friend, whose name I am ashamed to say, I cannot remember. I'm finding it very strange; I'm having vivid memories of events but not people's names, it's quite disturbing. The wedding took place at '*St Michael and All Angels*' Birchwood Avenue, Hatfield, the reception was held at home, No 1 Greencroft. The weather was absolutely perfect, warm, dry and very sunny. To make more room for all the quests, the settee was taken out into the garden and used as an overflow extension. To ensure we had the support of our closest neighbours they were all invited and joined in with all the loud singing and laughter that was created by the family being together again.

Uncle Wal and Auntie Vicky stayed on at our house with Mum and Dad for a week and let Michael and I have the use of their home in Southend-on-Sea for our honeymoon. We travelled there on the Lambretta as we had no money for anything else. The weather continued to be unbelievably kind to us and we spent hours walking along the beach and sun bathing. The week passed far too quickly and it was time for us to travel back to our new home.

We had rented a small two up two down terraced cottage called Roe Green, in Chantry Lane, on the outskirts of Hatfield. It did have running cold water but the outside toilet left a lot to be desired. We were very happy in our cosy little nest for a short while but sadly, it didn't last for long as it soon became apparent I wasn't getting pregnant and Michael wanted a large family. The disagreements became more frequent and very heated; we went for various tests and in the end were told it was me who would be unable to have any children due to the illness and operations I had already been through. It was a devastating blow and one that was incredibly difficult to come to terms with. In those days there weren't the options that couples have now; it was just something you had to get on with in the best way that you could, which was so much easier said than done, there was no such thing as counselling in those days.

The rows escalated, intimacy became increasingly difficult as Michael's desire for a baby was greater than any love there may have been. We both found that distressingly difficult to cope with. I felt guilty and not

159

loved for myself, he wanted children, and eventually frustration became the over riding emotion as neither of our needs were being met. This frustration eventually spilled over into some physical abuse, I found this to be very distressing and demoralising. By that time we had been married for just over a year.

After a twelve year gap Doll had become pregnant again then a few days after my birthday in September 1960 gave birth to another beautiful baby daughter Vivien. I travelled to Addington to look after them both on their return home from hospital. Doll had been through a very difficult birth and I was more than happy to care for her and Vivien. She became my baby for a while and I loved every minute of being with them all. I was asked to be one of the godmothers which I was absolutely delighted about. Unfortunately the time soon came when I could no longer stretch out my stay or use the excuse of caring for Doll and Vivien any longer and had to return to the unhappy and difficult circumstances I had found myself to be in.

As time passed and as a distraction to how we were living, I used my time creating clothes for Vivien, I loved knitting and sewing clothes for her. In particular I remember an angora bolero I knitted, it was pink, soft and very pretty, but now I think about it, I wonder if it tickled or irritated her, poor lamb, what she must have suffered. To go with the bolero I made a pleated skirt, they were specific items that stand out in my mind although I can't explain why.

Because of my taking so much time off, with hospital visits and my prolonged stay at Addington etc, I lost my job in the Welwyn Dept Store. I then applied for and got a job working in the fabrics section in the only department store in Hatfield. I had just settled down and made some very good friends when the next blow hit me with the full force of a sledge hammer.

Whilst struggling to deal with my own traumatic circumstances relating to my inability to bear children, the strained atmosphere this had created in our marital relationship, another scenario was taking place in my parental home. My brother David had fallen out with Dad, a regular occurrence at the time, he had turned up on our doorstep asking to stay for just a few days, his plan was to move to London to live. On returning home from work a couple of days later I found a note saying that both Michael and David had left, gone to seek their fortunes in London. On investigation I found all the utilities money had been taken, not one single penny had been left. There were incriminations all round from Michael's family members; I felt the impact of them all. I was specifically blamed for having allowed David to stay in the first place thereby putting temptation in Michael's path! Somehow I weathered the storm, was just getting used to the peace and quiet of being on my own, when a very disillusioned Michael returned home full of apologies.

Shortly after Michael's return, I think sometime in July1961, we travelled up to London on the Lambretta to see Johnny Mathis in concert. What an incredibly fantastic evening that was, for the first time in ages we were as one in our appreciation of someone we both loved. On the way home it poured with rain, we were not only soaked to the skin we broke down as well, overall though the evening had been a wonderful success and for a short space of time we experienced a closeness we hadn't felt for a very long time!

By this time I was approaching my twenty-first birthday, Mum and Dad had given me a choice of having an electric sewing machine or driving lessons, I eagerly plumped for the latter as I knew I would never get another chance like that again. I was duly enrolled at the British School of Motoring (BSM) at St Albans and was one of the very few women on the course. My instructor's name was Roy and I loved every minute I was in the car. I was quite used to cars as Dad had always had one when times were good for him; he'd always taken us out on weekend trips or holidays whenever he could.

My marriage being extremely unhappy at that time I found Roy was like a breath of fresh air, he was fun to be with and very likeable. After a while his attentions became a great temptation, however both my birthday and my driving test were just around the corner, planning for both events, fortunately, kept that temptation at bay.

I decided on having a fancy-dress party for my birthday and hired the village hall; just a stone's throw away from the cottage. I dressed up as a bottle of 'Squeazy' washing up liquid made of cardboard; there were some exotic and outrageous costumes, the show of the moment on TV was the 'Flint Stones' and yes, they turned up to the party, along with monkeys and a vast assortment of animals. We had the Police visit us at least twice as the neighbours were complaining about the lateness and noise levels we were generating. My work colleagues had been very supportive during the previous extremely difficult months and they clubbed together and gave me a beautiful enamel broach which I still have and wear it often, it's not only one of my favourites but it also reminds me of what it was like to have so much love and support shown me during a time of great unhappiness. Michael, by way of apology, had bought me an old Austin seven car, unfortunately it didn't work and I never drove it.

A few weeks later, after a particularly bad situation had arisen (I had taken another beating), I took an overdose and landed up in St Albans' A & E. My Doctor, who had been aware for some time of what had been going on, contacted my parents. On my discharge from hospital they took me back home, I never returned to the cottage or the marriage. Now that I am a lot older and wiser I can look back and feel desperately sorry for both of us, as neither was capable of satisfying each other's needs I couldn't give him the children he desperately wanted and he couldn't give me the love I needed, neither of us had the wisdom, age or experience to cope with the challenges we were faced with, particularly at that time in our lives.

Late September 1961, not long after the separation, I passed my driving test at the first attempt, I was very nervous but Mum told me to dress up and wear my white fluffy fur hat, knowing that if I felt good in myself and my appearance, it would settle my nerves and impress the driving examiner. I was delighted to have passed first time and put it all down to the hat! It wasn't of course, I had been well taught and I was determined that Mum and Dad were not going to be put through any more expense. I have already said that very few women drove cars in those days even though, out of necessity, many had done so during the war, driving and owning a car was for the better off, I certainly didn't fit into that category. Dad was one of the very few, from the working class, to own a car and it seemed perfectly natural to me, we always had a car when times were on the 'up' as Dad would say.

I started going out with Roy on the odd date, he was very funny and cheered me up. After a while the dates became more regular, he visited my home and got on well with my parents. Through him I got to hear of a driving job, it entailed delivering and collecting spare parts for a car repair shop in a large garage in St Albans, I applied for the job and amazingly I got it. I was an attractive novelty that the powers that be decided would be an asset to the company. I had only passed my test three months previously and hadn't been in a car since that day, so Dad, bless him, decided I needed to get some practice in before I started. The garage where he kept the car was in a block just around the corner from where we lived in Greencroft, I backed out of the garage, straight into a concrete boulder, and damaged the underside of the car; it was a blue Ford Prefect. I made my way back home again and, as I walked through the front door Mum jokingly said, 'what's up have you crashed the car?' I promptly burst into tears and vowed never to drive again. They were very supportive and understanding, after I had calmed down, they talked me into starting my new job the following day.

I turned up for my first day at work and was presented with a gleaming red Comma Cob van; I immediately fell in love with it. I was sent out on my first assignment and on the way back to the garage I ran out of petrol, I was horrified and at a loss, what on earth could I do. Mobile phones weren't around at that time and not many homes owned a telephone, I got out of the van and frantically looked for a house with a telephone line running to it. I was very lucky to find one not far from where I had come to a sudden juddering halt, the lady of the house very kindly let me use her phone. You cannot even begin to imagine the reaction I got from all the mechanics when I returned to the garage; it took months of jokes and ribald remarks before I proved my worth. From that day onwards, I vowed I would never get myself into a situation that would necessitate calling them out ever again. Winter arrived, thick snow and fog in plenty, and every time I left the garage they took bets as to how long it would be before I got stuck and would be calling for help. I couldn't have had a better training in self preservation, not once in all the time I worked there did I call anyone out, in fact I ended up by going out with the mechanics to rescue customers who had got stuck in the snow. I had finally become one of the 'boys', and a valued member of the team.

My first task of every day was to collect the breakfast orders for everyone, there would be an assortment of freshly cooked egg and bacon sandwiches, made up in thick slices of newly baked crusty bread, there was also egg and sausage, black pudding or thick slices of ham. Every combination was delicious and we all had something different every day. The shop which produced those fabulous creations was very small and in a position where parking was extremely difficult. I would phone the order through and, by the time I arrived outside, everything was ready waiting for me, all hot and wonderfully delicious. While I was gone the boys had prepared the tea and coffee and everything came to a halt for our twenty minute break.

One of my responsibilities was to travel up to London about three times a week to collect spare parts from a variety of Motor Factors, it was an absolute pleasure. I was treated like a queen and without fail got to the front of the queues; I always made sure I wore high heeled shoes and looked smart and feminine, no trousers in those days, at least not for me. It worked like a dream; I was very slim and did get a lot of attention, which was a great boost to my morale!

The journeys, particularly to London, could sometimes be a bit hairy, due to very thick fog; it was before smokeless fuel became law. I always made it back to the garage, even if it did take me much longer than usual. The main landmark to keep an eye out for was the Hendon Police Training centre, it was like a half way point on my journey and, as long as I could find that complex in the fog I always knew I could make it back.

Before passing my test Mum had vowed she would never to get in a car with me as the driver, she was very nervous in cars, but one of the things I had learned during my lessons was that a 'good' driver always makes sure their passengers feel at ease. One day I turned up on the doorstep and asked her if she would like a trip to London. She was so excited she didn't give any thought to her fears and off we went, we never looked back after that and over the years travelled many hundreds of miles together.

My dates with Roy were becoming more frequent, I was happy about that as he made me feel good. One of the local garages I had to visit on a regular basis had a very nice young man behind the counter, when he found out that I was going out with Roy he approached me one day and told me that Roy was married. I was devastated at having been made a fool of and confronted Roy, he was adamant it was untrue and that the person in question was either trying to make trouble, or was aiming to have a date with me and wanted a clear field. He was so sincere I believed him and carried on seeing him, until the day came when the same young man approached me again and said that Roy's wife had just given birth to their first child. He knew of the event because she was his cousin. I wasn't just devastated, I was extremely angry, at both myself and Roy, for having been so believing and being made such a fool of. I never saw him again and felt very sorry for his wife as I felt certain he would find another gullible idiot like me to take for a ride. I was so worried about facing that kind young man who had told me but I needn't have been, he understood perfectly, he felt I had been an innocent victim, and always treated me with respect. Apparently Roy had a reputation and I hadn't been the first to fall foul of his very slick and proven approach to vulnerable women; however, it was a very hard lesson for me to learn. Needless to say, I was very wary after that and I wouldn't go out with anyone without finding out something about them, especially if they were married or not.

After a while we had a new mechanic join the team in the garage and, would you believe it, Michael number three entered my life; he was very tall, with dark hair and a beard, good looking and unmarried, an irresistible combination. Mick liked the 'good life', he wined and dined me and took me to all the best places. He seemed surprised, and quite pleased, to find I had the ability to get on with anyone I was introduced to. Life with him was always in the fast lane and very exciting. Bearing in mind my background of ill health and incapacity, I felt as if I was in another world and I loved every minute of it. Our relationship was very exciting and eventually very passionate. He drove around in a variety of impressive, large American cars; being allowed to drive them gave me even more experience of handling different vehicles, which was a valuable asset, adding to my credibility as a competent driver.

Unfortunately it wasn't long before I had another relapse and went into hospital again for more surgery. At the time I thought that would be the end of our relationship, but it wasn't, he regularly visited me, eventually collecting me and taking me home. I was realistic enough to know I would be off work for some months, and wouldn't be able to return to the garage, so with a very heavy heart I had to give in my notice. They were all extremely kind but I knew that period of my life had come to an end, it turned out to be the happiest and most satisfying job I ever had, with the exception of my time with my first employer Mrs Schmeler in Cambridge.

While I was in hospital Mum took it into her head to buy a shop, I have no idea how or where she got the money from, but buy it she did. The shop was one of four in a small precinct at the end of Birchwood Ave, not far from where we lived. It was ideally situated as it was next door to the post office and a few doors away from a grocer which meant lots of passing trade. The premises had previously been a shoe shop, Mum bought all the left over stock, had a sale, and with the money she got from it, set up a wool and baby linen shop with a three bed roomed flat above. She named the shop 'Fran's' and kept saying she had bought it for me. I wasn't the grateful or happy individual she expected me to be, it had happened without any consultation of any kind and was definitely not something I wanted to do. A period of bad feeling erupted between us as she expected me to be an unpaid assistant working for her, I rebelled, big time, I wasn't prepared to fall at her feet and be compliant to her wishes or decisions. The day eventually came when Dad was called upon to be the intermediary. In the end I reluctantly backed down, but not before telling him how trapped and unhappy I felt, I didn't like the situation one little bit. I did work there and made the best of a bad job by becoming the chief buyer, in effect, if not name. We used to go and visit all the warehouses in London and give her, her due; Mum was expert in getting a good bargain. I think Nan's association with her Jewish employer and her less salubrious acquaintances during the war had rubbed off, as Mum certainly knew her stuff, I was just as quick to pick it up. Dad, on the other hand, didn't have a clue and fell into a number of costly traps. It was at that point I came to understand why his business had gone bust; he just wasn't a business man, his attitude and approach put people's backs up, just as it had done when they were on the market selling china.

After a very long time, it must have been three years or more, of having made no contact with any of the family, David had suddenly turned up on the doorstep one day with his girlfriend, Kathy. Mum got very emotional and cried for a long time, I got angry and said a lot of things that would have been best left unsaid, all in all it wasn't a very pleasant homecoming for the prodigal son. David and Kathy wanted to marry but he was under age and needed parental consent. Dad wasn't happy with the situation but knew he had effectively lost his parental rights on the day David had left home, Mum didn't want anymore friction, and the relevant forms were duly signed. The wedding was arranged at the Brixton Registry Office in London and Dad paid for us all to enjoy a family meal afterwards. When Kathy gave birth to a beautiful baby girl, they experienced a great deal of hardship and after some time of moving from place to place they found a flat in Brixton on the outskirts of London. The flat was not really suitable for a small child and left a lot to be desired, after a while Mum and Dad suggested they move into the flat above the shop.

Using Dad's car, Pearl, who was staying with us at the time, and I made a number of trips between Hatfield and Brixton, moving all their belongings back to the flat and they came to live in Hatfield. I can't remember the details of how it happened but, after another stay in hospital, for what turned out to be a ruptured ovarian cyst, a decision to swap accommodations had been made and we had moved into the flat. David, Kathy and the baby moved into the house. I think they must have put in for an exchange straight away, as it didn't seem very long before they moved into a new flat not very far away.

Living on the premises of a shop brought its own special challenges as Dad was always very happy to open up at any time for whoever knocked on the door asking for a ball of wool or a packet of sanitary towels. I used to get very annoyed about it as our meals were frequently interrupted, or our Sundays disturbed. Dad used to open up the shop and then have to call Mum or me to get whatever the lady wanted as he didn't have a clue about the wool and embarrassed about dealing with sanitary towels!

Early Sunday mornings were our re-stocking days, our trips to London to visit the various warehouses had to be sharp and early as the Jewish traders opened very early in the morning and were closed by twelve noon. Mum had asked around as to who was the best traders to go to and we very soon got ourselves known and respected.

As we were open six days a week, with a half day on Wednesday when we used to clean the flat/shop, do the grocery shopping and change the window display, etc. time to myself became very precious, I deemed any out of hour calls as a intrusion upon my time and space. When we arrived home every Sunday there was all the unpacking of the items we purchased to sort and pack away, cooking a Sunday roast, eating it and clearing up etc. That was of no consequence to Dad whatsoever, he hadn't been involved with any of it, he simply couldn't bear to turn business away and Sunday afternoons became increasingly fraught and very bad tempered.

A series of events which took place during that period of time was at first funny, later becoming less so. Someone kept stealing my underwear from off the clothes line. The thefts had happened a few of times in

Greencroft and although I had reported it no one had been caught. But then it started occurring from the garden at the back of the shop. As I have said it started off at first by being funny but, as each set went missing, I became more and more annoyed. I used to wear very pretty, lacy, all matching sets in a variety of colours. In the expectation of catching the culprit, the police decided to set up a twenty four hour watch. My bedroom was the only room that overlooked the back garden and a police constable was stationed there even though I found the young policeman being in my bedroom extremely embarrassing. I had put three matching sets out on the line but no one turned up. After a couple of weeks 'Operation Panty Picker' came to an end!

However, a few months later the local police did catch someone, a man who used to steal women's clothing, hide them in a trunk in his garage, and wear them whenever he could, completely unbeknown to his wife and children by all accounts. I was called in to the police station to go through all the clothes in the trunk to see if any were mine as they were very distinctive. It was horrible in the extreme and totally disgusting as a lot of them were covered with semen, the whole thing made me feel sick. I had to go through every item as the police needed to know if they could close my case, or if they were looking for someone else besides the man they had caught. Not one item of my underwear was found and so their investigations continued. To my knowledge no one else was ever caught. It made me wonder if the person responsible had personal knowledge of my day to day activities, had found out about the police etc. and was scared off. I became more convinced with that idea as time went by as no other theft took place. The whole experience was particularly unsettling and not very pleasant in the end.

While we were living in the flat I decided I wanted my bedroom decorated, Mum said that was fine, as long as I did it myself. As it wasn't something I had ever done before Mum showed me how, including papering the ceiling. That task was achieved by putting a line of dining room chairs across the room, then walking across them, while holding the pasted paper in place with the head of a large broom, brushing it up to the ceiling at each stage of the journey across the chairs. It was an excellent lesson to learn, I have been the main decorator ever since. Dad wasn't very good at wallpapering and would invariably get it wrong. When he papered the hall and stairs he put a few pieces of paper on the wrong way up. It wouldn't have been so bad except there was a very definite pattern to it, there was a lady sitting in a rose arbour, and she was upside down in some very prominent places. It was one of those situations where you either laughed or cried, much to Dad's annoyance we choose the former, the more upset he got the more we laughed.

Another incident occurred, which turned out to be even funnier, was when one of the water pipes burst one night and flooded the shop to about eighteen inches deep in water. Dad got in a total panic, running backwards and forwards in his socks and pyjamas achieving very little. Mum and I could only see the funny side of this demented person running amuck in his socks, the more we laughed, the more he thought we had lost our minds, and so it went on. In the end Mum and I sent him into the kitchen to make a cup of tea while we got things under control. The first thing I did was open the shop door and let the water out while Mum found the stop cock to turn the water off. The shop was in a mess, but fortunately the water didn't get into the living area, we soon had everything mopped up as best we could. Amazingly we lost very little stock, as the majority was on shelves, well above the level the water had risen to. I can't remember how we knew there was a problem with the water in the middle of the night, I can only guess one of us had got up to go to the toilet, heard something suspicious and investigated where the sound was coming from. It took a few weeks to get over laughing every time we saw Dad in his stocking feet, he wasn't very happy with us at all.

One of our visiting reps was a very good looking salesman from a lingerie Company called 'Martin Emprex'. They sold the most beautiful underwear and nightwear imaginable, I simply fell in love with the nightwear, they were of the softest fabrics, in all the most delicate colours of the rainbow and simply stunning. I was able to get whatever I wanted at cost price, much to Dad's dismay, as he thought I should pay full price. As I was already feeling very aggrieved at being a low paid skivvy I stuck to my guns and bought them at cost price. I decided it was all Mum's fault as she had started me off loving beautiful nightclothes and underwear; with all the exceptionally pretty things she had bought me in hospital in an attempt to lift my depression.

There were days when I was bored out of my mind in the shop, with little or nothing to do, so I decided to start knitting with any of the new wool we had bought in. I made up all sorts of garments from small baby wear to ladies' suits, I used to display them in the window or wear them. Surprisingly, we managed to sell quite a lot of the wool, along with the patterns to go with it. It was so much easier to see how the wool would look once it had been made up. Dad thought I was taking advantage of what was in the shop and tried insisting I paid for the wool etc. As you can imagine, another argument would erupt, I would threaten to leave and he would eventually back down, no one else would work for pocket money and board and keep and he knew it. He appeared to be totally blind to what was going on; I dressed the window with the knitted items and, more often than not sold them. We also sold a lot more of the wool than we had done previously, it was the ones I didn't sell he objected to.

My divorce was going ahead, albeit slowly and Mick and I had to be very careful not to been seen alone together at any time. That did sometimes prove to be difficult but fortunately we had a lot of friends who were willing to be chaperones which meant we could still go out and be together socially but nothing more. At the time it felt like forever but lasted for about six months in all. Mick, in his own time, had come to the conclusion that I was a great asset in his life, I got on well with people, I was slim, attractive and well dressed, I made all my own clothes and continued to be quite innovative in putting together the smallest pieces of material and ending up with something smart but unusual. I was a good cook and our physical relationship was fantastic; and most importantly I wasn't able to have children, what more could someone, who loved the social life as much as he did, ask for, he eventually asked me to marry him.

During our courtship I was rushed into hospital and had more surgery, more adhesions and a cyst on the ovaries were found and removed, being realistic I had to finally come to terms with poor health and its limitations. The most interesting occurrence had taken place just prior to my going into hospital; Mum and Dad had gone away on holiday leaving me in charge of the shop when I started getting severe stomach pains and being sick. I did my best to carry on and then suddenly they turned up, completely out of the blue. Mum had been convinced something was wrong; as those feelings strengthened she talked Dad into returning home. I was rushed into hospital a few hours later. Surprisingly, my being ill didn't seem to faze Mick in the slightest, he had made up his mind he wanted to marry me, we seemed to have everything going for us, including the fact he didn't want children and I couldn't have them, perfect!

To return to the divorce, days before it was due to be heard in the courts in Cambridge my ex-father-in-law came to visit me and pleaded with me not to go through with it, he wanted me to try and make a go of it with his son. I tried to make him see it wouldn't work, I couldn't give his son what he wanted and he had found someone who could, a baby was expected, it may even have been born by then, I don't remember. He was very upset and told me he had come to love me as a daughter-in-law and would miss me. For everyone involved there was no turning back, the divorce went ahead. Divorce, in those days, was extremely difficult to obtain, proof for grounds of infidelity, abuse or indeed anything, had to be obtained and that involved private investigators and photographers, etc. Proof of adultery was submitted and, considering their baby was a few months old by then, it went through reasonably quickly. The court appearance, during the summer of 1964, was degrading and humiliating for all concerned, I was extremely glad when it was all over. I was awarded the princely sum of one shilling a year as a settlement which I found to be insulting in the extreme, but which was considered to be justice in those days. I was single and theoretically able to work and they had a young family to support. Rumour had it they went on to have five more children; I could only feel inordinately pleased that his dream at least had come true.

Pearl had travelled with me to add support on that difficult day. While we were in Cambridge we called in to see my old boss Mrs Schmeler who was delighted to see me and Michael number one, who still worked in the cycle shop on the other side of the street. He was married, but had just lost his beloved sister, as I have already indicated they were a very close family; she had tragically died on her way home from the hospital a few days after giving birth to her first child. It was a bitter sweet meeting as I'm sure we both wondered, momentarily, how our lives would have turned out, had we stayed together. We also called in to see my friend Joy on the way home and I was able, at last, to say goodbye to a dear friend and the village of Melbourn where I had been so happy. A closure to another chapter of my life had reached a final, albeit sad conclusion.

Later that year my parent's twenty-fifth wedding anniversary was due to be celebrated at Christmas on 23rd December 1964. I had arranged a family dinner in a smart restaurant and as the day progressed I became rather anxious as it was developing into a night of thick fog, however Mick was driving and he wasn't at all concerned. We managed to find our way there OK as we were driven in style in Mick's posh American car. We all enjoyed an evening of rich food and a lot to drink, much more than had been planned. When it was announced a special wedding anniversary was being celebrated a number of bottles of champagne arrived, courtesy of other party revellers. True to the spirit of our partying family we soon became the life and soul of the evening, we were more than a little the worse for wear by the time we were thrown out. We emerged from the restaurant to find the fog had got a great deal thicker we even found it difficult to find the car in the car park. To this day I will never know how we all made it back to the shop as apart from the fog we were all rather inebriated. Neither do I know how David and

Kathy got home! It had been a pretty good evening, certainly one we would remember for many years after. As an anniversary gift we gave them a canteen of silver cutlery. Looking back, I think that was another reason why I became such an attractive prospect as a marriage partner for Mick, he loved partying and our family had it down to a fine art. He asked me to marry him and we were engaged on Christmas day and made plans for the wedding the following March.

In those days we used to have some particularly severe weather to contend with. Snow would be one of the most difficult as it was heavy and could build up to drifts of six feet or more. Mick lived on the outskirts of St Albans and would use a narrow back lane to travel between us. I remember one night the snow was so deep it reached above the roof of the car, I can only presume a tractor or such like had been through to clear a way because we drove through it with only inches to spare on either side. The whole experience was magical as the headlights reflected millions of sparkling diamonds in a world of purest white. It was freezing cold and the snow had held the various shapes created by the vehicle that had previously pushed its way through. We had found ourselves in a world of absolute beauty, pristine sculpture and sparkling gems, cocooned within the muffled sounds that you can only get when surrounded by deep snow. However beautiful we found it to be we were sensible enough to know we were in an exceptionally dangerous situation and didn't dare stop in case the snow collapsed on top of us.

As we talked about what would be our ideal wedding I really wanted it to be in a church, unfortunately, that wasn't an easy option in those days, as I was a divorcee! A good friend of Mick's put us in touch with a vicar in St Albans; the Reverent Hart Synott, who tended to be very liberal. We went to meet him and he agreed to marry us on the condition we could 'prove' we lived within his parish boundary. The same friend agreed to us using their address, albeit we didn't actually move in and live there. On the surface everything fell into place, even if there were a great many question marks against it being totally legal, the liberal vicar didn't seem to think it mattered! During one of our interviews with him Mick had only one request to make; he wanted the hymn '*For those in peril on the seas',* a strange hymn for a wedding, but that was what he wanted.

The date was 29 March 1965, we paid for the wedding ourselves, I had been married before and felt it wasn't fair on Mum and Dad to foot the bill all over again. We had the reception in our favourite public house by the river on the outskirts of St Albans, I can't remember the name; we were blessed with an unbelievably warm sunny day for the end of March. My two piece suit I made in oyster damask satin, the dress was straight and knee length, with a matching long sleeved jacket. To finish the outfit off I wore a cerise pink pill box hat, with matching gloves and shoes. I'm not one hundred percent certain, but I think Len made me another beautiful cake. It was a happy day with friends and family joining in the celebrations and wishing us well.

We spent our honeymoon at Horner, a tiny idyllic village in Somerset; we stayed at Mick's auntie's who owned a cottage and tea rooms. In the summer she had a thriving business, selling tea, home made scones, jam and double cream, to all the walkers and visitors. It was so beautiful, old, interesting, and very tranquil, even the chiming clock added to the peace. His auntie let us stay there on our own while she visited with her sister, Mick's Mother. The tea rooms were set in a valley with rolling hills on every side. The bedroom window overlooked green fields with grazing cattle and was the first thing we saw on waking every morning, it was completely serene and very beautiful; we loved every moment of our stay there. Every morning I would cook a full English breakfast on the Aga cooker, we would eat it outside in the courtyard in the morning sunshine. Our days were spent exploring the area, walking in the woods or on the beach near Minehead, in the evening we would read in the warmth and quite solitude of the cottage, with the ticking clock in the background. We could not have wished for a more perfect time together, it came to an end far too quickly.

On our return home I stopped working in the shop, 'alleluia'. Mick and I had moved to St Albans to stay with friends of his, an elderly couple. It was to be for a short duration while we were waiting for our new home to be built in Newent, Gloucestershire. Living with friends as newly weds wasn't the best of arrangements, I was a guest in someone else's house and wasn't allowed to do anything. As a new wife there were things I wanted to do for my husband, such as cooking a special meal, but it wasn't to be. We also felt very inhibited in other ways, the bed we had been allocated made a dreadful noise. The iron springs would creak as soon as we sat on it, which wasn't conducive to, quietly, making love.

One thing I do remember, very clearly, was the four of us sitting up one evening listening to the *Mohammad Ali v Sonny Liston* fight on the radio, which was broadcast over the air waves from Madison Square Garden in New York USA, the date was 25th May 1965. We were in a fever of excitement as the build up to the fight progressed, we had been avidly listening to the pre-fight hype and thought Cassius was a mouthy individual. Because of *Sonny Liston's* unexpected (if not controversial) ending of a previous fight, boxing authorities ordered a second bout, this time with *Cassius Clay* (now *Muhammad Ali*) as the defending world champion, and Liston as challenger. The bout was scheduled for November 1964, but Ali needed emergency surgery for a strangulated hernia. The fight was postponed until the following May. It proved to be one of the most controversial fights in history. Midway through the first round Liston fell to the canvas, in what many have argued was not a legitimate knockdown. Referee *Jersey Joe Walcott*, a former world heavyweight champion himself, seemed to be confused after he had sent Ali to a neutral corner. Ali refused, instead he stood over his fallen opponent, yelling at him to get up and then posing over him, with his fists in the air celebrating the knockdown. Walcott took 20 seconds to figure out what to do, and by then Liston had gotten to his feet and resumed boxing. Walcott was advised that Liston had spent more than the requisite 10 seconds on the canvas; Walcott stopped the fight awarding Ali a first-round knockout. The blow that ended the match became known as 'the phantom punch' since most people at ringside didn't see it. Many continue to claim that Liston had bet against himself and 'took a dive' because he owed money to the mafia. It is said that slow motion replays show Ali connecting with a quick, chopping right to Liston's head as Liston was moving toward him. They also show that Liston was unsteady when he finally got to his feet (Ali appeared to connect with four additional unanswered punches before Walcott belatedly declared the knockout and an end of the contest.) The comentaters were hysterical and we were equally so, jumping up and down in our seats, with so much excitement we were worn out the following morning.

Earlier I had very quickly gained employment as a driver for another Motor Factor company, driving a fifteen hundred weight van; they already knew me from my old job as they were one of the many companies I had visited. I enjoyed my job and appreciated being out on my own again, but it lacked the camaraderie of my job in the garage. Eventually it had to come to an end as our brand new three bedroom bungalow in Newent was finished at last; finally we were ready to move in.

Me, 1957, my hair had started to grow again, after it had all fallen out while in Hospital, Mum had taken me to have a Bubble Cut (Perm).

After having been in Hospital for so long, my weight had dropped to 73lbs. Here I'm convalescing at Westgate-on- Sea

My first marriage 19 July 1959

My Bridesmaids were all dressed in Turquoise Satin with Deep Pink Velvet Ribbon Trimmings

My Bridesmaids were all dressed in Turquoise Satin with Deep Pink Velvet Ribbon Trimmings

Me, 1963, with my favourite family, Doll; Pearl and Vivien

The only photo I have of me at my second marriage, 29 March 1965, wearing the Cream Brocade Dress and Jacket I made, with a Cerise Pink Hat

౻ఴ౼ఴ
Chapter 7
"Motherhood"
Newent and Redmarley
1965 ------ 1972

Our reasons for moving to Gloucestershire were two fold; economics, property was so much cheaper, and Mick had friends there. Bud and Wes lived in a tiny village called Minsterworth; they had a number of children and a dog called Bengi. He was the nuisance of the village! As soon as a bitch came into season he would take on a very destructive character. Washing would be pulled off the washing lines, door mats ripped to pieces, toys destroyed, in fact anything that got in his way of reaching the object of his desire. It was how he took out his frustration when not being able to get to his chosen partner, needless to say he wasn't popular with the neighbours. Bengi was as gentle and placid as could be at any other time, but suddenly it was as if a switch had been turned on and he would disappear for days. I could never understand why they didn't send him to the vets for the operation that would have controlled those frustrations.

We had stayed with the family a number of times during our courtship, which had given us ample opportunities to explore the area very well. We decided, after a great deal of thought and investigation that Newent was where we wanted to live. We settled on buying a newly built bungalow in Ackerman's Orchard and Mick managed to get a job straight away as a mechanic in a cement company in Quedgeley on the outskirts of Gloucester.

Newent or 'Noent' was first mentioned in the Domesday Book as a sizeable town, but it was generally thought to have been a settlement many centuries earlier, perhaps even in Roman times. It was

186

and still is a pretty town although, to me, coming from a considerably larger town, it was only the size of a village. I understood it was called a town due to there being a Magistrates court, which apparently allowed it to be classed into a town status. The old railway line was known as the daffodil line as acres of wild daffodils could be seen on the route through Newent. For many years people would volunteer to pick the flowers that were then sent by train to be donated to the hospitals in London. Lord Beeching closed the line in 1966 along with many others over the country.

Our new next door neighbours were a local couple, we had heard all the stories of having to live in a place for twenty years before anyone accepted you, so I was a bit apprehensive as to how we would take to each other. I had been worrying for nothing as Chris and Geoff were fantastic and I very soon became the best of friends with them both. They had two daughters at that time, Heather and Trudy, and they all helped me settle in very quickly. Mick wasn't a gardener and I wanted to get it dug over and planted, so rather than wait, I set to and started digging. Geoff was horrified that I should be doing such hard labour and took over the heavy task for me, it didn't help that Mick was sitting in his chair reading a book and smoking his pipe! Geoff was a very down to earth lorry driver and didn't mince his words but he was very controlled on that day and set to work muttering under his breath during the whole operation. With his help we levelled off both the back and front gardens and laid down some turf, my favourite flowers were roses and I planted some around the edges, I didn't know a great deal about gardening back then.

Mick was a motor mechanic and for him the essential item for any garden was a garage where he could work on cars. He eventually set too and built one, with help from his brother John. He also put up some brilliant washing lines for both Chris and I, they worked on a pulley system which meant we could get our washing extremely high up in the air where the wind would dry it in double quick time. I have never had or seen another washing line since, as good as that one proved to be. It may seem strange to be waxing lyrical about a washing line but it was pre tumble dryers and the only way to dry your clothes was out on a line. In the winter if you could catch the wind or sun, if it showed itself, you could usually get two loads dry, when the weather turned very cold the washing would be stiff but it did dry, I'm not sure how or why but it did. Mick's clothes line was definitely in a class of its own.

As in all newly built homes there was a lot of cleaning to do after the builders had left. The floors were tiled and I scrubbed and cleaned them until they shone like glass, it was my first home to make my own, I didn't count the rented cottage in Hatfield as a home due to being so unhappy there, I wanted everywhere to shine like a new pin. As we were very short of money Mick found an army surplus store up in the Forest of Dean and it was there we bought our first set of furniture, a three seater settee and two armchairs. They were something to sit on, they were cheap, but not very comfortable. We also bought a table and chairs and a few other bits and pieces, I soon had them all cleaned up and shining like new.

We weren't there very long before the summer really set in. Chris who had become a close friend, something I hadn't had for a number of years, and we were saying how nice it would be to go to the seaside. Geoff was extremely careful with his car, cleaning it at every opportunity, even after a relatively short run. Completely out of the blue one day he said we could use it to go to Weston-Super- Mare, I was absolutely astounded; he trusted me with his baby, his pride and joy! I was very touched at the confidence he was showing in me and my driving. That day out was one of many and a landmark for me, Chris, Bud, another friend, and all the children, we all had a fabulous day in Weston. The kids loved being on the beach making sand castles and paddling in the sea, although it isn't the sea at Weston-Super-Mare it's an estuary of the river Severn and mostly mud if you go too far out. The picnic lunch we had packed between us got slightly sandy but everything was eaten down to the last crumb, along with the ice creams etc. Children, sand, sea, sunshine, buckets and spades were an essential part of a fabulous, typically British day out, we all made the most of every glorious moment. When I think about it now, regarding all the laws and restrictions of today, we would have had to hire a coach, it was so much simpler then as we had crammed into the car three adults and seven children and not a seat belt in sight! On the way home, at the end of an exciting and sun kissed day, it was decided to go back over the newly built Severn Bridge; I don't like heights and wasn't aware of just how high it was until I had driven on to it. I was terrified, but there was no going back, no one else could drive and the car was full of people dependent on me! I pulled over to the side, lit a cigarette to steady my nerves but it never went near my mouth, I found I couldn't take my hands off the steering wheel. By the time we got to the other side of the bridge the cigarette was completely squashed, I then had to pull over for a while to stop from shaking; that was the first of many journeys over the Severn Bridge but none ever proved to be as bad as on that day.

Chris, as a friend in a village new to me, was invaluable in helping me get to know a lot of the local people; she quite often stopped me putting my foot in it by making comments that could have got me into trouble! Everyone seemed to be related to each other and it was difficult to know who belonged to which family. Chris also helped me out by letting me use her washing machine as I didn't have one. Her support and friendship helped me cope on a day to day basis as there were days when I was particularly homesick and missed my family. Mick also worked long hours so I had a lot of time on my own, a situation I had never experienced before. In a way I was surprised at how well we did get on as I wasn't used to having friendships with another woman. Because of spending so much time in and out of hospital, having female friends wasn't something I had been able to develop, the ones I had made in the Welwyn Department Store had only lasted for a short duration and it wasn't on a social basis only at work.

My turn to reciprocate her support and kindness came when Chris had her third daughter Mandy at home; I had the pleasure of looking after her and the children. I loved that short period of time; I enjoyed the children and absolutely adored the baby. As the months passed by I used to have Mandy in my home in the afternoons, she wasn't good at sleeping but for some reason I could always get her off to sleep, it gave Chris the chance to rest for a while before the two girls arrived home from school.

Chris went through the usual laying in period of two weeks, which was quite normal then; her Mother-in Law wouldn't visit her until she was up and had been 'Churched', a church ceremony new mothers were expected to go through after giving birth. It was considered by some of the older generation, to be bad luck to go near a new mother until after the ceremony had been performed. My understanding of it was that babies were born out of sin and the churching redressed that sin and made you clean and whole again!

Geoff, bless him, was a very down to earth big gruff bear and soft as could be, I loved them both and we are still good friends some forty plus years later. One of Geoff's favourite foods was a local delicacy called *Elvers;* they are transparent baby eels with black eyes staring at you as you eat them and are caught in the river Severn. I did try them once but wasn't particularly impressed they were a bit tasteless as far as I was concerned; Geoff loved them and was more than happy to eat a plate piled high of glassy eyes! Chris cooked them in her own special way.

As Mick and I didn't have a lot of money or much in the way of mod cons; we decided it was time for me to look for a job; I secured one in the local grocery store dealing with the money, counting up the takings etc. I wasn't very good at it; maths had never been a strong point of mine. I did manage to survive and stayed there for quite a while, the bonus I enjoyed every day was interacting with the rest of the staff and customers; it definitely helped lessen the loneliness and homesickness I had been experiencing.

Mick loved dogs and had set his heart on a having a German shepherd bitch he had heard was for sale. We visited the breeder and fell in love with an older bitch that had been returned by her previous owners. We concluded the sale and gave her the kennel name of Lady Rebecca of Horner; we called her Beauty for short as she was so beautiful. She was my dog in the home and obeyed my every word; outside she wouldn't do a thing for me, once through the back door she was Mick's dog and obeyed his every word. If I took her for a walk and passed a man who, out of politeness would raise his hat to me, that still happened in those days, Beauty would think he was about to attack me and in her efforts to protect me would appear very aggressive. I had to be very careful and choose a walk where I hoped we wouldn't pass anyone, at least not the polite older man! I could have done with some advice from Cesar Millan the 'Dog Whisperer' but I don't think he was even born then!

There was a male *Daschund* dog that lived a few doors away from us and every time Beauty came into season that little dog would come out in warts in his frustration at not being able to mate with her; he was an absolute pain but extremely funny with it. His owners weren't very happy about the situation as they had even more trouble trying to control him. Even if we had wanted her mated we couldn't imagine what a cross German shepherd/ Daschund puppy would look like, assuming that he had been able to reach that far without a ladder! Our home and driveway always smelt of citronella in an effort to put him off the scent, it didn't appear to have much effect, in fact it seemed to be the invitation he had been waiting for. We did try a couple of times to mate Beauty with another German shepherd, but she got very upset and agitated about it all, yelping and crying in distress, we couldn't cope with seeing her so unhappy and decided not to put her through it anymore. The strange thing was she used to have phantom pregnancies and would try making a bed ready for her puppies at the back of the garage. After a few days of frantically trying to get it finished she would suddenly be back to normal again, it was like a switch being turned on and off, very much like our female hormones making us act strangely at times!

We also had a black and white cat called Scamp who wasn't too overjoyed at first about having this rather large intruder invading her space; however, it didn't take long before they became firm friends. Some time later Scamp had a litter of kittens and Beauty became their ever vigilant guardian. She didn't think Scamp was a very good mother to those tiny babies, if they cried Beauty would go and find Scamp, take her very gently by the scruff of the neck and drop her into the basket, as much to say 'now get on and feed your babies' it was just wonderful to see it happening. Although Beauty and Scamp had their bedding in the kitchen, when we were around their favourite spot would be curled up together in front of the fire, we had a job getting our feet anywhere near the fire.

At one stage Mick got involved with stock car racing and became a mechanic for a man I didn't trust one inch. He would call to see Mick when he knew very well he was at work, I would have to hold Beauty back as she didn't like him either and would continually growl until he gave up and left, it was obvious she was picking up on my negative energy. I always kept him at the door as I didn't trust him or Beauty around him. I was extremely grateful when Mick finally gave that interest the thumbs down.

In October 1968 I was asked to be the matron of honour at Pearls wedding. My dress was a long A-line style Magenta satin. I felt very regal and delighted to have been asked. After the wedding, Mick unfortunately got together with Mum's brother Mick and they went off together somewhere and got happily drunk, I saw nothing more of him. We were staying in a hotel in Addington and I had to make my own way back to it having no idea where he was, I wasn't very happy to say the least. I was careful not to let Pearl know as I didn't want it to spoil her day. The atmosphere on the journey home was rather strained. We had taken Mum, Dad and Keith, Mum, in particular, was particularly vocal about her brother's behaviour; Mick bitterly resented her interference and was not at all happy.

I'm not certain when Mum and Dad sold the shop but it wasn't too long before they moved to Bristol and finally bought a house in Chalford Close Yate. Other than the shop it was the first and only house they ever owned. Dad's brother, Uncle Wal, and his family were living in Downend, just on the edge of Bristol, they had moved there because Uncle Wal had got a job working for a newspaper wholesalers in Bristol.

Mum and Dad's move to Yate was a wonderful bonus for me; it was only an hour's drive between us which meant I was able to see them fairly frequently. It did cause a few problems in our marriage, they were aware we didn't have much and would bring us gifts of meat, or clothes for me etc. I was grateful for anything to ease the strain, but Mick sadly resented it!!

After I left the grocery store I applied for, and got, a job in the local 'Bennions' Garage, a family run enterprise. They had decided to open an adjoining shop selling car accessories and spare parts, my past employments qualified me for the position and I got the job. It wasn't the success they were hoping for; there were very few customers, except for one particular gentleman who was a member of the local Plymouth Brethren. He visited me nearly every day with offers of a good time if I would go out with him, the fact that he was married and had a family didn't appear to bother him, he found great difficulty in understanding why I refused his offers. To make matters worse he would leave me, then go and stand on the street corner spouting off about giving up our evil ways and turning to God, a complete hypocrite of the first degree. I used to feel like standing next to him and telling everyone the things he had just been saying to me, I never did of course, but I did pity his poor wife.

Mum and Dad had decided to pay a visit on one of my afternoons off and had arrived at the bungalow before me; Mum was dying to go to the toilet but was scared of Beauty. Need overcame caution and they let themselves in assuring Beauty that all was well and all Mum wanted was the toilet, that lovely gentle dog took her by the hand and showed Mum where the bathroom was, they became the best of friends after that.

We had lots of our family and friends to stay, two particular couples were friends of Mick's from back in St Albans, they came on a regular basis and I was in my element with cooking special meals etc. I did a lot of baking in those days, mouth watering cakes, pastries and pies and I loved having lots of people around me, a throw back to my childhood family get-togethers I think. We also spent quite a few evenings down the local Pub 'The Black Dog', we were always strapped for cash but the social life had to continue.

Mick's brother John came on a regular basis as well and helped Mick with building the garage and constructing some built-in wardrobes for our bedroom. Not only were they needed to house our clothes but we wanted a barrier between us and Chris and Geoff's bedroom, we were always aware of disturbing them with our passionate love life!

The day eventually came when the owner of the shop decided to close due to the very poor sales. Fortunately I was promoted to working in the spare parts department alongside the man who ran it, as I had a fair idea of what was expected of me I soon settled down and found my way around all the stock they held. I was once again doing a job I enjoyed but still had problems with the same pestering customer. He had to be more careful as most of the time I had someone quite close I could call upon to pass him over to, but he timed his visits well, it was as if he had been keeping an eye on all that was going on. In retrospect I should have reported him but, at the time, I wasn't in the least frightened or intimidated by him, I just thought he was sad and pathetic. I'm not sure I would be quite so trusting or dismissive in today's society.

During one night there was a tremendous storm and tons of mud and rubbish came down from the hills and made its way into the centre of the high street. The garage was in its path and when I eventually got into work everywhere was in chaos, inches deep in horrible thick mud. I had to go back home and change into some suitable clothes and footwear ready to get stuck into the cleaning up process. It was extremely hard and filthy work but everyone set to with a will and we all did the best we could to get everything into some semblance of order, at least sufficient to carry on serving the customers.

Each day on my way to work I became friendly with a young lady named Frances, we immediately hit it off and became firm friends, another friendship that lasted for many years. At first it was quite confusing for everyone as we were both called Fran, but she was Frances Mary and I was Frances Ann, family and friends found that easier to deal with. Fran and I spent many hours' together sewing and making ball gowns as she was in the local Ladies Circle. Her husband John was in the Round Table, Newent had had their own group newly inaugurated on 7th Oct 1965 and he eventually put Mick's name forward to be voted in as a member. Mick was in his element as it suited his personality down to the ground, unfortunately it became very expensive and we didn't have the money; however, this was of no concern to him at all, he was thoroughly enjoying the high life. Fran did her very best trying to talk me into joining Ladies Circle but I resisted for a long time, in the end I did join I think it was due to a feeling of self preservation, on the 'if you can't beat them join them' principle. Mick was becoming more and more involved and I was spending a lot of time at home on my own.

Although lack of money was a constant worry to me we were in the cycle of 'eat, drink and be merry for tomorrow may never come'. A great deal more was being spent than was coming in and I felt that the responsibility for paying the bills had fallen on me as I was the only one concerned about them. In the end I became very unhappy and resentful and rather stupidly gave up my job thinking it would make him see sense, which it did for a short space of time, but in reality it became increasingly harder to manage. I really don't know what possessed me to do it but at the time I did feel resentful, I felt as if the whole burden of responsibility was too much and it was time Mick started taking some over himself.

Fran and I worked in a fruit picking market garden during the summer season, I found it exceptionally hard work and nearly passed out during the strawberry picking especially when it was hot, I'm not good in the hot sun. The only good thing about it all was the camaraderie amongst everyone and I ended up with a lovely suntan. The worst possible job was gooseberry picking as the bushes were lethal, covered in extremely sharp and painful thorns. We would cover ourselves with as much padding as we could which would allow us to work but, by the end of the day, my hands were sore and covered in cuts, it paid well but I hated it.

Our circle of friends was widening all the time and we became very friendly with a younger couple, David and Vicky we saw a lot of them, they were great fun to be with. I had also been attending the local St Mary's Church as I had the strong feeling of needing to be confirmed. We become friends with the Rector and his family as well and our social life became even more hectic, we mostly saw all our friends at the same time so we never felt as if we were neglecting anyone and we always had an open house. The Black Dog Inn was a favourite meeting place, invariably ending up in someone's home afterwards.

My time in Ladies Circle was interesting in many ways. I got involved with meals on wheels and enjoyed visiting the housebound; we had some very interesting speakers from various organisations covering a wide variety of subjects. I learnt a lot about planning and organisation with all the different fund raising events we were involved in and got to know some of the local poor and needy who were helped in a variety of ways, I also enjoyed dressing up for all the balls. Fran and I would scour the shops for cheap interesting materials that we could make up into ball gowns; there was also a good second hand shop in Cheltenham that sold beautiful clothes which were of excellent quality and as good as new. Mick didn't dance but there was never any shortage of dance partners for me and I loved dancing. At every dance there would always be some form of entertainment and one year Newent Round Table was asked to put a skit together. It is very difficult to explain without a visual picture but in essence three men striped down to the waist and had a face painted on their torso with the lips surrounding their belly buttons and the nipples were the eyes. Extra large top hats that I had made were placed onto their shoulders and stabilised. Dinner jackets were arranged around their hips, with a made to measure shirt front and collar and large bow tie around their waists. I can't remember the actual piece of music but they used their tummies as if they were whistling in time to the music, it was very, very funny. Fancy dress parties, cheese and wines and any number of activities were organised to raise money, all of which were great fun. While all this was going on we unfortunately got deeper and deeper into debt. One year we went to Brighton to attend a Round Table/Ladies Circle conference, we had a fantastic time but I ended up feeling as if we were supporting the National Debt. I will apportion some of the blame to myself, but Mick would have gone without me and I didn't see the sense of missing out on all the fun!! Mum would have been very envious as Acker Bilk was the main entertainment and, as I have said previously, he was one of her favourites.

One very tragic event we were involved in was directly related to the Aberfan Disaster

'At 9.15 am on Friday, October 21, 1966 a coal waste tip slid down a mountainside into the mining village of Aberfan, near Merthyr Tydfil in South Wales. It first destroyed a farm cottage in its path, killing all the occupants. At Pantglas Junior School, just below, the children had just returned to their classes after singing All Things Bright and Beautiful at their assembly. It was sunny on the mountain but foggy in the village, with visibility about 50 yards. The tipping gang up the mountain had seen the slide start, but could not raise the alarm because their telephone cable had been repeatedly stolen. (The Tribunal of Inquiry later established that the disaster happened so quickly that a telephone warning would not have saved lives.) Down in the village, nobody saw anything, but everybody heard the noise. The slide engulfed the school and about 20 houses in the village before coming to rest. Then there was total silence. George Williams, who was trapped in the wreckage, remembered that 'In that silence you couldn't hear a bird or a child'. 144 people died in the Aberfan disaster: 116 of them were school children. About half of the children at Pantglas Junior School, and five of their teachers, were killed.'

As many of the Round Table and Ladies Circle members who were available went all round the town with collection boxes raising as much money as we could to send to the stricken village in Wales, it was a particularly upsetting time for all concerned and although we managed to collect a considerable sum, we still somehow felt inadequate, it just didn't seem to be enough.

As time passed by Fran, sadly, found she couldn't carry babies' full term and had a number of miscarriages. I felt desperately sorry for her and did all I could to support her and help ease her pain, but no one can feel someone else's pain or take it away or make it any easier, she just had to work through it in her own way, again, I felt totally inadequate. The most surprising effect it had on me was to want a baby of my own. Knowing it was impossible didn't take away the longing, having daily contact with Chris's three girls didn't make it any easier either; it was like a constant numbing ache inside me! I knew it was how Fran felt as well but I didn't have the miscarriages to go through and come to terms with. I suddenly found myself unable to go near new babies and tried desperately to convince myself I didn't want children, but the longing and constant ache continued to grow within me.

Just a few doors away from where Fran and John lived was a woman who had adopted and fostered some children, they were a family who stood out, mainly because of how the husband dressed, he was very theatrical and wore an assortment of cloaks and trailing scarves. It was said he was a permanent student and they were also reputed to be Mormons, whatever that meant. Mormons were those strange young men who stayed at the Black Dog periodically; it was the only place in the village that did B&B. Every time they arrived in the village, which was approximately twice a year, word would be sent out and everyone kept their doors shut or else they were sent packing, sometimes quite aggressively. The story was that some years earlier Mormon Missionaries had arrived in the village, had been tarred and feathered and sent packing. Although I thought it was brave of the young men to dare to be there again I was one of the people who wasn't interested in what they had to say and would send them on their way, an action I regretted many years later. However I started taking notice of this lady although I wasn't quite sure why at the time.

Then one day on my way to or from Fran's I instigated a conversation with the lady, asking her what adoption involved. She gave me the name and address of a Church of England adoption society based in Gloucester, the office was yards away from the Cathedral down a narrow alleyway. After talking it over with Mick and various friends we decided to make contact. Deep down in my heart of hearts I knew Mick wasn't totally sold on the idea but I chose to bury those thoughts as it was something I desperately wanted. Amazingly, after a number of in depth interviews, we were accepted as prospective adoptive parents and Mick requested us having a baby boy. We were told it would be a long wait so we didn't feel in any hurry to prepare for the forthcoming event. The hardest thing I had to do was tell Fran and John, but like all true friends, they were delighted for us. Pearl was another person I was extremely worried about, but for a completely different reason, once again she was delighted for me as well.

One very significant event took place during that summer of 1969 on the 21st July Neil Armstrong and Buzz Aldwin landed on the Moon. A large group of us gathered together and watched it on television at some friend's house, which was the largest and easily able to accommodate us all. It was great party atmosphere with lots of food and drink. We all stayed up and watched the whole historic event and felt part of the history in the making, it was a fantastic night and one I shall always remember.

It was around that time that Beauty was taken ill and died twenty-four hours later, we were absolutely devastated. She had shown no signs of anything being wrong and suddenly she was no longer with us, our beautiful gentle dog had died. With the help of his brother John, who was staying with us at the time, Mick buried her in the garden at the back of the garage. It was the only time I ever saw him cry. Every time I vacuumed the floor and rugs I cried, I was upset because there weren't any dog hairs to vacuum, I missed her so much as she had been a joy to have around. Someone else who was missing her just as much as we were was Scamp the cat, she went off her food and only moved from the spot Beauty had made her own in front of the fire place when she needed to go outside. It took months for us all to go through the grieving process. Unless you have lost a beloved pet it must be difficult to comprehend how much it hurts to have them no longer around you, or appreciate just how painful the grieving can be!

A few months after being accepted by the agency as prospective adoptees an elderly lady knocked on our door and asked if we would be interested in selling her the bungalow as it was exactly what she was looking for. We gave it a great deal of thought and decided to go ahead and sell, by that time Chris and Geoff had moved to another part of the village and it just wasn't the same without them being next door. We found a house out in the country just on the outskirts of a village called Redmarley; but unfortunately it wasn't going to be vacated for quite a few months. David and Vicky, bless them, invited us to stay with them so that the sale of our bungalow could go through as quickly as possible.

I finally made the momentous decision to be confirmed into the Church of England sometime in late 1969 after having attended confirmation classes for a number of weeks. When the day finally arrived, the Bishop or Dean of Gloucester, I can't remember which, attended St Mary's Church in Newent to perform the service. I couldn't explain why, but I didn't experience the warm feelings of acceptance I had been expecting and hoping for. In fact, I felt confused and uncertain about what I had done. I talked it over with our friend the Rector, all he could say was give it time! I did continue attending church each Sunday; I loved the sound of the church bells calling us to church and the wonderful feeling of reverence as I walked through the doors, but the feeling of acceptance eluded me.

We were just weeks away from completion and moving out of the bungalow when a letter arrived that turned our world upside down. There was a four week old baby boy, born on 24th February 1970, for us to go and see. Mick was at work when the letter came and I couldn't stop crying. I eventually made it to David and Vicky's, they only lived down the bottom of the road and we were all in a state of excitement, it must have been a Saturday morning otherwise they would have both been at work. Mick worked on Saturday mornings and when he eventually walked through the door on returning home he was nearly knocked over with the welcome he had and I promptly burst into tears yet again. Once the initial excitement had calmed down practicalities took over and we decided it wasn't going to be possible as we had nowhere to live. David and Vicky wouldn't hear of it and immediately said that the baby would be just as welcome as we were and of course we had to see him. The next problem to overcome was that we had nothing prepared, except for some romper suits I had knitted; we had decided to wait until we had moved into our new home. David and Vicky convinced us that none of those minor details mattered; they certainly shouldn't stop us from going to see the baby.

We arrived at an unremembered building in Cheltenham where we met a lady from the adoption society, we were shown into quite a small room, at least that is how I remember it. I was very nervous and worried as I didn't know what to expect. The lady from the adoption agency asked us to take a seat and wait a few minutes, it seemed like forever before another lady came in holding a sleeping baby, as she placed him in my arms he woke up and smiled at me, no one will ever convince me it was wind, in that instant I fell head over heals in love with that precious bundle of joy and I knew for certain he was meant for me, invisible threads had been woven between us and I had this overwhelming feeling he was a very special gift from God. His given name was Matthew Robert McKinnerny but Mick wanted him to be called Ian Andrew Norris, IAN. Because of the circumstances we were in, moving house and having nothing for him, not even a napkin, it was agreed for the foster mother to keep him for a further two weeks to give us time to get everything sorted out. Every one of our friends and neighbours rallied round and were incredibly supportive and wonderful in what they passed on to us, including a nearly new Silver Cross pram, cot, and carry cot etc. There were a hundred and one things we still had to get but all the large things were very kindly given to us. Mick and I went into Gloucester on a shopping spree and returned home with a car full of a vast array of necessary baby paraphernalia.

I cannot remember very much about the day we went to collect our beautiful baby, which may seem surprising, all I can clearly remember is taking him into my arms and being overwhelmed with a variety of emotions. Would I be a good mother, would I know what to do if he was ill, would he be happy, etc. etc. So many thoughts flying about in my head, I was worried, nervous, ecstatic, and consumed with an overwhelming sense of joy and love. We eventually arrived home with our precious bundle of joy and were visited by all our friends and neighbours. However, baby Ian wouldn't settle and we could not stop him crying, I felt distraught as one of my worse fears was being made manifest, I didn't know how to make him happy. In the end someone suggested a dummy, kindly went to the chemist and bought one back and, low and behold, Ian settled immediately and went off to sleep.

Mum and Dad came over to see their new grandson and a short time later we took him back to St Albans to meet his other grandparents. My Mum was worried about how I would cope if he woke during the night as I was a heavy sleeper and can take at least 20 minutes to come to. However an amazing thing happened that very first night, my whole being tuned into that baby, if he cried I was instantly awake and up out of bed in seconds, which has continued to this day, I still subconsciously listen out for him.

A week later we moved in with David and Vicky and spent the next few weeks in blissful contentment, it only took a very short time for Ian to sleep through the night and, as I didn't want Mick to feel left out in any way, I made absolutely certain he was satisfied in every way possible, it was a period of great joy for us all.

As they all went out to work I more or less took over the running of the house and would have a meal waiting for them when they arrived home, Ian would be bathed and ready for bed all ready for play time. David in particular loved playing with him and it was hard sometimes to put my foot down and insist on bedtime.

We were staying there during the 1970 World Cup series and every evening we would be glued to the television, the famous footballer Pele had come out of retirement to play for Brazil. In the Brazil v England match Gordon Banks made an amazing save against one of Pele's shots but sadly Brazil did go on to win the game. Those were the days when I enjoyed football, I lost interest when big money and the arrogance of certain players became more important than the game!

The only difficulty I encountered during that time was, Ian had a crying period every afternoon between two and four, it didn't matter what I did, he would not stop crying. The longer he cried the more concerned I became, however once bath and tea time arrived he became a different child and by the time everyone arrived home he was an absolute angel. I used to take him out every day in his pram down to the main high street to get the fresh vegetables, bread and groceries etc. One day I got carried away with what to have for dinner that evening and I completely forgot about Ian, arriving back home without him. I had left him outside the 'butchers shop'. Fortunately everyone knew me and he was kept perfectly safe until I turned up to fetch him, it took a while to live that one down, I was ribbed about it for weeks after, every time I went out there would be calls of 'don't you forget him'

A few months later we moved into our new home, it was an older style semi-detached farm type cottage, 'Down Cottage', Redmarley D'Abitot, Gloucester. It had a Rayburn cooker in the back room leading off to the kitchen. By today's standards it was quite big and certainly not your usual square box. There were three main rooms downstairs. The front door was in the centre of the house and as you went through it the large dining room was off to the right. The stairs were straight in front and they went part way up before splitting and turning back on themselves. Turning left at the split took you to the bathroom and separate toilet, turning to the right took you to the landing and three large bedrooms. The main sitting room was on the left with a smaller room at the back which was where the aga cooker was and where I did most of my cooking. It also had a huge floor to ceiling Welsh dresser with cupboards and shelves along one wall. A long narrow kitchen had been built at the back, it had two doors leading off, one out to the back garden and one leading to a covered outhouse, the window at the end spanned the width of the room and overlooked the garden and fields full of black and white milking cows. Both the back and front gardens were huge I never did get them up together. As soon I had worked from one end to the other the first part had overgrown and it became a never ending chore in the end. There was a cooking apple tree in the front garden, raspberries in the back and in the hedgerows were blackberries, elderflowers or berries depending on the seasons, and cob nuts, I felt as if I had suddenly been transported back to my childhood in Noons Folly.

I loved our new home and the first room we decorated was Ian's bedroom. We papered the walls in a pale blue nursery print with clowns, balloons and animals on it. Mick also attached to the lower part of one wall a blackboard for Ian to draw on when he was older. We got that room finished and Ian settled in before we tackled anything else. Ian loved being out in the garden under the trees and would be perfectly happy in his comfortable coach built pram. He would be awake bright and early in the morning and would be ready for Mick to give him his drink and bring into bed with me. Mick's morning routine was always the same, he was an early riser and would start each day with breakfast, coffee, his first pipe of the day and a book to read, all while I continued to sleep, he would always bring me a cup of tea in bed before he left for work. As Ian had been up bright and early since 5.30am he was always ready to go down for a sleep by 10.00am, I would put him back in his cot and he would sleep for a couple of hours and be perfectly happy upon waking and ready for his bottle, then suddenly no matter what we were doing as soon as 2-00pm arrived the crying would start and last for at least two hours.

However much I loved the house it needed some work doing on it but, as usual, we had no money to do very much. I had never lived so far away from civilisation before and became quite low and lonely, my only visitors were the lady from the adoption society, another lady who was Ian's Guardian ad Litume and a social worker, I can't remember their names, and a friend called Margaret who used to deliver my meat once a week from the butchers in Newent. We were friends with Margaret and her husband Arthur through all the activities in Round Table, I had also worked with Arthur in Bennions garage, he was the manager there. Margaret would invariably turn up during Ian's crying time and sometimes I was at my wits end, not knowing what to do with him. She would always manage to quieten him down for me before she left.

Ian then went through a period of not sleeping very well and I rang the doctor, who knew me very well, and said if he didn't do something for this child I would end up by throwing him out of the window. He saw us both and put me on a course of tranquilizers. I hadn't had a child before and was unaware of how we can transmit our feelings through to them. I was unsettled and lonely, feeling the strain of having no money and constantly worried in case Ian's birth mother would change her mind about agreeing to the adoption. It all had an adverse effect on me and consequently on Ian. Once I had been made aware of what was happening and the tablets had calmed me down I began to cope much better. Overall he was a contented and happy baby, as the weeks went by and the tablets had apparently taken effect Ian settled down again and all was well for a while.

As time passed by Mick's brother came to stay again and between them they converted the Rayburn from a coal to an oil burning stove, it made the heat easier to regulate and as previously stated I used it all the time for the majority of my cooking. Bread was a great success and I never seemed to make enough of it, along with all the cakes and pies etc. Because we were so far away from anyone we had a telephone installed and placed on the Welsh dresser. Unfortunately the bell was very loud and whenever it rang we had to rush to answer it as Ian would get into a hysterical panic, he couldn't stand the noise. We were to realize later that was the beginning of what became increasingly a collection of strange and unaccountable fears and behaviour patterns, however, we were new and inexperienced parents and it didn't register that there was anything unusual in his behaviour. He was late in his development but I wasn't aware of that either, not having had any children to compare him with, he never made any attempt at crawling but did eventually shuffle around on his bottom. Aside from his many fears he had a mischievous sense of humour and one day I couldn't find him anywhere. I suddenly heard strange noises coming from the Welsh dresser, I opened the door and there was Ian covered from head to toe in flour with a great big grin on his face. All he needed was a black bowler hat on his head and he could have been mistaken for the little man in the 'Homepride' flour advert. He couldn't stop giggling as I worked my way through clearing up the mess he had made, I didn't think it was quite as funny as he did; he had to have his bath early that day!

I was occasionally allowed to have the use of the car and travel over to see Mum and Dad at Yate, on one of our visits Mum expressed concern at Ian's late development and in particular she felt certain there was something wrong with his eyes. I had noticed his eyes rolled and flickered a lot and had asked the doctor and a friend, who was an optician, about them and was told not to worry as it was just the muscles taking time to settle down. Mum persisted in her concerns as Ian was beginning to show other signs that certain things weren't quite right. He found play difficult and was becoming very withdrawn, his fears of sudden noises were increasing and his behaviour was erratic, but once again the Doctor assured me he couldn't find anything wrong.

The court hearing for the adoption kept being cancelled or delayed and I was getting extremely concerned as Ian must have been approximately seven or eight months old and I was convinced it was his natural mother delaying it. Then, one day, I got a phone call from the adoption agency asking me to take him for a medical at the Gloucester Hospital. I was told it was a routine check prior to the final papers being signed. The lady from the adoption agency, Mrs Holland, met me at the hospital and we went in to see a lady paediatrician. She was very tiny in statue but not quite so much in build, I was asked to undress Ian and then lay him a huge examination bed/table. After what seemed like an eternity and carrying out a variety of tests, which Ian ferociously protested to, the doctor stood back and said, quite matter-of-factly "this child is being placed for adoption isn't he?" when the affirmative answer was given she then said, "It has to be cancelled as this child is severely handicapped and blind".

It was as if a bomb had been dropped into my very soul, I simply could not take it in. I just stood there as if I was in some sort of time capsule where everything had frozen in a micro second of time. I felt as if my heart had stopped and I was paralysed. It must only have been seconds before returning to some sort of normality as I heard the Doctor being insistent that the adoption must not go through. She walked out of the room and I was left to calm Ian down and dress him, I left that building in a complete daze desperately trying to assimilate the information I had just been presented with.

As we arrived at the car Mrs Holland asked the following question "Could you have Ian ready by three o'clock tomorrow afternoon?" on asking why, she said that "someone would collect him at that time and take him away". I then asked where he would be taken, she replied "He will be placed into a children's home". What on earth was she talking about, he was my baby, I couldn't give him up just like that it was unthinkable, how could I live with myself not knowing where he was or what would happen to him? I was adamant no-one would be collecting him the next day or any day and I would fight tooth and nail to keep him. It had been a double body blow, to be told he was severely handicapped and blind was more than enough to take on board, but to have him taken away from me was more than I could cope with.

After an exceedingly difficult journey home, crying all the way and hardly able to see or concentrate on my driving, I rang Mick and asked if he could get home early. I was too distraught to tell him why over the phone but it was obvious I was in a bad way. After finally settling Ian, who was very fractious obviously picking up on my distress, Mick and I began talking it through in great depth and detail, we covered every aspect we could think of and finally reached the decision to fight the powers that be. I don't remember getting much sleep that night

The following day, while Ian was asleep in his pram out in the garden, I wrote a poem called 'LISTEN MY SON', for some unexplainable reason I had dismissed his other handicaps from my mind but felt an overwhelming sadness that he couldn't see.

LISTEN MY SON

Listen my son to what I say,
Listen to the noises as your play,
Feel the sun on you warm and bright,
Listen my son, let ears be your sight.

Listen to the many sweet songs of the birds,
Listen hard and you will hear their Words.
The songs they sing are clear and bright,
Listen my son, let your ears be your sight.

Listen to the soft wind in the trees,
To the gentle rustling of floating leaves,
To the kitten chasing them with all his might,

Listen my son, let your ears be your sight.

Listen to the rain as it thunders down,
Listen, it's stopping, it's quite gentle now.
The earth needs water, for without it, it dies.
Listen my Son; let your ears be your eyes.

Listen as I get on with my work in the house
Listen at night when it's quiet as a mouse
I'm always here, there is no need for fright,
Listen my Son, let your ears be your sight.

While you are still young, listen hard and learn,
So that when you grow up, there will be no need for
concern.
But for now, use my eyes, and together we'll fight,
So listen my Son, let your ears and my voice, be
your sight.

The following morning we contacted our friend, the vicar of St Mary's, and arranged to have a Healing Hands service performed especially for Ian. I cannot find the words that adequately express the depths of anguish, despair, worry, fear and concern I was experiencing at that difficult time, but we were doing the only thing that I, in particular, thought would help and that was to turn the problem over to the Lord.

The healing hands service took place a couple of days later, it was held in the early evening so that as many of our friends could be there without having to take time off work. It was a beautiful service and I had the deepest feeling that everything would be all right, no matter what the future held, God would be at our side. The very next day, with the service still fresh in my mind, the Rector called to see us and spent hours trying to talk us into giving Ian back to the agency as he felt we had no concept of what bringing up a handicapped child would entail or how difficult it would prove to be. Although I knew that what he was saying was correct, indeed I didn't have any idea of the difficulties the future could hold for us. However I was more than a little dismayed at his attitude and asked him if he had no faith in the service he had performed the previous evening. He glossed over that extremely well, but it left me feeling very disturbed, I knew deep down inside of me that God would be with us, no matter how difficult it proved to be. The results of that meeting left me with a strange a feeling of spiritual insecurity, I believed totally in God but I started doubting the church and his servants.

Mum and Dad came to visit as soon as they had received my letter, having written to tell them about what had been happening. After going through everything again Dad took me into those comforting arms of his and asked me if I was absolutely sure about what I was taking on. I looked at him and asked him if he had ever considered giving me up when I became ill. He said "My darling girl of course we didn't, you were our very precious daughter". My reply to that was, "Dad now you know how I feel about Ian, he's my very precious son and I cannot give him up just because there is something wrong with him". With tears in their eyes they both replied, "If that's how strongly you feel we will support you in every way we can" Mum, Dad and I were in floods of tears but, what none of us knew at that time was, how important for my peace of mind that statement came to be, or how prophetic.

Everyone in Round Table and Ladies Circle thought we were very brave and many of them slapped Mick on the back and told him what a wonderfully courageous fellow he was, taking on the challenge of a handicapped child! Overall it was a mixed response from those who knew us, but our close friends were like rocks and totally supportive,

Within a very short space of time the battle to keep Ian started with a vengeance; we spoke with the Guardian ad Litume, who was responsible for Ian's welfare, various doctors, including one who diagnosed Ian as having super sensitive hearing, an eye specialist, who said Ian wasn't blind but he did have very poor sight with limited tunnel vision, he also had Nystagmus which is a rapid movement of the eyeballs from side to side. He registered Ian as blind as he felt that would allow us to get more help in the long term. We also saw the adoption agency hierarchy etc, the list of people was endless. After what seemed forever we saw an eminent paediatrician, a Dr Gryspeerdt who spent a very long time assessing all of us and our interaction with Ian. He saw Ian and I separately then Mick and Ian, he finally concluded that there was a very special bond between Ian and me and, even though Ian seemed to be withdrawing from everything around him, he wasn't withdrawing from me. He was absolutely certain that Ian had lacked oxygen for a period of time at birth but the adoption agency refused to give him or us any details, I had the very strong impression they knew about it when placing him with us but took a chance on him being OK. That lovely man advised us to stick to our guns and continue the fight to keep Ian; he promised to support our petition and definitely recommend that the adoption went ahead. On the strength of that one report we won our case and on 4th December 1970, we attended the court in Gloucester and Ian became our legally adopted son, he was ten months old. As we left the court Mick turned to me and said, "Well, now you have what you wanted", I don't think he meant it quite like that but it gave me a very strange feeling of being on my own.

We left the courts and straight away travelled down to St Albans to stay with his parents who weren't at all convinced we had done the right thing! His auntie in particular thought we were downright stupid and raving mad.

Listening to the radio had been an every day occurrence throughout my life but during the weeks and months to come it took on an even more important role, it became a close friend and companion which sound's really silly but it was true. I was desperately lonely, with no one to talk through all my fears and anxieties, so the various characters on the radio became my imaginary friends. Women's Hour, Desert Island Discs, the afternoon play etc. took me out of myself for short periods of time, helping me hear human voices and about other people's lives. Those programmes allowed me to view my own life from a different perspective. I can fully understand how the lonely and housebound people become personally involved with the television personalities and characters in all the soaps, from my own experience I can easily see their need for a friend who asks nothing back from them!

Life with Ian went on more or less as it had always done, except for the fact we were able to tap into a few helpful agencies, play therapy was the first activity to be organized and Ian and I were shown different ways to overcome his lack of sight. He was prescribed glasses that were kept on with elastic around his head. I became much more aware of everything around me and started breaking everything down to find ways of helping him.

Then, one day, I suddenly realised he was responding to the colour red. Different toys, clothes, food, anything I could find that was red, which I thought would stimulate a response, were introduced every day. He very soon had his favourites and we would work with whatever it happened to be. However his all time favourite was a bunch of my car and house keys, he would lie on the floor and swing them within a fraction of an inch in front of his face. I will never know how he missed hitting himself but he never did, I came to the conclusion he went by the strength of the draught on his face, his other senses were coming into play.

We then started on things with different sounds, but we had to be extremely careful about that as some noises would send him into a panic, phones ringing, dogs barking, balloons going bang etc. It took a long time but, very slowly, we started making progress, introducing even more colours and sounds as we went along. He was a strange mixture of mischief and panic, he would do something he thought was very funny and giggle endlessly, then the next minute something would frighten him and he would be screaming the place down. He disliked change of any sort and was extremely rigid in his routine, but he loved going anywhere in the car and would happily sit for hours on a journey and enjoyed every minute of it. As long as we kept to a very strict routine each day of eating, sleeping, bath and bedtime, we could take him anywhere and he would settle.

Getting him to progress onto solid food was a major challenge as he was frightened of the spoon going into his mouth, after a number of aborted attempts and trying to ignore the screaming I suddenly hit on an idea that some would say was cruel, when he screamed he had his mouth open so I got Mick to hold him tight while I put a spoonful of food into his mouth, immediately followed by his bottle. It took a number of attempts but suddenly the taste of the food took over and his fears left him, tins of stewed apple baby food quickly became his favourite, he didn't mind if it was warm or cold. Since that very difficult start Ian developed a very healthy appetite, wasn't at all fussy and enjoyed everything he was given.

After having bathed him and preparing him for bed it was time for Mick to have his dinner, Ian would shuffle over to him and patiently wait to share a few mouthfuls together, rather like some dogs do when they look longingly at their masters at meal times.

Of necessity our social life suffered and Mick wasn't too happy about that, babysitters found Ian difficult and, although we did manage to find one young girl to sit with him now and again, it wasn't very regular. Friends were happy for us to take him to their homes if they were having a dinner party or social evening but it was the big events we found hard to cater for, more often than not I stayed home. We still didn't have enough money to go around, I was lonely for most of the time and I very soon acknowledged I wasn't cut out for the country. I was a people person, a townie; I needed the interaction and stimulation of human beings around me.

Mick joined the Territorial Army which meant even more time on my own and Ian was getting more and more withdrawn. Mick had met a chap who offered him a job installing swimming pools, I hadn't taken to this man and felt very uncomfortable around him, what he was offering sounded as if there was something not quite right about it. Mick ignored my opinions and went ahead and took the job. He was travelling away more and more and I started having suspicions that there was something not quite right going on though there was nothing I could prove. He was very much a ladies man and, although up to that point our physical relationship had been brilliant, everything that was happening around us at that time was taking its toll and our relationship was no longer cohesive.

My marriage was falling apart, Ian was getting worse, and I was desperately lonely and unhappy. Looking for solace I turned to an unmarried friend who was in the Merchant Navy, during his times at home he had spent a great deal of time with us, taking Ian and I out to all sorts of different places. We were extremely relaxed in each other's company and I chose to see more into the relationship than there was. Ian seemed to blossom on those days out, he loved the attention and travelling around and I suppose, because I was happy seeing Ian happy and was in need of attention myself, I found myself unable or unwilling to get him out of my mind. He finally realized what was happening and backed off and our days out came to an abrupt end.

It was during that difficult time Mick's Mum became ill and I went and looked after her and his Dad for a few weeks. It wasn't the best or easiest of visits as I had to be very careful around his Dad, they didn't have a bathroom and I would have to take a bowl of hot water up to my room to wash, I had to lodge something against the door as he would try and get into my room whilst I was washing. His Mum had her bed downstairs as she had phlebitis in her legs and was on complete bed rest, bless her. I'm certain she knew what he was like but was helpless to do anything. I stayed there for approximately four weeks then her sister arrived and took over.

As Ian became progressively worse our Doctor recommended we see a children's specialist at the 'Children's Hospital' in Bristol. As we were virtually passing the door we called in and picked up my Mother before attending the appointment. We were kept waiting for what seemed like an interminable length of time, Ian wasn't at his best as everything was new and different around him, sudden noises and movements frightened him and he was out of his routine. The nursing staff had tried unsuccessfully to acquire a urine specimen and the more they tried the more upset Ian became. When we did eventually see the specialist he gave Ian a cursory examination stood back and said "This child is severely handicapped, he will never be able to walk, talk or feed himself, he will be a vegetable for the rest of his life, put him into a home and forget he ever existed." I thought my heart had stopped it was as if I had been knocked out cold with a sledge hammer, I couldn't think, move or speak, I suddenly became aware of my Mother angrily telling the specialist how utterly insensitive his approach was. As we left the hospital Mick said "I will leave you at your parent's house for two weeks during which time you will have to decide if it's him or me!" I cannot find any words that can adequately explain the emotions that were overpowering me at that moment in time, on what had become a significantly momentous turning point in our lives. Over the following two weeks every micro second of time was crammed to capacity with a jumble of conflicting emotions, a deep intense pain, fear, hate, anger, confusion and above all an overwhelming feeling of love and sadness for this special child who God had blessed me with.

My parents did their level best to encourage me to talk it through with them but I was locked within myself, rather like Ian when he was faced with something he could no longer cope with. Every fibre of my being screamed out to me to follow my heart and innermost instincts which were to continue to keep my precious, albeit damaged, child. My common sense was asking 'how on earth could I do that on my own?' I also knew that whatever decision I came to my marriage was over, I was being held to ransom and love cannot flourish under those conditions. Both decisions were extremely painful in their own ways, but in the end I finally concluded it had to be based on which one of the two paths that lay before me was the one I could live with for the rest of my life. I went with my heart and instincts and choose to keep Ian.

Everything was very strained between us when Mick arrived to collect me at the end of the two weeks and I had told him of the decision I had reached. There wasn't time to go over anything in depth as we were going on to a Round Table dinner and dance that same evening and had to leave straight away, my parents had kindly offered to have Ian over night. We were late arriving at the venue, by which time the dinner was over, and completely ignoring my presence or indeed my need for sustenance, he went off to find something to eat. Although deep inside I was extremely hurt and upset I was determined to enjoy the dancing as they had a steel band playing and I loved the sound and rhythms they made. It was blatantly obvious to everyone that there was something very wrong between us and, surprisingly, I got a lot of attention that night. Looking back I dare say they wanted to find out what was going on, but we both kept it to ourselves, it was still too raw and not something to be shared until we had processed the inevitable outcome ourselves.

After enduring a couple of months of a very cold and distant relationship, I finally had to reiterate the reasons as to why and how I had arrived at the decision to keep Ian. However, Mick was very complacent and sure about my always being there with him, I had repeatedly said that my first divorce had been too horrendous for it to ever happen again. He was absolutely certain I wouldn't leave and knew I was in a total quandary as to which way to turn. I knew we couldn't go on as we were but what could I do and where could I go, I had no money but I did have a little car. The final decision as to what I was to do solidified on the day I found out he was having an affair with our next door but one neighbour. I also knew deep down inside there were other women he was seeing as our physical relationship had ended some months before, and I knew Mick. I already felt utterly degraded but coming so close to home was the last straw.

By that time a very cold December had arrived and he had gone away again and left us without money, oil for the Rayburn or coal for the fire, he had finally pushed me too far. I did all the washing, cleaned the house, packed our bags and set to and ironed all his shirts, all the time crying my eyes out as I knew we had finally come to the end. I had loved him with a passion but I could no longer fill the role required of me. I had become a mother and, because of his handicaps, Ian's needs had become paramount. I could no longer be the social wife Mick needed. I don't blame him in any way as I'm certain I must have proved to be a great disappointment, I could also understand him not being able to cope with a handicapped child who would ultimately become a man, especially as he wasn't his own. Once again I felt sorry for us both as we each had our own needs which couldn't be fulfilled for a variety of reasons.

I packed the car and made the difficult journey to Yate, Ian and I turned up on my parent's doorstep. In floods of tears I explained what had transpired and asked if we could stay, and so began yet another period of my life!!

**I was Matron of Honour at Pearl's first wedding
in October 1968**

Ian was six weeks old in April 1970, the beautiful
baby boy we eventually adopted!

I was overjoyed to become a new mother; this
was when my life was irrevocably changed forever!

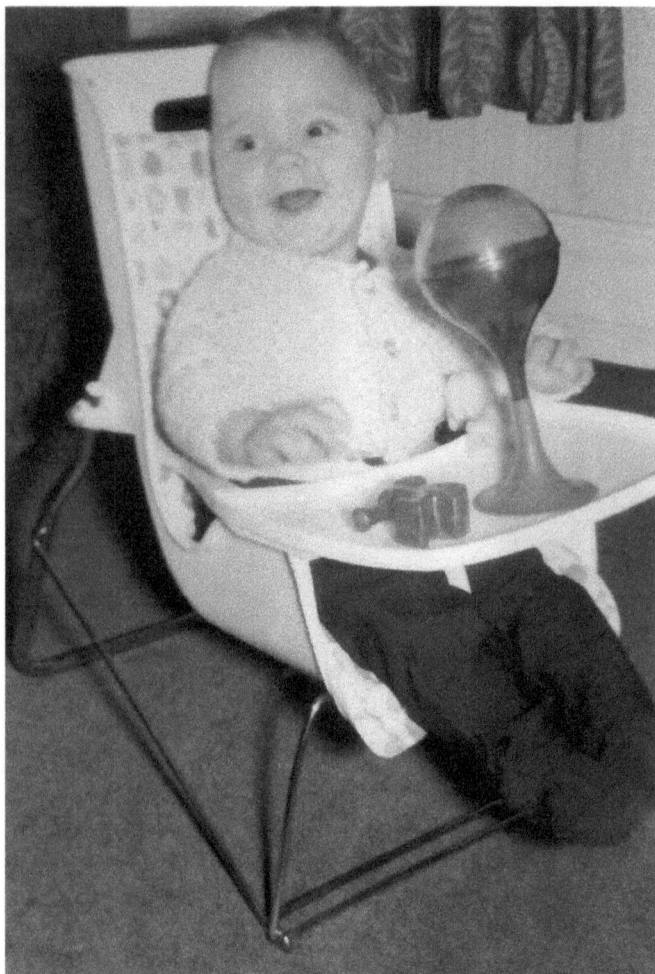

Ian 1971, taken before we found out he was Handicapped!

Chapter 8
"Emotional Turmoil"
Yate
Bristol
1972 ------ 1975

After talking everything over in great detail with Mum and Dad and settling ourselves into the smallest bedroom, the biggest question and obstacle to overcome was what was I going to do for money? I went to see a solicitor the following morning and the first step in the legal process for claiming maintenance for Ian and me had began. We didn't end up with a great deal to work with but, with the help of my parents not asking for too much towards board and lodging, we somehow managed to scrape by. The next thing I did was visit the local council offices to put my name down for a council house, I was added to the waiting list but they couldn't tell me how long it would take for us to get a home of our own.

Needless to say, because of all the change and upheaval, plus all my emotions being heightened, Ian withdrew more and more into himself. Mum, Dad and Keith decided that if he could progress in small ways they would be happy. Keith wanted him to kick a football down the hall, Mum wanted him to learn to walk and Dad wanted him to respond to him as well as to me, I didn't mind what he did as long as we could get through to him and help break the barrier he had retreated behind. Sandy, the dog, wanted someone to play with and would lick Ian whenever she got the chance. The very strange thing was he was frightened of every other dog he came into contact with, Sandy, for reasons we were never able to determine, managed to overcome his fears and her very presence would make him laugh. She was a very excitable, sandy coloured mongrel, a Heinz 57 variety as the saying goes, and she seemed to understand Ian and he adored her.

To say that going back home wasn't easy, would be an understatement of the highest magnitude. Mum, in particular, treated me like a child, at least that's what it felt like. She vetted anyone who came to visit, in her opinion nobody ever gave anything without wanting something back and that included so called friends. She stipulated times for me to be in and if or when I could go out. I was 32 years old and had successfully run my own home but she made me feel like a teenager who knew no better than to be kept under control. Was all that in my imagination? No it wasn't, but there was nothing I could do about it I was utterly desperate and totally dependent.

We went down to stay with Uncle Wal and Auntie Vicky for that first Christmas 1972, by that time they had moved down to Wivelsfield Green, Sussex, due to uncle Wal gaining a long awaited promotion. I hadn't been feeling well but put it down to all the stress I was going through, I felt very sad and lonely but did enjoy being with all the family again.

A few months later Mick, for whatever reason and known only to himself, bought me a new car, new to me that is, a pale blue Ford Escort Estate, I loved that car and called it my little road runner. However back in Newent I heard, via the grapevine, that everyone in the Round Table/Ladies Circle groups thought I was absolutely dreadful leaving Mick the way I did, they couldn't begin to imagine how I could do that to him when he was so good to me! The car of course added to that misguided concept, but what did that matter to me, I had the car and that was a wonderful, a totally unexpected bonus. It was quite obvious that no one knew what the true story was behind the break-up of our marriage! If that was what he wanted that was fine by me.

Around the end of February 1973 I decided to go and stay with Doll and Len, Pearl was back home living with them after her marriage had come to an end and we spent hours talking. We also went dancing at the Streatham Lacarno where I was able to let my hair down and get rid of all the pent up frustrations that were festering away inside me. Doll, Len and Vivien were perfectly happy to look after Ian who seemed a lot happier while he was there, maybe because I was more relaxed and at ease and able to be myself.

One of Ian's most annoying and disturbing fixations was banging his knuckles on a door; it could, and did, drive you mad. Wherever we went the first thing he did was verify where all the doors and windows were, he wouldn't settle until they were all checked out and then would begin banging on any door that took his fancy, the banging continued until eventually his knuckles were covered in horrible warts

While I was staying with them I started getting very severe abdominal pains, I rang The Gordon Hospital and arranged an immediate appointment. I was taken in on 15th March 1973 and after having another dreaded sygmoidoscopy, was operated on the next day when they found a cyst and rectal bleeding. Pearl, bless her, looked after Ian for me while I was in hospital and then us both during my convalescence. I must have been with them for over two months or more, as I was admitted again shortly after my release after experiencing excruciating pain and nearly passing out while out on a shopping trip with Pearl in Croydon. Acute cystitis was diagnosed and I spent a few more days in the Gordon.

Vivien would take Ian down to the local park where he loved going on the swings, and with her help his mischievous personality started to show itself. Doll, unfortunately, couldn't get around too easily, due to having a calliper on her leg as a result of a stroke which had left her partially paralyzed down one side. Ian would hide things from her; in particular her walking frame! You always knew he had done something naughty because his giggles would give him away. There were constant cries of "bring that back you perishing nuisance you" when Doll was unable to do, find, or get to, what she needed.

He loved listening to 'Tweety Pie' the budgie, just as long as he stayed in the cage, then one morning tweety pie was found lying in the bottom of his cage, he had fallen off his perch and sadly died!

I had put it off for as long as I could, nevertheless the time finally arrived when I knew I had to return home to Mum and Dad, but it was one of the most difficult things I had to do, as both Ian and I were so much happier and more relaxed with my wonderful family in Addington. However we couldn't impose on their kindness any longer, I had to return, regardless of my feeling the need to be constantly on guard regarding everything I said and did, I never felt able to relax around Mum. The only way I can explain it is, that she didn't trust me or my judgment and appeared to be jealous of anyone I had any contact with.

Through the National Health Service I managed to get a physiotherapist to visit Ian at home. Her name was Pat Austin, a very practical, fantastic person, more than able to cope with Ian's screams. She showed me how to do all the exercises that had to be done every day in order to strengthen the muscles in his back, arms and legs, slowly but surely we began to notice a difference. He still shuffled about on his bottom and we were told, by other well meaning professionals, that unless he crawled he would never be able to walk. Pat, bless her, said that was rubbish, all we had to do was strengthen his leg muscles. So each day I would go through all the exercises she set out for him, while Ian screamed and fought me. The process would start with a warm bath to relax the muscles then I would lay him on the floor while systematically going through the exercises for his arms, hands, legs and, finally, feet. The paralysis was all down his right side very much like a stroke victim. He enjoyed the baths at first until he realized what the inevitable outcome was going to be, the screaming would start as soon as he heard the water running. He screamed and fought me and became extremely distressed and I cannot find a word descriptive enough to describe how awful I felt for having to put him through that torture, but the exercises had to be done twice a day and it was all down to me to do them! The day eventually arrived when Mum couldn't stand it any longer, shouted at me to stop and accused me of being very cruel, I was desperately upset as all I was trying to do in the long term was to help strengthen him. I could perfectly understand how distressing it was to hear his constant screaming but she couldn't see beyond the moment and I was trying to work towards a day when he had grown so big I wouldn't be able to handle him on my own. Needless to say, Mum called upon Dad for his support and I could do no more than stop the exercises.

Pat visited once every two weeks and, when she found out what had been going on, with all guns blazing she came to my rescue, telling me to take no notice of anyone and carry on with all that I had been doing. She spent a long time explaining to Mum the long term benefits we were working towards and that I needed their support, not condemnation. In an attempt to ease the situation she arranged for Ian to have a swimming lesson in a hydrotherapy pool, somewhere near Frenchay Hospital, as she felt it would have an overall benefit. The water was warm and the exercises could be done without Ian noticing too much. The first few weeks we went he screamed the place down, terrified of everything around him. I would hold him tight and very slowly walk into the water, his arms around my neck were like a vice, but it was the only way I had found to get him over his fears. It took a few times, but persistence paid off until he finally realized there was nothing to be frightened of and started to enjoy himself.

Because a lot of the stress had been diverted the atmosphere at home settled down and they decided to put a new floor down in the kitchen. We talked it over and agreed the best time to do it was after Ian had gone to bed and Dad and I set to, cleared everything out and laid the new floor. We were very late getting to bed as it had taken longer than expected and the next morning I was taking longer than usual to wake up. Ian and I were in the small front bedroom where we slept in bunk beds, Ian on the bottom and I was on the top. He had found a way to get out of bed and down the stairs on his own by going down on his bottom. I was suddenly woken up by a piercing scream and nearly fell out of bed. Ian had reached the kitchen door and horror of horrors, everything was different, and he was absolutely terrified. It took me all day just holding him, with his vice like grip around my neck, literally taking one step onto the new kitchen floor, retreating, then going over the same process over and over again until he finally quietened down and allowed me to walk across the floor to the back door. It took a couple more days before I could get him to go in on his own but we did eventually succeed and he overcame his fears. Even the promise of food couldn't break through the barrier of fear, considering we had to go into the kitchen to get the food, we all felt rather hungry by the time he finally calmed down.

I didn't know anything about autism at that point in time, that knowledge and understanding came much, much later, he had been conveniently 'boxed' as multiply handicapped and the only professional help I got was from Pat. Her constant advice and support was like the safety of a life jacket to a drowning person; however many times I went under, she pulled me back to the surface again.

Pat put me in touch with another parent with a handicapped daughter, they lived out in Pucklechurch. She was part of a group of mothers who had set up a play group of their own because, like me, they had found 'normal' play groups wouldn't take handicapped children in. The group had the use of a building within a complex on the outskirts of Bristol which I believe had been a Dr Barnardo's Home that had closed down a few years before. I haven't been able to find any information about that so I can't confirm the validity of its previous use, however, it was a very large complex and the group had the use of a big room. Ian and I were invited to join the group, after seeing what they had to offer, we were more than happy to get involved. It was a very small group of concerned mums wanting their children to have the same opportunities of play and interaction with each other as 'normal' children had in the community.

The play group became so successful that they started getting referrals from the professionals, of children with a variety of disorders that didn't quite fit into the main stream of education. Eventually the success of what they were doing spread and the local authority finally concluded a great need was being addressed, they then decided to set up an official play group for children with special needs on the corner of Blackhorse Lane, Downend. In the blaze of publicity, to my knowledge, not one of the mothers who had started up the original group, out of a desperate need to help their own children, got any recognition at all.

It was around that time I managed to get Ian admitted into a special unit attached to Culverhill School in Yate, Jo Marshall the teacher, asked if I would mind staying with Ian at first until she got to know him, I continued to stay on and became an unpaid classroom assistant enjoying every second of my time there. Although Ian was now in the system, so to speak, in my opinion my being with him all the time wasn't very beneficial for him or his progress, however, as that was the only way I could get any sort of agreement from the powers that be, it was something I had to work with.

All in all we had a busy round of activities. He still had his swimming, attending school, having his daily exercises, attending a variety of clinics and a toy library, where he was able to try out a variety of toys that I simply couldn't afford to buy him. After a while I was approached to be part of a parent support group as it was felt that my experiences could be a help to other parents. I only attended one session, that was more than enough for me, the attitude of a lot of the parents were at opposite ends of the spectrum to mine. The main difference was that I had a pro-active approach of how best to help Ian; their idea appeared to be to sit back and let someone else do the work for them. It didn't take them long to strongly disagree with my ideas. It finally came to a head when a little boy about the same age as Ian kept using the vilest of language, his parents thought it extremely funny and spoke back to him using the same sort of language. I put up with it for a while before saying I would rather Ian never spoke a word for the rest of his life than use language like that. Needless to say it didn't go down at all well and by mutual agreement we parted company!

Ian had by that time been referred to the children's eye hospital in Bristol and after numerous, very ingenious, tests it was decided he would benefit from wearing stronger glasses although to be truthful we'd had a great deal of difficulty getting him to keep the ones on he'd had from a baby and once again keeping the new ones on at first was a challenge but once he came to terms with being able to see more clearly he soon settled down. The diagnosis was that the Nystagmus had got worse which was even more noticeable when he was agitated, a frequent occurrence; he also had tunnel vision which made it even more difficult for him to see.

Although we didn't see her quite as often as we had in those early days another activity Pat arranged for Ian, at a much later stage, was for him to attend a *Riding for the Disabled* group near Warmley, Bristol. He loved it and did remarkably well, he wasn't frightened of the horses and his balance was exceptionally good, although he only had the use of one hand he coped brilliantly. What we would have done or where we would have been without that wonderful woman's support I dread to think, she opened up so many doors for Ian to try and progress in. Our life were a never ending round of things to do and places to go, some good and some not so good! However, life was soon to take on a much more frantic pace.

A break in the weather brought about some very welcome sunshine, after days of heavy rain, and it was decided to try and get some washing dry out on the clothes line. Towards the end of the afternoon Mum went out to get the washing in, fell over on the damp grass and broke her leg. I rushed out to help her but it nearly proved our undoing as Mum was quite a heavy person to lift. Sandy the dog was barking and running around in circles trying to get in on the act and I was trying to stay upright on the slippery grass. After a great deal of effort I eventually got her indoors and, while doing my best to make her comfortable before sending for the Doctor, she started gesticulating and trying to say something to me very, very quietly. I couldn't make it out at first until she pointed to Ian and said, "Look" and there he was, taking his first steps across the room. We both burst into tears; her leg was momentarily forgotten in the excitement and wonder of this walking miracle of mine. Sandy not to be out done she was so excited wanting nothing more than to lick him to death, which made him lose his balance and he ended up on his bottom again. Nevertheless it was the beginning of his determination to walk and nothing was going to stop him.

I had called the Doctor in to see her and I drove Mum to the hospital shortly after, she was X-rayed and had a full length plaster cast put on her leg. I can't remember how I got her home as Ian was all stressed out and screaming but, get her home I did. She coped as well as could be expected for a few days. Like Ian she dragged herself up and down the stairs on her bottom, there were no toilet facilities downstairs.

The highlight of everyday was Ian's progress in walking and finding he could reach places that had previously been out of bounds. His sense of fun and mischief knew no bounds and I was constantly checking to see what trouble he had got himself into. One favourite was the control knobs on the washing machine, he could not only reach them but he could turn them on as well, all accompanied by hysterical laughter.

After a few days had passed by it was obvious Mum wasn't feeling well, she had gone off her food and didn't look or sound right. She assured me she was fine and I was to stop fussing. Two or three more days went by before Dad came into me in the middle of the night saying he wasn't happy with the way Mum was breathing and that she had a pain in her chest. She was adamant there was nothing wrong but I didn't like the look of her and her breathing was very shallow. They didn't have a phone so I quickly got dressed and went round to the next street to the phone box and rang the Doctor. After explaining all her symptoms it took approximately ten minutes for him to arrive, having phoned for an ambulance before he left his house, she was rushed into hospital with a blood clot on her lung. It was touch and go for a number of days; they put her on oxygen and Warfarin to thin the blood down and fortunately after a few days of rest and treatment she did eventually pull through and returned home once again. Apparently it was quite common for a clot to travel to the lung with a plastered leg, the Doctor felt certain that if we had left it until the morning before phoning him she would most certainly have died.

I was totally exhausted, what with visiting and worrying about Mum, having all of Ian's clinics to attend (they all seemed to fall while Mum was in hospital), doing the shopping and making sure Dad was OK as well. It was during that time David and Kathy had travelled up from Welwyn Garden City where they lived and, once again David and I fell out. There were a number of issues he didn't agree with, how things were being run etc. How he had the audacity to criticize when all he had done was cry over Mum was more than I could stomach. I was extremely tired, not necessarily in control of my emotions, upset and annoyed and, sad to say, I lost my temper and found myself saying things that were best left unsaid. Dad acted as the intermediary but the atmosphere was more than a little uncomfortable until they finally left.

There followed a never ending round of hospital visits for Mum's blood to be checked, along with all Ian's various appointments at different places. For a number of weeks I felt as if I was on a merry-go-round rushing from one place to another on an extremely strict time table. Ian was more than a little unsettled and tended to be totally uncooperative and screamed a lot, Mum's plaster eventually came off, her blood levelled out and everything did finally settle down and we all survived to tell the tale.

I don't remember how I got to know about it but someone had told me about the 'Gingerbread Association', a club for one parent families. I started attending but found myself in deep water after a very short space of time. One of the men seemed to take it for granted that I partner up with him and we had a few dances together which I enjoyed. It didn't take long before he started expecting much more, when I told him I didn't want to get involved he accused me of leading him on only to let him down badly. Going steady with anyone had not been in my plans, I had no desire to form a relationship and he got pretty upset with me. I felt rather sorry for him as he was obviously very lonely, but he had totally misinterpreted my intentions. All I had wanted was to have a drink and a dance but nothing more, he was very harsh and aggressive in his opinion of me, which completely knocked the stuffing out of me for a while.

I was working myself into the ground doing all that I could, tapping into anything and everything in order to help and stimulate Ian, however, underneath it all I was deeply unhappy. I missed my own home, my friends (who I thought had been my friends from

Ladies Circle), but most of all I missed the love, warmth and passion of the relationship Mick and I had had before everything had gone sour. I found myself disliking my Mother intensely as she seemed convinced I was up to no good as soon as I was out of her sight and was very vociferous in her opinion of me. I reacted by losing my patience with Ian and his continual screaming; he was going through a phase of getting out of bed within minutes of my leaving the bedroom and bumping his way downstairs again, and Mum was getting more and more critical with me. At the end of another day of criticism, Ian screaming and not staying in bed and having put him back in it for the umpteenth time; I completely lost it and proceeded to smack him a number of times. I suddenly came to my senses and promptly burst into tears asking Ian to please forgive me over and over again, I was so close to breaking point and I was taking it out on him. My distress caused Ian to be more distressed and so the cycle continued, he was a reflection of my unhappiness and expressed it in the only way he knew how, by screaming and withdrawing into himself. At that stage I didn't know how I could achieve it but I knew that something had to change.

I was in that cycle of depression and deep unhappiness when I met up with this chap who was a prison officer at Leyhill Prison. He was charming, attentive and separated from his wife and made every effort to court me. He assured me the divorce was going through and had applied for married quarters for us to live in on the Isle of White when his transfer came through. I fell hook line and sinker for the story as I saw it as my life line to sanity once again and started making the necessary preparations. A week before we were due to leave he wrote and told me it was all off, he had decided to try and make a new start with his wife! I had been exceptionally foolish, extremely vulnerable and desperately unhappy.

After being subjected to another lecture a few days later on how I should or shouldn't be behaving something snapped inside me and there followed a period of time during which I can only describe as having engaged a self destruct button within me. If she was to keep making these unfounded accusations as to the type of person I was then why not prove her right, she accused me of being a tramp, as had the man from the Gingerbread club, so why not be one! There followed a very long period of self harming. I abused myself spiritually and emotionally, I disregarded any code of ethics I had previously lived by and went from one man to another. I had convinced myself that I wanted to use them as I had been used, but underneath it all I was in the cycle of destroying myself. I was still quite slim and attractive and had no trouble at all getting men to fall for me, but they were all the wrong type of men. Over the years and certainly during that period of time, I heard all the heart stopping stories that I'm certain many women have heard upon finding themselves alone, the 'My wife doesn't understand me!' crying on the shoulder stories, I'm sure you know what I mean. I remember one man I met kept a certificate of his having been sterilized in his pocket, to supposedly reassure you it was safe to have sex with him and not become pregnant! I treated him with the contempt he deserved. It was as if a boil was festering inside me, getting bigger and bigger filling with revolting, pulsating puss ready to erupt.

Events over the following months have no logical cohesion to them as they are all blurred and interlinked with each other in my memory. Time, length, space, objectiveness or even accuracy I can't confirm but I can only tell the stories as they come into my mind.

I had met up with this chap who was another prison officer at Leyhill Prison. As it was close to Christmas, he invited me to his parents' home up north somewhere, Newcastle rings a bell but I can't be certain. I had arranged to spend Christmas at Addington and contacted them to ask if I could take him along as well. We made the trip up north, spent two miserable days there and then set off down the A1 to Addington in time for Christmas. We were in my car and for days previously I had been getting severe stomach pains which got worse as the journey progressed and he had to take over the driving even though he wasn't insured. I somehow managed to get through the holidays, I was in a lot of intermittent pain, but also the more I got to know the said young man the more I disliked him and couldn't wait to drop him off at Leyhill. I had proved to be a convenient form of transport for him to get home for Christmas, ending in a cheap holiday with very generous people!

I was coping with my daily life in the best way that I could until the day came when the pains I had periodically been experiencing started up again. I had started feeling unwell then crippling pains, low down in my stomach, would suddenly grip me and I would be doubled over in the most excruciating pain imaginable. It was in early 1974 before I went to see Dr Hall my GP, he sent me for an emergency hospital appointment at the Bristol General and, after tests and X-rays had been completed, another ovarian cyst was found to be on the point of rupturing. The hospital doctor wanted to keep me in there and then, but that was impossible as I had Ian to sort out. They told me to make arrangements for him as soon as possible and not to lift anything, again another impossible thing to ask as Ian was still in napkins and also needed his exercises etc. What was I to do, where was I to go for help? Mum and Dad couldn't cope with him, he was too difficult to control as well as having to change his napkins. I contacted the social worker and arrangements were made to send him to a 'Sunshine House for Blind Children' for a short period of time. It was to give me time to have the operation and time to recover from the surgery. Mum and I took him to a place called Ogmore- By- Sea, Glamorgan. It was the first time Ian and I had ever been separated and I felt dreadful, how could I explain to him what was happening? I was being forced into a corner with no way out. It was the first time I had met the staff or visited the Home and I can only describe it as extremely imposing, large rooms with high ceilings with no feeling of homeliness about them. When I saw the dormitory where he would be sleeping all I wanted to do was bundle him up and take him back home again. I didn't want to leave him in their care but I had no other choice. He was four years old and, to all intents and purposes, lived in a world of his own, but how I hated leaving him. Mum and I cried all the way home again.

I went into hospital the very next day and ended up having a total hysterectomy as a number of cysts and a mass of adhesions, which had completely worked through my womb, had been found. I was 33 years old and any hope of having a baby of my own, which had been buried deep down inside my consciousness, was finally crushed. I became very depressed again and went through what I can only describe as a bereavement; I felt less of a woman, totally unattractive and unwanted! It's one thing to go through life knowing you couldn't have children but when you have a period each month, at the back of your mind you always believe that a miracle could happen, and quite another to suddenly know for certain that miracle will never happen. It sounds silly when I think of it now but at that time I suddenly felt less of a woman. All the reproductive organs that identify you as a woman had been removed and I was having a hard time coping with that.

I developed a severe chest infection a few days after the operation and was very poorly for some time. Mick visited me on a regular basis and, when the hospital decided to send me away to convalesce, he bought me a sheepskin coat, it was March and very cold. I remember the women on the ward saying I had to be mad to have left him. They saw him as being very attentive and caring, which he was, but sadly I no longer trusted him or believed in myself.

As soon as I returned home to Mum and Dad's, Ian had to come home as well, in those days if he was away from home for any longer than six weeks I think it was, he could be taken into care permanently. It is going to be impossible for me to describe the emotions that were enveloping me on the day we were going to bring Ian home, due to all the complications and extended convalescence, what should have been a six weeks stay had turned out to be nearly three months and even then he was only going to be home for two days. Mick drove Mum and me to Ogmore to collect him. With difficulty I knelt down on the floor, as I still had to be very careful, and called him. We could see a mixture of emotions flitting across his face, as soon as he was certain it was me he rushed across the room and threw himself at me and we both cried and hugged and cried some more, it was all highly emotional. As I was still unable to lift him, the manager of the home decided that he could go home over the weekends only, as I didn't have any able or permanent help to assist me care for him.

Mick once again came to the rescue and came every day over that, and subsequent weekends, to do all the major tasks of bathing and changing Ian etc. as well as transporting us backwards and forwards to Sunshine House. I was very, very tempted to try and make another go of our marriage but something inside me said no, even though he was being his wonderful, charming and attentive self and so much like the person I had fallen in love with.

At the conclusion of his time at home every Sunday we were left in no doubt at all that Ian did not want to go back. He cried and fought us as soon as it was time to return. We tried different routes but he always knew it was time to go back and the nearer we got to Ogmore his crying would become even more pitiful, I couldn't bear seeing him so distressed and I would start crying as well. My distress didn't help the situation but I simply couldn't bear the pain he was going through on sending him back to a place he quite obviously didn't want to go to. Those separations were so painful for us both but, at the time I didn't think it would be too long before he would be home for good, how wrong that misguided belief turned out to be.

In the opinion of the manager of the home and a number of, so called 'qualified experts', I was deemed to be an unfit mother, who was living my life through Ian. I was aggressive, self opinionated and selfish and unable to give him the quality of life that was available to him in the home for blind children. I did everything I could think of to get him back home but, the more I fought them, the more I fitted into their perceived opinions of the type of person that I was. Nothing I could say or do made the slightest bit of difference, they had made up their minds that they knew what was in the best interest for Ian. He became more and more withdrawn and distressed and there wasn't a thing I could do about it. They eventually let him home for weekends and school holidays, it wasn't ideal but it was all we could get. I was so distraught over the whole situation and set of circumstances that had brought us to this point; I couldn't understand why it was happening after having fought tooth and nail to keep him in the first place. I couldn't bear the thought of his being put into a home and my losing him. (Many years later Ian was able to tell me how unhappy he had been there, although I did my best to explain to him, at that time because of the circumstances we had found ourselves in I hadn't been given a choice, I felt a deep intense pain all over again of having let him down.)

One of the stipulations I was required to fulfil for having him home during the summer holidays was, I had to take him to a centre somewhere in Downend for us both to be assessed. The first time we went there we were booked to see a child psychologist, I can't remember her name, which is just as well as I could end up with having to go to court for defamation of character. Her room was full of toys but Ian's first need was to check out all the windows and doors, once he was satisfied they were all secure he turned his attention to a dolls house which of course had more windows and doors but he wasn't allowed to go anywhere near the said dolls house or any of the other toys. He became extremely frustrated and erupted into one of his screaming sessions. Nothing was achieved and we were asked to leave. The following report stated that I was uncooperative and had no control over Ian. Had he been allowed to work through his anxieties of having all the doors and windows checked he would have happily settled but she didn't allow that to happen, her toys were more important than the child. I was fighting a losing battle and I knew it, I had no redress whatsoever.

One of the weekends Ian was home Mick decided he was going to make a determined effort to get me back. He arranged with Mum and Dad to baby-sit while he took me out to wine and dine me. We had a wonderful, expensive evening and when we returned home he took me into his arms and kissed me. I have already said ours had been a very passionate and exciting union, but on that night I felt nothing and couldn't begin to imagine myself sleeping with him again. I tried telling myself that maybe, if it had been a less expensive evening, I might have felt differently, I kept wondering how he could afford to pay for it and what bills weren't being paid. Whatever it was, I knew I couldn't take the chance of him hurting me again. Dad decided to have a long talk with me the following day, he knew what Mick's intentions had been to take me out on my own but I had spent all night going over everything in my mind and knew it just wouldn't work. I think it was the following week he told me he had just got engaged to someone he had been seeing for some time, she was very well off and financially that suited him perfectly! It may seem a strange thing to say but I felt deeply hurt and upset, not because he had met someone else, but that he had tried to court me only the week before. I asked him what he would have done had I said yes, he didn't have an answer for me. It left me wondering if he would have carried on seeing her if we had got back together. Once the pain had subsided I just felt glad that, at last, I was released from it all.

Towards the end of my convalescence, during which time I was unable to drive, Pearl had been arranging her marriage to her boyfriend Phil. Mum, Dad and I had been invited to the wedding. I approached my GP and asked if it would be OK for me to resume driving again, I didn't want to miss the wedding. I was delighted when he agreed but I had to promise to take it very easy as the internal wounds would still be vulnerable. The wedding took place in Croydon in May

1974 on a beautiful sunny day. As I was still in a post operative recovery period I wasn't able to be quite as active as I would like to have been, but it was a good day and we all had a great time.

When my three month recovery period came to an end I found it difficult to be positive about very much at all. I was still feeling very low about my perceived lack of femininity and the battles to try and get Ian home for good were wearing me down. Ian's continuing unhappiness and, as I saw it, withdrawing into himself, was hard to cope with. I felt totally helpless and didn't know where to turn and once again took myself off to Addington. I went out dancing with Pearls friend Sandy and met up with a sailor called Peter, he was fun to be with and for the first time in months I was made to feel like a woman. It must have been during one of Ian's holidays because I know he was with me and being looked after by Len and Vivien. For a very short time Ian and I were free from all the aggro going on around us as we found ourselves in an all encompassing bubble of fun and laughter.

One day we had gone to see Jim; Dads brother who lived close by in Biggin Hill, and Ian fell down the steps in the back garden, that same evening I decided it would be best if I took him to the hospital as his leg became was very swollen. I was put through an intense grilling and treated as if I had injured my son on purpose, it was awful. Ian had a plaster put on his leg amidst much screaming and we were eventually allowed to leave, Peter who had taken us in his car, took us back to Addington, stayed for a meal and that was the last I saw of him. I don't know why but it had come to a sudden and abrupt end, with no explanations. The suddenness was difficult to cope with and left me feeling even more depressed than before, what on earth was wrong with me?

By that time I had reached the stage of hating myself, my life, my circumstances, my mother, for she hadn't let up on me, the authorities and the faceless powers behind the scenes who had determined I was an unfit mother, with such intensity it went beyond an explanation that I can verbalise. A few months later while staying once again with Doll and Len, I came to the day when I simply could no longer tolerate any more pain; I had met up with a young man some years younger than me who was very inexperienced in the art of sex so I took it upon myself to teach him. It was at that point of total despair and self loathing that the boil which had been festering inside me for a long time erupted. I knew exactly what I had to do! I planned the day very carefully; as I was more than familiar with everyone's routine. Doll had been collected and taken to a day centre (she'd found each day difficult since her stroke), Len and Pearl were at work and Vivien at school, my mind is a total blank as to where Ian was. This is one of the events that are very mixed up in my head. I assume he must have been staying at Sunshine House because I cannot bring him to the forefront of my mind! I had saved up some pain killers, took some of Doll's tablets from her cupboard then took all the tablets washing them down one by one with a bottle of whisky. If I had any rational thoughts at all I felt certain Pearl would look after Ian for me as I knew I couldn't cope any longer with this sex crazed monster that I had become or with the life I had been dealt with.

Pearl didn't work very far away and I found out, much later, that she'd had this urgent feeling she was being told to go home as something was wrong. Her first thought was to ignore it as common sense told her that everyone was where they were supposed to be, but the promptings became stronger and she acted upon it. What she found was me, I thought she must have phoned Philip her boyfriend as I vaguely remember them both making me sick and walking me non-stop across the bedroom, endlessly backwards and forwards. I've recently learnt that it wasn't Philip; it was Vivien who was helping Pearl. I cannot begin to explain how horrified I was when she told me that, as Vivien couldn't have been much more than twelve years old at that time, what a dreadful burden I had placed upon their shoulders. I've no idea how long they worked on me or how long it took to bring me round, all I can remember clearly of that time was it left me with an all consuming hatred towards them both for having brought me back into the world I no longer wanted to be in. It took me a very, very long time to finally come to my senses and acknowledge how utterly selfish I had been to all concerned, especially to my beloved Pearl, for expecting her to take on the onerous burden of Ian without so much as a by your leave. You may be wondering why they didn't send for an ambulance, that is very simple to explain. It was against the law in those days to attempt to take your own life. To this day I don't know how they explained away the events of that day to Doll and Len on their return home, I only know I was particularly unwell for days after as a result of everything leaving my system!! On reflection, I'm pretty certain I have a number of things mixed up over that devastating event. My only excuse is the state my mind was in during that period, it blocked a lot of things out and I don't seem to be remembering the events in any particular order, what I do know is it all happened.

I eventually returned home to Yate and whilst I was in the depths of a deep depression Mum said "for goodness sake pull yourself out of it, life isn't and never has been, a bed of roses you know". I remember feeling like wanting to hurt her as much as she was

hurting me and replied, "Don't you think I know that!"
A few days later I wrote the following poem

Living Hell
Is this what they call a living hell?
Sinking into a deep, dark, dirty well
Dropping fast into a murky slime
Drowning slowly, erasing time.
I've reached the bottom,
What can I do?
I'm choking, reaching out for whom?
There's no one I know, who can help
To take away this pain I've felt.
I've no fight left anymore,
I'm groping blindly behind a thick closed door.
The unbearable torment closed within
I wonder, what has been my sin?

Months of deep depression and self pity followed, I don't know where the strength to look after Ian came from but, fortunately for him and all concerned, I struggled through somehow. It was as if my mind was encased in an unyielding vacuum, but my body worked as an automated machine. It was the blackest period of my life but I did eventually come through and an inner, self healing process started working within me and fortunately I began the slow process of emerging from the deep dark abyss I had fallen into. Unfortunately however, by the time that process had begun I had started drinking more than usual whenever the opportunity arose and that did get progressively worse, I wasn't consciously aware of it at the time but I was emerging from one dark place and walking blindly into another. Where the money came from to purchase the cigarettes and alcohol I consumed I don't know, Mick had increased his maintenance but surely that didn't allow for what I was consuming, it is something I simply cannot explain.

During those months of depression and upheaval I threw myself into attending church, any church, it didn't seem to matter, all I wanted was to feel close to God in order to try and understand why all these challenges were being thrown at me. I don't remember how I heard about it but Ian and I started attending Pip and Jays in Bristol. It was a 'happy clappy' type of church and nothing like the quiet, reverent places I was used to. We settled in and quite enjoyed it there for a while, but something inside me was missing. Years later Ian and I were reminiscing one day and he told me exactly how we got there, where the door of the room he went into for a children's meeting was, what the colours of the walls and carpets were, etc. He was only four years old at the time and everyone around me was telling me he wasn't taking anything in!! He loved the singing and would happily rock backwards and forwards in his pushchair. All the members were wonderful, embracing both Ian and I, however I still had this all consuming feeling that something was missing, although I was unable to put in plain words what it was.

Mick and his new fiancée wanted our divorce to go through as quickly as possible as she had older children. I was never quite sure why that mattered, but apparently it did, although I was given to understand they wanted to go on holiday as a family and wanted everything in order! I was more than happy for everything to go through, nevertheless everything took its usual slow course, nothing could be brought forward and they had to wait. In early June 1975 Mick and I had to go back to the Gloucester Divorce Courts for the hearing. We certainly didn't have any hard feelings towards each other and ended up going out for a coffee afterwards, all we wanted was for each other to be happy, which was the nicest way to end it all. It was shortly after the divorce that a light bulb suddenly switched on in my head, I realised my drinking was being used as a crutch to get me through each difficult situation I had to face. I was no longer in control of myself and hadn't been for a very long time however in this instance I knew the only way I could get any form of control back was to give up drinking altogether while I still had the strength and awareness to succeed. Not one drop of alcohol has passed my lips from that day to this.

During all this time of turmoil many events were taking place that kept me somewhere near sane. Over the years Ian and I had made many visits to our fantastic friends Fran and John Gardner. John was one of those people who were expert at buying houses that needed a lot of work doing to them. They would buy a house, renovate and decorate it to the very highest standard then sell it and start the process all over again. That meant we had the opportunity of visiting and getting to know lots of new areas. If I remember correctly they moved from Newent to a variety of places in Wales. One of their many homes was in Abergavenny where Fran and I frequented the local market stalls always looking for materials to make up into clothes, etc.

Interspersed with all the moves, Fran, Ian and I spent quite a lot of time together visiting different places. One of our favourites was Fran's parents' home; they lived in Margam, near Port Talbot in Wales. I would strap Ian's cot onto the roof rack and the rest of a small child's paraphernalia and our bags, etc, packed into the boot of the car and off we would go. We had some brilliant times together and as I've said before, as long as I kept to a strict routine, Ian loved every minute of it. He was thoroughly spoilt by everyone and, as always, as long as I was relaxed he was fine, for most of the time anyway!

There came the time when Fran hadn't been well again and asked if I would go over and stay for a while. At the time I rather assumed she had had another miscarriage but, when I arrived at her home, she told me she had been passing out a lot and the doctors didn't know why. I hadn't been there more than a day when we found out what it was all about. John had gone out in the evening, Ian was in bed asleep and we were sitting catching up on each other's news when she said she had to go to the toilet. A few minutes later I heard her call out and then a lot of banging. I rushed upstairs and she was in the bathroom in the throes of an epileptic seizure, I eventually got her into bed and then had the unpleasant task of telling John on his return home. Fran and I went to see her GP the next day and I had to explain all that I had witnessed, he put her on medication straight away. It was very distressing for her but they did at last know what had been happening and could deal with it as and when the need arose. I think the hardest thing to come to terms with was the ban on driving; it subconsciously took away her independence and made her feel like an invalid. I can't remember how long it took but after quite a long time the seizures did eventually stop and she was able to come off the medication. It was unexplainable but we always seemed to be with each other during our times of need; it was like some sort of sixth sense between us, we each knew when the other was suffering in any way. I don't know how I would have coped without their support Fran's in particular, when I was at my very lowest she would be there giving encouragement and taking Ian off my hands so that I could rest.

One summer Fran, Ian and I travelled to Addington to stay with Doll and Len, stopping off on the way to have lunch and visit the town of Windsor. We parked the car, went off to investigate and when we eventually got back to the car it had been broken into and my suitcase stolen. Fortunately Fran's and Ian's were still there, but I was left without any clothes to wear. We reported it at the local police station but nothing was ever found, I had to buy new knickers, bra and a few tops to tide me over until I returned home, I haven't been back to Windsor since.

As I have already mentioned, Fran had suffered a great many miscarriages and, by the time they arrived at Ragland, she had finally come to terms with not having a family. They set up home in a caravan and, while John worked on the house, Fran set about creating a small market garden as she was very good at growing vegetables. Ian loved visiting them wherever they lived, Fran was an early riser and would quietly take him downstairs, give him his drink and breakfast and have some play time while allowing me a much needed lie in. He adored John as well, but for a completely different reason, John tormented him mercilessly and between them there was a lot of laughter whenever they were together.

When we stayed with them at Raglan they had a smaller caravan that we slept in and Ian was always eager to be up and about as there were so many adventures to be part of. John had a small tractor that he would give Ian a ride on, that was the ultimate treat of the day. Then one day we found him climbing a ladder to get up to John on the roof, we all nearly had a fit but Ian never did anything he wasn't sure about and we had to wait until he carefully made his way back down again. On one occasion when John was nearing completion of the renovation and, having made a start on the interior, Ian got into big trouble during one of our many visits. John had started painting all the white gloss paint and Ian decided it was great fun putting his fingers all over it. John didn't think it was so funny on that particular occasion and neither did I as we had to set to and get all the paint off of Ian and his clothes, the atmosphere was a little strained for a while!!

The record of events aren't in any order during that period of my life as I have no way of being precise, I think my extreme state of mind at the time has blocked a section of memory that is not allowing me to get the events in order of occurrence, so many things were happening they all seem to have merged into each other. At this point I'm recording stories that happened over a wide period of time that relate specifically to people who were the rocks that kept me going. Fran and John, like Pearl, were a major part of my life for many years and we supported each other through many trials and illnesses as, like me, Fran was in and out of hospital on a regular basis.

Although this next event came to pass much later and during another part of my life, I feel the need to include it now, as it adds a happy note to events that had been out of our control for such a long time. Fran had finally come to terms with not having a family, was working hard on her garden, and John on the renovations, when completely out of the blue she suddenly found she was pregnant again. With a mixture of delight and concern we all waited for her to pass the danger point of her previous miscarriages, she went on to successfully carry the baby until their longed for daughter Hannah was delivered, strong and healthy!

Pearl, Fran and Chris in Newent, were like threads of gold that weaved their way through the tapestry of my life, each one special in her own way and without whom, I'm certain, I would not have come through the blackest periods of my life.

To return to Ian's progress in life, every time he was allowed home for a weekend or holidays it always took a while for him to settle down again. For the long holidays, once we got the weekend over with, he seemed to know that he would be home for a while and it didn't take many more days to pass by before he was up to his old tricks, he had some very definite windup favourites. His best one was rolling up the carpet runner in the hall and hiding it; we would hear his giggles and knew he had been up to something, the amazing thing was it was quite heavy and he found some ingenious places to hide it. On hearing all the giggles one of us would go out to see what he had done and he would laugh so much it was hard to keep a straight face and not join in with the fun, however no matter how much we told him off it made no difference, it was a game he loved to play. The dining room and kitchen had a large serving hatch and cupboard between them and on the dining room side was a pair of very heavy glass doors, Ian found a way of taking the doors out of the runners and hiding them behind a chair, we never knew where he got the strength from, but that was another wonderful game, until in the end Dad became so worried he boarded it all up as he was certain Ian would eventually hurt himself. Then there was the twin tub washing machine, as I have already said the controls were just at his height and he loved the sound of them clicking, as well as the noise driving you mad Mum was convinced he was going to break it. Mum's treasured treadle Singer sewing machine was another favourite, he would work that so hard we thought it would go through the floor. Ian thought it all very funny but Mum and Dad didn't, consequently I was constantly on the alert in case he broke something and upset them further.

He would be this totally, unpredictable enigma, laughing, giggling and into all sorts of mischief one minute, and then without any warning whatsoever, he would be screaming but we could rarely identify the reason why. I remember one particularly bad day we were having with him, he was screaming about something that had frightened him but we didn't have a clue what it was, it so happened that was the day when a children's social worker called to see us. She had only been with us for a very short space of time trying to fill in all the numerous and statuary forms when she suddenly said, "For goodness sake can't you shut him up?" I had been at my wits end all day trying to do just that. Mum got on her high horse and told the lady in no uncertain terms that if she couldn't offer any constructive help and couldn't cope with the crying, hadn't she better consider doing a different job? We later heard she had gone into some type of office work. Over the years we have had contact with dozens of social workers, I can count on one hand the ones who were incredibly wonderful and helpful, the rest have been, quite simply, useless and a waste of space. I could always tell who would be brilliant, or not, at the first meeting. On the whole I don't have a lot of time for them, however, the exceptional ones have moved mountains for us over the years and I will be eternally grateful to them and all they did for us.

Ian was frightened of so many things; he was terrified of a wide expanse of grass, I couldn't walk across the grass in the park to get to the swings and had to find another way. We went a lot to *Page Park* in Staple Hill, Bristol, it had a tarmac path that went all the way round and ended up at the swings, it became a favourite place to go as long as we stayed off the grass.

In the end I did what I always did with him during one of his 'being frightened sessions', I would take him into my arms then one step at a time take him unto the grass until he finally overcame that fear, we were then able to picnic on the grass as long as we sat on a blanket. Going into large shops, such as 'Marks & Spencer, for instance, was a nightmare as he screamed loud and long, we could never see what it was that frightened him but we very slowly got him through those fears one at a time, going through the same process of holding him in my arms and making him face whatever fear it was. The big stores did prove more difficult until we hit on the idea of promising to take him for something to eat if he was good. 'British Home Stores' in Bristol had a restaurant upstairs and he soon cottoned on to having fish and chips, followed by a pudding of his choice. We would gradually lengthen the time walking round the store before taking him to eat until in the end the fears left him. Mum usually paid and however much we said we didn't have time for a pudding he refused to leave without having one. Over the ensuing years we have found food to be a great incentive to overcoming his fears but, even today, we cannot get him to go to a party where he thinks there might be balloons or to the Pantomime where there will be sudden loud bangs. Going back to those early days, any planned outings invariably ended up in a restaurant, he played up to Mum and her generosity to the full, he had got it all down to a fine art. It was often remarked upon how well behaved he was and how much he loved his food. On many occasions he was given a free pudding by a member of the staff for having been so good!

There was only one occasion when he let me down in a restaurant, which was on a day trip to Weston - Super - Mare. We had been invited to go on the trip by the local Blind Association; afternoon tea had been booked for us all at a big hotel on the sea front. As I have already said, Ian had a fixation with doors and windows and the hotel we were booked into sported two, very large, revolving glass doors. Ian had never seen anything like them before and made an immediate beeline for them. It was out of the question for him to stay and play with them, however much he kicked and screamed to get to them. After threatening him with a good hiding and dragging him kicking and screaming into the restaurant we were escorted to a table for two that was beautifully set out with all the china, sandwiches and cakes etc. Ian determined to get back to the doors, put his feet behind the table and promptly kicked it over. Everything went flying, china crashed to the floor and smashed, sandwiches and cream cakes splattered everywhere, Ian was screaming and I lost my temper. I did no more than march him outside and gave him the hiding of his life, it was then he came to his senses and realised how much trouble he was in. There were a number of elderly ladies in the restaurant, who were absolutely horrified and very loudly berated me for what I had done to that poor child. I would probably have been arrested and prosecuted if it had been today. However, at that precise moment in time, I had reached the end of my patience and Ian knew it. The restaurant personnel were very kind; they straightened everything out and set before us some more tea. We were both very quiet for the rest of that day. Ian has never ever done anything like that ever since, the threat of a good hiding had materialized into something he knew he didn't like. I used that threat to good advantage on many occasions after that, it always had an immediate effect.

Christmas 1974 was once again spent with the Overall clan we travelled down to stay with Uncle Wal and Auntie Vicky at Wivelsfield Green, Sussex. After the holiday was over, on the way back home, Ian started being sick and a couple of days later we realised he had whooping cough. Because of him being classified as mentally handicapped he hadn't been given all his injections in case further damage was done, which meant he went through a very bad time. He was very poorly and violently sick every time he coughed. He slept in my bed for quite a while so that I could see to him immediately he coughed or was sick. It took the stuffing out of both of us, but he eventually come through it. Then within days of his recovery, he came out in a rash which turned out to be measles. We were both exhausted and slept when we could, but that was a very difficult few weeks. Keith had left home by then and I had moved into his room, it had a double bed which enabled me to have Ian in bed with me.

We had just recovered from all of the sickness and exhaustion when Ian had to return to Sunshine House, once again kicking and screaming, they had been happy to leave him home with me when he was ill!

It was at that stage I received a letter from the local council saying they had a ground floor flat vacant and could I make arrangements to collect the keys to view it. I couldn't get down to the council offices fast enough; Mum and I went to have a look at it. We had to go past some not so nice, buildings on the way and I was feeling rather apprehensive. However, when we found the address I was pleased to see it was in a block of four flats, two up and two down. We let ourselves into the empty two bed roomed ground floor flat and found it was more than I could ever have wished for. As I went from room to room it suddenly struck me that I had never lived on my own before and I found myself subconsciously saying, 'This will either make you or break you'. The more I thought about it the more excited I became as I began to realise that, at last, I could be my own boss, have a key to my own front door, invite in anyone I wanted to. If I accepted tenancy I could be free from past husbands and out of my mother's control, what an incredibly exciting prospect that was. I made up my mind there and then that I was going to love being on my own and immediately went to the Council Offices and signed the necessary paperwork. Two weeks later I moved into 1 Blenheim Drive, Yate.

I had nothing except a bed, bunk beds and linen, plus a radiogram I had bought off Dad's brother Jim some time previously. What was I going to do for furniture? I used one of the bunk beds as a settee, some kind person gave me a chair and Dad got me a cheap cooker from Parnell's where he worked. I had a carpet square off Mick, plus a few pots and pans and I set up my third home. It wasn't much but it was mine and I set to with some elbow grease and worked until the flat was spotlessly clean, the tiled floor gleamed with polish and I made some curtains and a few gay and colourful cushion covers for the settee out of some very inexpensive material off Eastville Market in Bristol, which sadly doesn't exist any more.

My favourite pastimes were listening to classic FM or playing my records whilst reading all sorts of books, *Vivaldi's* Four Seasons, *Beethoven's* Pastoral Symphony etc, and all the wonderful music I loved, but hadn't had the freedom to listen to. I didn't have a television and I didn't miss it. Because I was living on my own with a handicapped child to care for, a charity, I think it was the Blind Association, kindly had a telephone installed for me. She didn't say a word, but I'm as sure as I can be that Pat Austin had instigated that important lifeline for me.

It was during those early weeks of freedom that I read two particular books that were to have a lasting effect upon me; one was 'For the Love of Ann' by James Copeland which was based on the diary of Ann's father Jack Hodges. It's the story of an autistic child and her father's love and determination to break through the barriers of fear she had built up around her. I had never heard of autism before but that story was almost like reading a carbon copy book of Ian and explained so many things, to me it was as if I was suddenly walking into the light, that book was totally inspirational, Ian had autism of that I was absolutely certain. I immediately starting making enquiries with the health professionals and social services but they did not want to know, he had been neatly boxed as being mentally handicapped and nothing else mattered. In the end I went with my instincts and using the book as a guide I set too and started making some changes in the way I handled the screaming sessions which were so much easier to cope with now that I understood.

The other book was called 'Tongue Tied' by Joseph John Deacon, another inspirational book but for very different reasons. It's a story of a Joey, who was severely handicapped and unable to communicate in any way. He spent the greater part of his life in a subnormality hospital but with the help of three of his mentally handicapped friends wrote the story of his life, they had somehow broken the barriers of communication and each used their different skills and strengths to tell Joey's story. I cried and laughed all the way through but it left me with a deep feeling of thankfulness and conviction that I had made the right choice in keeping Ian and refusing to have him put into a home, I didn't know how I was going to achieve it but somehow I knew that one day I would be able to have Ian home again permanently.

Ian settled into our new home quite quickly even though he was still only allowed home at weekends and holidays. I had hoped having our own home would make a difference to the powers that be, but no chance, they still wouldn't budge an inch. In fact in some ways it became worse as they continued to think that it confirmed their opinion about my wanting to live my life through him.

Sadly it wasn't long before reality of the real world finally set in. I had very little money coming in, the utility bills started dropping through the letter box and I started to get pretty desperate. I was still attending church, not any one in particular, whatever took my fancy on the day. I was also reading the Bible given me for my sixteenth birthday and somehow felt there was a message in there that I couldn't, at that moment in time, see. My prayers became more intense, I was in a total quandary and needed to know what more it was God wanted from me.

Mum was still in a controlling frame of mind and would keep dropping in to see what visitors I had, if she did find any she would be very rude to them. I have thought long and hard wondering why she was like it but I still continue to think she was jealous of anyone else having my attention. As I've recapped on all that I've said I must now say, although she was more than difficult to get on with, she also had a heart of gold, during that difficult period of my life; I loved and disliked her in equal measure. What I couldn't deny was Mum and Dad's love and generosity in taking both Ian and I into their home, it wasn't the easiest time for any of us, but for them the peace of their home had been invaded with nothing but screams and challenges, each day was like a battle ground. I could never repay all that they did for us but, towards the end of their lives, I gave all that I had to give nursing both of them in the last stages of cancer, fulfilling their wish to die in their own home, feeling it an honour and a privilege to do so.

If I can now go back in time to 1957, when I made the decision to be christened from my hospital bed prior to my expected death, the experience I had of feeling a hand being extended out to me and hearing a voice saying, "Frances you know I am here now go and find me" had set me on a journey which had many diversions and crossroads to negotiate.

I cannot say with any honesty, as you can judge from my story, that I was particularly diligent in trying to find God. I allowed the events in my life and a worldly perspective to take control of any spiritual thoughts I may have had. Periodically an inner voice called me to look for something special but I didn't know what it was or where to find it, the inscription in the front of the bible those two nurses had given me which says *'To Frances, with love from Susan and Elizabeth... "Thy word is a lamp unto my feet, and a light unto my path." Psalms 119: 105* would pop into my mind every now and again. The threads of gold they planted in my heart by that simple act of kindness to a very sick sixteen year old, had proven to be a lifeline I had striven to hold onto even during my hours of darkness and despair.

Over the years there were occasions when I truly felt close to God and knew without doubt he was watching over me, then there were other times when I felt completely deserted and on my own in a morass of spiritual darkness. I clung on by an invisible thread, using prayer and poetry to vocalise my innermost thoughts and feelings, using both as a poultice to heal the wounds.

The never ending sequence of events of my life now brought about a sense of desperation which finally brought me to my knees to pray, pleading with God to help me. I loved having my own home at last but how was I going to be able to keep it if I had very little money coming in, in the depths of despair I asked God why had my life been so hard? Why did I have to have an incurable illness? Why did he give me the incredible gift of a child only to find out he had multiple handicaps? Why had both my marriages gone wrong? The first because I couldn't have children, the second because with his help I had become a mother! Why had he brought me back from the brink of death on more than one occasion then to be constantly bombarded with trials to get through? Why had he blessed me with my own lovely home then make it impossible to keep it because of having no money? As all those thoughts became prayers of desperation, throughout it all just one word kept coming back to me 'Commitment', but what exactly did that mean, how could I commit myself to God? Commitment to me meant becoming a Nun and that was impossible as I had Ian to look after.

I talked to a variety of religious leaders and the only advice they could give was to attend church on Sunday and to live a good life. I knew deep down there was more to it than that; I had been down that road before and felt very strongly God wanted more from me. My prayers became more intense as I needed to know what it was God wanted from me and finally I asked him to "please send your Minister to my door so that I would know what he had to say is from you!"

It was around that time I had some friends come to visit for a few days bringing with them some bottles of alcohol ready for having a good time! As I hadn't had a drink in nearly a year that didn't interest me in the slightest but they carried on drinking and got slightly the worse for wear. In a rather inebriated state the 'gentleman' put forward the suggestion that what I needed was a man and he was offering his services! I told him that was the last thing I needed and picked up my Bible and said, "I know the answer to what I am looking for is in here, but I don't know where to find it" He thought that was very funny and highly unlikely. At some point over that weekend Mum called in to see who it was visiting me, she had convinced herself she would find me in bed with someone. To say I was annoyed with her would be a gross understatement, I was furious, what right did she have thinking she could rule my life or be rude to any visitors I cared to have in my own home. She wasn't at all happy when I insisted she leave.

What with one thing and another the weekend wasn't going too well and my mood was very quickly deteriorating. The door bell rang and on answering it found two 'Mormon Missionaries' standing there, I was very short with them and said, "Thank you, but no thank you" and shut the door. After my 'friends' had left I got back to praying again and as I asked the same question of having God's Minister call on me, the faces of the two 'Mormons' came into my mind. What had I done, was it them I was supposed to listen too? I asked for them to be sent back if indeed it was them who had a message for me. I kept seeing them in the streets wherever I went but I didn't dare approach them, if they were the messengers from God they had to come back to me. Four weeks later the door bell rang, I opened the door and, with a sigh of relief said, "Come on in I have been waiting for you to call." I think they were just a little taken aback at the response they received. The interesting thing was in those days they didn't go back to an area they had already 'tracked' (knocked on doors in a given street) for at least six months and neither of them had any record of having called on me four weeks previously, but it was definitely the same two young men I had turned away,

Elders Michael Dinnell from Nevada and, Ronald Holberg III from Salt Lake City.

What an incredible message they had for me to digest. It answered all the questions I had been pondering over for years, where did I come from? Why was I here? And where was I going? I don't think I thought in quite that specific way but the questions I had fell into those three categories. As I read the 'Book of Mormon' I was given, I became very excited and had a million questions for them every time they visited me. One of the things that impressed me the most was, if I asked a question they couldn't answer they would freely admit to not knowing, went away and always came back with an answer that was completely logical and made total sense. The more I read the more thrilled I became as suddenly God was no longer the faceless person I had been talking to, Jesus Christ was a person in his own right, the Holy Ghost was the comforter and guide, also suddenly for me the 'Trinity', as I had previously known it, took on a completely new dimension.

After a few days they challenged me to attend their church, so I decided I would go and find out where it was the day before the planned date that had been agreed upon. It was approximately eight miles from where I lived. Before setting out I felt the need to ask God to show me a sign if it wasn't what he wanted me to do. I wasn't able to find the church and decided that was the sign and decided to return home, I had travelled about three miles into the journey home when I had the very strong impression to turn back, I ignored it at first but as the impression got stronger I made the decision to turn back. I found the chapel straight away but the building was securely locked and I couldn't get in, again was it the sign I had asked for? Downend Chapel in Bristol had some lovely grounds and I found a seat situated beneath a tree. To my shame I sat there smoking whilst talking to God pleading with him to let me know for sure if this was the commitment he wanted from me?

That same evening there was a severe thunderstorm, lightening flashes, incredibly loud bangs and all the fury imaginable was being released and it felt as if it was immediately above me, was this God, trying to tell me something? In the midst of the storm I picked up my Bible opening it at random and read Proverbs 3: verses 4 & 5. *"Trust in the Lord with all thine heart, lean not unto thine own understanding, in all thy ways acknowledge him and he shall direct thy paths."* I was willing to commit myself to the Lord, I trusted him completely and when I was with those two young men I experienced a feeling of peace never before felt in quite that way.

I attended church the next day which was the first Sunday in August 1975. I had never experienced a church meeting like it before and had never heard of anything referred to as a *'Fast and Testimony'* meeting. It was certainly different but actually quite interesting, I was particularly moved by a young boy, approximately 12 years old, who went up to the stand and expressed how much he loved the church, his parent's and teachers etc. It surprised and inspired me that a boy so young could be so positive about what he believed in, he had given me a great deal to think about. The Elders were very attentive and kept calling members over to introduce me, everyone took me under their wings and supported me in every way possible and in particular, they took Ian off my hands so that I could concentrate on everything there was to learn. Ian loved the attention and was soon being thoroughly spoilt.

I knew from everything I learnt, saw and heard that this was what I had been looking for since 1957, I had found the God who had spoken to me and allowed me to live, I made my decision and was baptised two weeks later, three weeks from the day those two wonderful young men had followed the promptings of the spirit, knocked on my door the second time and filled my life with an unexplainable joy.

As soon as I had made that momentous decision and informed my parent's, opposition came at me fast and furiously. My Mother was horrified, she was adamant it was the church of the devil, as were my Pentecostal neighbours who lived in the flat above me. More neighbours kept telling me I was inviting evil into my home, and so it went on from all different quarters. The only defence I had was feeling a lovely warm spirit every time the Elders visited me and feeling bereft after they had left as I felt the warmth had left with them, no one could convince me they were agents from the devil. The only one who was happy for me was my cousin Pearl, when I told her I had given up smoking, drinking tea, coffee and alcohol she wasn't at all surprised except for not drinking tea anymore, between us we could have filled a major reservoir the amount we had consumed over the years, it's very much a British institution, we could survive any crisis and had won two wars on cups of tea!

No friends or family attended my baptism on 11 August 1975, but all my newly found friends were there to support me, as I went under the water I felt I wanted to stay there forever as I had so many sins to wash away. I don't remember very much about it and nothing at all of the confirmation, I was very nervous and worried that I wasn't good enough. I had done so many terrible things in my life, how could the Lord possibly forgive me?

When Mum found out I had gone ahead and been baptised against her wishes she was so upset she turned me out of her house and told me never to darken her doorstep again. She had gone to the local library and taken out everything she could find about the church none of which was good. I asked her if she had read the 'Book of Mormon' and when she said "no" I said she really didn't have a case, how could she make a judgment with only one side of the picture to base it on. She refused to speak to me but kept accosting the Elders in the street accusing them of not only taking her daughter away from her, but they had stolen her best friend too.

As the weeks passed by with her refusing any contact I finally wrote her a letter explaining how sad I felt that she couldn't be happy for me after I had been through so much sadness. Being baptised into the church was the best thing that could have happened to me, for the first time in my life I was at peace with myself and very happy. I received a very short note back saying, "I miss Ian bring him round to see me." That first meeting was very strained but I persevered and we got back to a better relationship in the end.

As I have already said I had very little money coming in but I had made up my mind to pay my tithing, (10% of what I had coming in) I was beginning to learn and accept, what commitment truly meant and paying my tithing for me was a spiritual necessity. In those day's church meetings were twice a day, Sunday school in the morning and the Sacrament meeting in the evening. The day very soon arrived when I had to make a choice which one to attend as I only had enough petrol in the car to get to just one. I didn't have any money to get me through the week but felt it was important to at least attend the Sacrament service. On my arrival Bishop Derrick Ireland asked me if I had any money on me, he did it in such a way as to imply he wanted to borrow some, without thinking anything about it I replied "No sorry I don't have any at all" he said "I didn't think so" and gave me an envelope. Inside was enough money to get me through the week and fill up the car with petrol. I refused point blank to take it but he insisted. That was my first experience of a Bishop in the church being directed by the Holy Ghost to help someone in need and having the right amount of sensitivity to not make me feel like a charity case.

That wonderful man gave me a job of assembling picture frames so that I could earn a little extra money, it wasn't a lot but enough to make all the difference to my getting by without accepting welfare, something I was determined I wasn't going to do.

The first responsibility I was called upon to do in the church was as a teacher within Relief Society (the women's organisation). Bearing in mind the low opinion I had of myself and my academic abilities I wasn't at all sure I was capable of such an undertaking. The subject matter was about the culture, traditions, food and history of the women of the church in other countries. The sister assigned to support me and help me get started was a woman named Ella Bressington; she must have been in her late seventies and an incredibly funny and outspoken character. On first meeting her I felt rather overwhelmed as she was larger than life, it didn't take long for us to become the best of friends and I loved her dearly.

There were other sisters who were to become very important to me as they took my hand, metaphorically speaking, and guided me through the various complexities of being a new member in the church. Every aspect was totally different to anything I had ever come across before and I was quickly learning that commitment came in many forms and was all encompassing. For the first time in my life I was being told that I was a very special daughter of God and that he loved me, nobody was making me feel inadequate or stupid, they were actually making me believe I had something special to give, it was a very heady matter to take in and digest.

I had no doubts whatsoever that the church was true but I couldn't get my head around the validity of the present day Prophet, why did he have to be an American? Some members loaned me a tape called *'Profile of a Prophet'* by Hugh B Brown and at its conclusion I was in streams of tears, pleading with the Lord to "please let me see the Prophet or one of the General Authorities!"

I had been in the church for approximately three months when the Missionaries asked me to accompany them to see a lady they were teaching who was in a similar situation to me, a single parent with a young son. I loved every aspect of the Gospel and felt like shouting it out to the world so I readily agreed. As they went through the presentation they had prepared I instinctively felt her situation wasn't quite as she had led them to believe, there was definitely evidence of a male presence in the home. At the close of the Missionaries presentation she asked me if I would stay on and visit with her on my own to which I agreed, more out of curiosity than anything else. I learnt that she was living with her partner who travelled to London twice a week, which was when she had the Missionaries visit with her. He didn't know anything about the visits and she felt certain he wouldn't listen to a couple of twenty year old Americans, she asked for my help by being there when she told him as she felt I had a certain serenity about me that would help the situation and I agreed.

It must have been towards the end of November 1975 when she invited me round for the evening to meet her partner who appeared to be a very nice man;

there was another friend of theirs present who was sat at a drawing board working, they owned a local printing company and he did some art work for them.

It was an interesting evening as the two men took great delight in making fun of me for not drinking tea and coffee etc. but it all washed over me as I felt very secure in my life and my beliefs. That was the beginning of a weekly get together as she had convinced me we were making progress in softening her partner up, she was continuing to be taught and I thought I was helping. They had also made the decision to employ me on a part time basis to work in the printing shop because she had been having some health problems, as it was nearing Christmas I could certainly use the money and I agreed to try it out.

Their friend John, spent nearly all his spare time at their house, he was married with three children but he and his wife had different interests and mostly went their separate ways. He was always there when I was invited round, even at different times of the day, as he worked shift work in the Post Office. I suddenly found myself taking an interest in his lovely strong hands and long wavy hair; I simply panicked and couldn't get out of there quickly enough. I told the lady I didn't want to visit any more, I felt she wasn't serious about what she was being taught and I wanted out. She pleaded with me to do one more thing for her, she was due to get the results of a series of tests she'd had done and would I take her to the Hospital as she didn't want to be on her own. What could I say! The results confirmed she had multiple sclerosis, she was absolutely devastated and I felt desperately sorry for her. She became very clingy, constantly phoning me for support of one kind or another, as I'm a naturally caring person I found it near impossible to say no.

I couldn't get away and knew I was heading into deep water; John was expressing an interest in me although we were never alone together and I felt trapped. It was close to Christmas when she asked me to help her with her shopping, when we arrived back at her house her partner had set out some drinks and sandwiches. That was the closest I ever came to breaking the *'word of wisdom'* (a church health code) because the drink was a very dry sherry, which had been my very favourite drinks, and everyone was smoking. I came within a fraction of an inch of accepting both and decided I had to leave immediately. John, for the first time, followed me to the car and asked me to go out with him, I explained about the strict rule of chastity I lived by, as well as pointing out about his being married, but he either didn't understand or chose not to understand what I was talking about. He didn't believe there was a God and found it impossible to see how anyone could think there was.

I immediately contacted Bishop Ireland and after explaining the whole situation to him his advice was to get out without delay. I had been trying to do just that for weeks but to no avail, I felt as if I was being hounded from all sides. I gave up the job and told them to stay away, unfortunately I was laid low with severe bronchitis (the clearing of my lungs after years of smoking), I was ill, very weak and unable to fight them, the three of them came round on a daily basis to feed me and look after me.

Christmas passed by and John started to write me letters, send me flowers and presents, leave records on my door step, write me poetry, phone me a number of times a day and so on and so forth. I had never dreamed it possible that anyone in there right mind would be interested in a twice divorced woman with a difficult handicapped child to bring up. The attention I received had the effects of heavy rain after a prolonged drought in the desert, I had lain dormant for so long I felt myself opening up like a beautiful flower which was how he made me feel. For the first time ever I was being seen as a person in my own right and not as someone who would be useful to bear children or to entertain.

My prayers were intense, why was this happening to me now? "Please, please help me, I can't fight this on my own," I didn't know what to do or which way to turn. In the end I arranged another meeting with the Bishop, I was absolutely desperate! John knew I was seeing him and expressed a desire to be present but that wasn't possible. Some way into the meeting Bishop Ireland, in frustration, said, "I wish I could meet this man, I would tell him where he stands," I immediately rang John and he arrived ten minutes later.

The Bishop wasn't at all complimentary about the situation and set out everything very clearly so there could be no misunderstandings, suddenly John burst into tears, totally distraught he put his head on my lap and sobbed his heart out. At that moment Bishop asked me to promise never to see John again, I would have given anything to make that promise but I knew I couldn't, by which time I was in tears as well. John was so distressed that Bishop Ireland suggested giving him a blessing, John had no idea what that meant but readily submitted to having it done, after I had assured him it would help him. I believe that blessing was the beginning of John's own spiritual journey he was about to embark upon!

The only physical evidence I have at that time is a letter I wrote to John in an effort to make him understand how I was feeling. Unfortunately there is no date on it but it goes as follows.

"My Dear John

This is going to be the first and last time that I will write to you. I just want you to know a few of my present feelings. I haven't been able to stop reading your poems and letters, oh! Yes confusion reigns! The more I read them I can see and feel a kindred soul who has suffered pain, joy, happiness, sorrow all of which have left there mark upon your heart.

You are a very loving and giving person, someone who wants so much to love and be loved. I have never met a man who is the reflection of myself. Oh yes! I've met some really wonderful people in my life but for the first time ever, I've met someone who can understand exactly how I feel about life and love, because I'm so sure that you feel the same way.

I have many times asked the Lord to send someone special, someone who can share my thoughts, feelings, faith. The last part you don't have, but I believe could. What I am trying to understand is why the Lord has allowed us to meet, as it would seem that we can't be joined together as one flesh, one heart, and one mind.

Nothing less will be good enough I've tried less and it doesn't work, not for me it doesn't. Maybe I've set my ideals to high but I don't think so, if I have then I'm defiantly destined to remain on my own.

I don't believe that love for someone else should be kept in check, because you are always in fear of rejection. That's how it's always been for me; I've been accused many times of loving too much and smothering. I wasn't prepared to chance it again, but suddenly I've found another heart that loves in the same way, at least that's how it seems.

John even if it takes a lifetime if it's truly meant to be we will one day become one flesh. I don't know if, when, or how all I do know is, that I'm prepared to wait for a perfect union, one that has the blessings of the Lord upon it.

If I am committing a sin now in the eyes of the Lord then I will have to answer for that sin, in the meantime I sincerely pray that he will be kind to me and help me through what I know is going to be a difficult time ahead. If love, true love is a sin then yes I'm sinning but it's a love of my heart, not of the flesh. Be strong my love and remember that nothing less than that perfect union will be good enough.

On having read my poems you must be aware of how deep my faith is, it isn't just a passing phase, it's something I've had for many years. Before I became a 'Mormon' I hadn't really lead a wicked live, I just bent the rules to suit myself, it didn't matter what church that I went to, they couldn't answer all my questions and they all bent the rules to suit society. In the end I asked the Lord for guidance and he directed me into being baptized into The Church of Jesus Christ of Latter-day Saints. I have always believed devoutly in the power of prayer and I have a very strong testimony of the truthfulness and doctrines of the church, for the first time in my life I'm not trying to bend the rules to suit myself, if I did then I would no longer be a member of the church. When I commit myself to anything I commit myself totally To the Lord, my son, and my partner in marriage (if there's to be one). I'm completely aware of the love that my Father in Heaven has for me and I'm completely aware of the love my son has for me also, I've committed myself to them, so please help me to keep those commitments.

A few days later the said couple came and asked me if they could stay with me, they had sold their house and the new one wasn't quite ready to move into. I explained the difficulties it would present to me as my flat was council owned and the policy was that visitors could only stay for two weeks, any more and I would lose my benefits. They assured me it wouldn't be for any longer than the two weeks and I very reluctantly agreed. They moved in with what seemed like dozens of black plastic sacks filled to capacity, I let them have my room and I moved into Ian's. That same evening Friday 12 March 1976 John turned up with a suitcase saying he had left his wife!

A roller coaster of emotions whirled around inside my head, absolute horror, disbelief, fear, anger and resentment, coupled with an incredible sense of joy that was overshadowed with an all consuming feeling of guilt. John and I sat up all night talking it through, I tried to talk him out of it but he had made up his mind, he wanted to be with me!

I rang Bishop Ireland the next morning (he must had wondered what he had done to deserve me) after a great deal of discussion he informed me a court would have to be held as I was deemed no longer worthy. He didn't put it across in the harsh way I've recorded it, in fact he was so gentle and kind I felt I had personally let him down, but I knew what the consequences of my actions would be and a few days later I was excommunicated. There are not enough words in the English language to even partially explain how I felt; I was numb and incredibly sad.

The next few days went by in a haze of emotions but one thing did stand out, every day John's wife would phone him relating in detail everything John and I had been discussing, how did she know? At first we didn't want to believe it had anything to do with our 'friends' but it soon became obvious it could only be them. We decided to make up a fictional story and talk about it at dinner that evening. Sure enough they left shortly after and a couple of hours later the phone rang.

I was absolutely livid, they were living in my home, sleeping in my bed and eating at my table, John was their friend and had invested money in their business and they were deliberately stabbing us in the back! By the time they had returned, all of their belongings were piled outside the front door. They were astounded, what was going to happen to them, they had no where to go. I told them in no uncertain terms they should have thought about that before abusing my hospitality and I wanted no more to do with them.

The next few days went by in a blur, although we were blissfully happy there was a constant cloud of guilt riding over it all. I missed attending church, but I was still saying my prayers, reading the scriptures and, much to John's amusement, I was also putting aside my tithing as I truly felt that the money didn't belong to me. All these events, I think, had taken place at the end of March 1976, everything happened so quickly it was difficult to take it all in. The more I got to know the real John, his gentleness and caring, the more the concept of a Temple marriage for time and all eternity, that the church taught, took on a very real and significant meaning, I wanted nothing less, but how could that be achieved when he didn't believe in God?

The couple who had loaned me the *'Profile of a Prophet'* tape called round to see me and told me that Mark E Peterson, a General Authority, would be attending a Conference at Wells Road Chapel on Sunday 4 April. It was an answer to my prayers and I knew I had to be there. Then started a see-saw of conflicting emotions, how could I go? I wasn't worthy to be in his presence, but I must go I had prayed for this to happen. I struggled with deciding what to do, until in the end I came to the conclusion that I simply had to go. I thought if I crept in at the last minute and left as soon as it ended I wouldn't be seen, I was too ashamed to face anyone.

John decided to go with me, not because he was interested, he just wanted to be with me. All through the meeting he kept muttering to himself what a load of rubbish it was. By the time it was the turn of Mark E Peterson I asked him to "please be quiet as this was who I had come to listen too," he did restrain himself and during his talk Elder Peterson announced that the Prophet Spencer W Kimble would be attending a Multi-Regional Conference at Wembley Stadium in June of that year, my immediate reaction was I had to go!

The meeting came to an end and before we had left our seats we were surrounded by members all keen to know how I was. I was suddenly surrounded by an outpouring of love so strong it was palpable. Ella Bressington said to John, "So you're the nigger in the woodpile are you? I hope you are going to do right by this young lady" he replied that if it was within his power to do so then yes he would. Everyone was taken aback by Ella's statement but we were fine with it. One of the members said she was giving a talk that evening in the Sacrament meeting and could I go. I said "no as John had already attended one meeting and I didn't think he would want to go to another on the same day". On our way back to the flat we passed Downend Chapel and as my head turned to look at it John said, "You really want to go there don't you?" with tears streaming down my face I replied "John, I may not be living as I should be but I haven't lost my Testimony, I know without any shadow of a doubt that the Church is true and yes that is where I want to be". We attended that same evening and I was made welcome in a way I could never have imagined possible. John told me later that he had never seen or experienced so much love extended to someone and that it had a profound effect on him.

We began attending Sunday School, held in the village hall in Yate, in the morning and the Sacrament Meeting in the evening at Downend. The routine was that after taking me back to the flat at the end of the evening meeting, John would go round to see his wife and children. One evening we had gone through the same routine but after John had left I was totally consumed with the unbearable feelings of having let the Lord down. He had blessed me with the magnificent gift of bringing the Gospel into my life and here I was throwing it back in his face, how could he ever forgive me. Those thoughts were so powerful I couldn't stop crying. I was still crying when John returned and he thought it was because I was convinced he wasn't going to return, but all I could say was that the Lord would never forgive me. Having tried everything he could think of to stop me crying and finding himself unable to do so he suddenly said "Get down on your knees, I'm going to talk to this Lord of yours and tell him what I think about it!" in a complete daze I did as I was asked and John said his very first prayer to a God he didn't believe in. It wasn't a very complimentary prayer and I have no idea how long it lasted but what was significant, as John got up from his knees his first words were "where's that book you keep on about? I'm going to take it into work tomorrow and start reading it instead of playing cards. I'll also give up drinking coffee and smoking." By that time I had stopped crying and looked at him in utter disbelief. He started to read the Book of Mormon the following day but found it quite ludicrous at first; however he persevered, along with not drinking his coffee or smoking his small cigars. He would phone me and say how ridiculous he thought it all was but he still kept reading, then he would bombard me with numerous questions most of which I couldn't answer bearing in mind I hadn't been in the church very long myself to have gained much knowledge.

I had continued saying my prayers, and even that he couldn't understand, who could I possibly be talking to, but gradually he started saying the Lord's Prayer and I left him to come to it on his own, I just kept doing what I needed to do which was read my scriptures, say my prayers, live the word of wisdom, and put my tithing aside.

As I have said we attended Sunday School in Yate and Easter Sunday 18 April 1976 was no exception. The Lock family had been assigned to do a presentation about the importance of the commemorations of Jesus Christ's Atonement in the Garden of Gethsemane, his trial and Crucifixion on the cross and finally his Resurrection. I cannot explain what happened to John during that presentation about Jesus Christ as that is part of his conversion story, what I can say is I knew that something significant had happened as his attitude and behaviour was different, he was very contemplative and fearful. After trying to explain to me what had happened my heart suddenly leapt for joy as I knew he had received a witness of the Saviour. All of a sudden he wanted to read all the Church publications he could, he devoured everything he could lay his hands on, the 'Book of Mormon', 'Jesus the Christ', 'A Marvellous Work and a Wonder', priesthood manuals, anything the members were willing to loan him. He thirsted after knowledge and the more he read the stronger his fledgling Testimony grew, at last he could understand how I was feeling and how his actions had caused me so much spiritual pain.

As we continued to attend the meetings it became clear to him that this was a family orientated church and what had he done? He had left his family! There followed a period of immense quilt and indecision, what should he do? Go back to his wife and children or stay with me. I had to stand back and let him work through it on his own, but I was quietly preparing myself for whatever the outcome was to be. He finally decided that his destiny laid with me but that we should do all that was within our power to heal the rift and hurt he had caused his wife and children. We were fully aware the process would not be easy but we did eventually achieve it and we finally became friends.

After all these events had taken place, June had arrived and it was time to attend the Multi Regional Conference at Wembley. The stadium was packed to capacity and we had a seat right up at the top, a very long way from the podium. I was very nervous and felt totally unworthy of being there but I knew this was an answer to my prayers; I was there for a reason. Suddenly everyone was on their feet and singing 'We Thank thee O God for a Prophet' and there entered a tiny, diminutive figure and I knew, with every fibre of my being, that he was indeed a living Prophet of the Lord. He hadn't said a word indeed I couldn't see his face but somehow I just knew and I rejoiced in that knowledge. The tears were streaming down my face as I bowed my head and silently gave thanks to the Lord for answering my prayers. We attended all the meetings over that weekend, Ian was with us and he was as good as gold, it was as if he knew the importance of the occasion.

John however had a difficult time, something that an Elder Bernard P Brockbank had said upset him and he found it difficult to let it go, he became difficult and quite aggressive, which upset me because I had found the whole event very uplifting. He did eventually calm down and we were able to discuss everything in great detail.

One thing we felt was very significant at the time, we had bought the newspapers to read as we knew the press had been in attendance at Conference, after reading all about the events of the weekend we were absolutely horrified, as every report was totally subjective and miss-reported. Our feelings of disgust were so strong we determined there and then to never buy a newspaper again, if the press could be so wrong because of their own prejudice at those meetings, then how accurate are they with any event they are assigned to report on.

When we finally arrived home we realized there was a great deal to think about, John had gained a Testimony and wanted desperately to be taught but because we were living together that wasn't allowed. He asked if we could see a President Knapp he was the Bristol England Mission President, he was the only one who could make the decision. That interview was one of the most difficult experiences we had to endure, President Knapp told us, in no uncertain terms, what we were doing was contrary to all the church's teachings. We were in floods of tears and felt as if we had just been beaten down to nothing. However as we were leaving he showed forth an increase of love and gave us Spencer W Kimble's book 'The Miracle of Forgiveness' and counselled us to read it.

Without saying a word we both knew we had to separate, but how on earth could we do it. Financially we were desperate; John was supporting his wife and children, paying the mortgage on their home, settling all their utility bills and paying maintenance for his wife and children. I had lost all my allowances when he moved in only having a very small payment for Ian coming in and John was paying our rent and all our utility bills as well. There was no way he had sufficient money to rent anything else for himself. On top of all that he was beginning to build up a relationship with Ian after overcoming his initial fear of being around a handicapped child. His most far reaching success with Ian was having taught him to go to the toilet, Ian loved having someone to copy and we were successfully on the way to getting him out of napkins, a miracle I had been told would never happen. He was worried about how Ian would react with him no longer being there. Putting all the challenges aside we knew it was something we had to do if we were to seriously stand a chance of putting our lives in order.

After a great deal of thought and prayer we decided to approach my parents and ask if John could stay with them until we could get married. They were absolutely speechless for a while, they had been delighted at him having taken me out of the church they were so against, they certainly hadn't bargained on him gaining a testimony and wanting to join the church! They discussed all the pros and cons with him and finally agreed to give him a home on a trial basis. John sweet talked my Mother round using all the charm he had used on me and, like me, she fell in love with his charm and gentleness, he had won her over. The utterly amazing and quite unbelievable event took place shortly after, they not only took John into their home but took in two Elders who had been persecuted and thrown out of their digs and John asked if they could stay as well. Elders Jared Weight and Craig Dean became part of the rapidly growing family, Mum was in her element, she had someone to spoil and cook for and all three of them became her adoptive sons.

I had put in for an exchange as the flat was no longer suitable and the neighbours were being difficult, I was approached by an elderly couple not very far away who had a two bedroomed house and we agreed to swap homes. The house was absolutely filthy but we set too and with the help of the members of the church we cleaned and decorated it throughout and fitted some new cabinets in the kitchen. Fortunately Ian was away all the week so I didn't have him to get under our feet while we were in such a mess, with everyone's help we got it done very quickly then Ian and I moved into 22 Fox Avenue, Yate.

John and I were determined to pay for all the costs of the divorce and as no one was contesting it in any way it went through quite quickly. As soon as the decree Nisi had been issued on 5 July 1976 John was, at last, given permission to be taught by Elders Weight and Dean which took place in his bedroom in the home of my parents! Six weeks later on Friday 3 September 1976 the divorce absolute was granted and we became officially engaged the following day, my thirty-sixth birthday.

John was on cloud nine as he had been taught well and was ready to be baptised. He wanted every one of his friends and family to attend his baptism on Tuesday 19 October 1976. His ex-wife, children, family, work colleagues and church members did indeed attend, he was ecstatic, but for me it was the most difficult time imaginable, naturally I was delighted for him but he was now a member of the church, but where was I? I was even more on the outside. I felt completely bereft and on my own, bearing in mind I had been told it could be years before I could become a member again, I simply couldn't imagine how I would survive. Within days John was ordained into the Aaronic Priesthood and was given his first responsibility within the church organisation, he became the assistant Branch Clerk. Yate had by that time become separated from Downend and was now a small Branch in its own right.

It has been difficult dating events with any accuracy, as neither of us kept journals and everything seemed to be happening all at the same time, but I think it was the second week of November that John told me I had to be at church a little earlier than usual but he wouldn't tell me why. When I arrived I was called into a small room that was used as an office to be interviewed by President Norris, the Bristol Stake President. Apparently Bishop Ireland had put my name forward to be considered for rebaptism, he felt I had consistently shown sorrow and repentance for all that I had done over the previous months. During the interview President Norris agreed to my being baptised then told me that I wouldn't be able to go to the Temple or be sealed to John for time and all eternity. My mind was in turmoil as that Temple sealing was the main thing that had helped us stay on the straight and narrow path during what had been a highly emotional and stress related time.

The main meeting had already started by the time the interview was concluded and I left that tiny room in floods of tears, not tears of happiness but tears of sorrow. John and Bishop Ireland were expecting to see my face shining with happiness, not the distress I was obviously in. A few minutes later Bishop passed a note to me which read 'Frances don't worry it doesn't apply to you!' I was in such a state it didn't mean anything, all I could think was 'what had the last few months been all about if I couldn't be sealed to John?' why had I suffered so much at not being able to take the sacrament or bear my testimony to the truthfulness of the Gospel? As all those thoughts were going through my mind the Sacrament (bread and water) was being passed around, as it came in front of me I knew within the very depths of my being that Jesus Christ was the living son of God the Father, he had suffered and died for my sins and no matter what he asked of me I would willingly submit to. That was the very moment I gained my full conversion and commitment to the Saviours teachings.

As soon as the meeting was over Bishop Ireland was the first person to see me and explained that President Norris had made a mistake, he had me mixed up with someone else. I had been in the church for less than six months when I was excommunicated and I hadn't been to the Temple. He was cross that I had been subjected to so much stress but I knew that was how it had to be for me, I had to submit to and accept the ultimate sacrifice in order to become converted, that sacrifice, I had thought, was not being married to John for time and all eternity. Thankfully the information had been incorrect.

John baptised me back into the church on Sunday 28 November 1976. The very first thing I did was pay in the tithing I had been faithfully putting on one side. Bishop Ireland assured me it wasn't necessary but for me it was essential as far as my spiritual well being was concerned.

One week later John and I were married at Downend Chapel on Saturday 4 December, so many people set to and helped us, and the sisters in particular prepared a fantastic hot meal for the reception. Nearly all of our family and friends made the journey to be with us even though a blanket of fog and ice greeted us on the day. We had one night in a nearby hotel, which was a blessing as the fog was even thicker by the time we were ready to leave. Our long awaited day had been a success and a new era was about to begin.

By that time, after numerous in-depth interviews had been attended to, John finally convinced the Social Services he was serious about his intention to marry me. Eventually they finally allowed Ian to return home, to live permanently, on Friday 10 December, six days after the wedding had taken place.

I spent the following year in a state of melancholy as I found myself unable to forgive myself for all that had happened, if I couldn't forgive myself I was unable to conceive how the Lord could forgive me.

Settling down to being a wife and full time mother again I found surprisingly difficult, John had become involved in fulfilling his church callings, we were having difficulties with his daughter, and he was feeling guilty for having let the children down. Whereas before our marriage and his conversion, his attention and total adoration had been on me, suddenly it wasn't there any longer he was busy with other things. And to cap it all we were desperately short of money and feeding us was a major challenge every day.

As I sank even deeper into the morose of guilt the idea of our being sealed together started to fade as we didn't have any money and felt we couldn't afford the travelling expenses etc. In the end John decided we couldn't afford not to go and arranged for the two missionaries at that time to take me through a series of planned lessons to help me overcome my feelings of guilt and prepare me for what was to come. Every lesson they gave me always ended in tears as the healing started to take place, I had come to realise that what would have been essential before I was re-baptised was to go through all the lessons again. However because it was felt that I already knew what the steps prior to baptism were I didn't need it. It is always easy to look back and see that in order to go through that final repentance stage, I had in fact needed those lessons in order to forgive myself. But it hadn't happened and here were two wonderful missionaries teaching me how to prepare myself for entering the Temple of the Lord

On 4 February 1978 John and I attended the London Temple, where we were sealed together for time and all eternity. As we looked into each others eyes across the altar I had the most beautiful feeling of being loved and accepted by this wonderful man who from all the women in the world had chosen me to go through life and into the eternities with.

I want to bring this part of my story to a conclusion by bringing together all the threads of gold which have encircled me through each and every aspect of my life, my family and friends who have travelled the road with me, who have loved and supported me throughout all the good and bad times. I feel as if I had been put through the refiner's fire in so many ways and I'm certain there will be more to come, but I will always be thankful that all those wonderful threads of gold and the special people at the end of them who enhanced the tapestry of my life and stopped it from becoming threadbare.

The rest of my story is another chapter and another book that can only stand on its own, I was now embarking on a different journey altogether.

Me 1974, although I was showing an appearance of happiness, but inside I was a maelstrom of emotion turmoil!

This was the man who swept me off my feet,
John Charles Lewis 1976

28 November 1976, the day John Baptised back
into The Church of Jesus Christ of Latter-day
Saints. The dress, I changed back into, was another
one I had made!

4 December 1976, this is the day I married my beloved John!

This being my third wedding, I choose to make my Dress in my favourite colour, Turquoise. It suited the weather which turned out to be frosty with a thick December fog

4 February 1978 was a day of joy and wonder when John and I were sealed together for Time and all Eternity at the London Temple Lingfield Surrey

.✒✑✒✑

Appendix

In an effort to give some historical background, regarding the circumstances surrounding the years both my parents were born, and later preparing to start work. I think it's worth highlighting some of the major events which had either taken place, or were taking place, during 1916 my Father's Birth; 1930 when he left school & 1918 my Mother's Birth

1916

January: Conscription was voted for in the House of Commons.

May: Clocks were put forward 1 hour for the first time as British Summer Time was introduced.

June: HMS Hampshire was sunk by the Germans and the defence secretary Lord Kitchener, who was on board, drowned.

July: David Lloyd George was appointed to replace him.

Sept: At the Battle of the Somme tanks were used for the first time. 1st Zeppelin crashed in Hertfordshire

Dec: David Lloyd George became the Prime Minister.

I think it's also worth noting some of the events that had either taken place or were taking place during the year my father left school, for the purposes of capturing a tiny insight of the conditions at that time and to show how far we have come in our country's development.

1930

February: the Zip fastener was invented

March: saw clashes between the Police and left wing 'marcher for work' on Tower Hill London

April: Amy Johnson completed her solo flight from England to Australia

June: Wimbledon begins, Bill Tilden and Helen Moody were the
Champions and in those days when men still wore long trousers playing tennis.

August: As the depression deepened in Britain unemployment exceeded 2 million and by December it had reached 2,500,000.

That same year Donald Bradman (batsman) had an aggregate of 974 runs in the England v Australia Test Matches, including 334 runs in the Leeds Test Match.

Again I think it would be interesting to note down some of the events taking place during the year my mother was born.

1918

January: Food rationing introduced.

April: British Royal Air Force formed.

July: Russian Royal Family murdered.

Aug: 2000 people per day died from a Spanish Flu epidemic.

Nov: End of the First World War.

Dec: Seven days after Mum was born the first women aged 30 years and over
were allowed to vote. To add to that only women of means or property were allowed to vote, not the ordinary woman, it took a few more years for that to come about.

www.ingramcontent.com/pod-product-compliance
Lightning Source LLC
Chambersburg PA
CBHW030819090426
42737CB00009B/796